SENECA'S TRAGEDIES

D1310951

OTHER TITLES IN

THE CLASSICS OF GREECE AND ROME SERIES

Dudley Fitts, *General Editor*

THE ILIAD OF HOMER

Translated by Alexander Pope.
Edited, with an Introduction and Textual Notes,
by Reuben A. Brower and W. H. Bond.

THE AENEID OF VIRGIL

Translated by John Dryden.
Edited, with an Introduction and Notes,
by Robert Fitzgerald.

OVID'S METAMORPHOSES

Translated by Arthur Golding.
Edited, with an Introduction and Notes,
by John Frederick Nims.

SENECA'S
TRAGEDIES

OEDIPUS
TRANSLATED BY ALEXANDER NEVILLE

TROAS
TRANSLATED BY JASPER HEYWOOD

AGAMEMNON
TRANSLATED BY JOHN STUDLEY

EDITED, WITH AN INTRODUCTION AND NOTES,
BY ERIC C. BAADE

THE MACMILLAN COMPANY
Collier-Macmillan Limited, London

Copyright © 1969 by The Macmillan Company

All rights reserved.
No part of this book
may be reproduced or transmitted
in any form or by any means,
electronic or mechanical,
including photocopying, recording
or by any information storage
and retrieval system,
without permission in writing
from the Publisher.

Library of Congress Catalog Card Number: 69-10506

First Printing
The Macmillan Company
Collier-Macmillan Canada Ltd., Toronto, Ontario

Printed in the United States of America

For
Clarence W. Mendell
Saepe in magistrum scelera redierunt sua

CONTENTS

——————————

PREFACE

IN PREPARING THIS edition of Tudor translations of Seneca's tragedies, it has not been easy to select three out of the ten plays; the criteria were numerous and somewhat conflicting. If the purpose of this book were solely to demonstrate the quality of Tudor translation and its effect on Elizabethan drama, it would be important that the three plays be by three different translators and that they exhibit the peculiar qualities, good and bad, of their period: the exuberance of language, fascination with horrors, reinterpretation of classical themes, and so on. If, on the other hand, the book were intended primarily to make Seneca available in English, the plays chosen need only be his best ones, provided that the translations are adequate. Furthermore, any study of Seneca's dramatic technique would be rendered more fruitful if the choice were restricted to those tragedies with extant parallels in Greek drama.

Of the tragedies chosen, the *Oedipus* and *Troas* show Seneca at his best and are adequately translated, while all three provide parallels to extant Greek dramas—the *Agamemnon* of Aeschylus, the *Oedipus Rex* of Sophocles, and the *Troades* of Euripides. Each play has been rendered by a different translator, and the three, Neville, Heywood, and Studley, are probably the most important of the five translators of the 1581 edition. Furthermore these three translations show various characteristics of the period, from Heywood's poetry through Neville's workmanlike verse to the bombast and bathos of Studley. The three plays also contain elements dear to Elizabethan dramatists, such as the detailed descriptions of bloody horrors and the appearance of vengeful ghosts.

My aim in this edition has been simple: to smooth the path of the modern reader by some modernization of the text without destroying the flavor of the translations, which (whatever their merits) are of great historical importance. To this end I have modernized the spelling and punctuation, provided some footnotes, and added a glossary of obsolete words (and of obsolete meanings of current words) and an index to all the proper names.

Beyond the obvious and simple task of standardizing the varied spellings of Tudor times to the accepted modern version, I have extended the modernization of the spelling to include the replacement of obsolete words by their modern cognates (e.g., "brast" by "burst"). My object throughout has been to prevent, where possible, the constant interruption of the flow of the plays by the appearance of totally unfamiliar words; but at some points the exigencies of meter or rhyme have forced me to leave a word in its old form or spelling, and there is also a considerable residue of words which have no useful modern cognate (e.g., "dor" and "rex"). Nowhere have I tampered with the text to the extent of translating it into modern English (*i.e.*, replacing obsolete words with current words of the same meaning but different derivation), though I have corrected some obvious typographical errors.

The modernization of the punctuation has presented fewer problems. The punctuation of the original printed edition is at best inconsistent and at worst actually misleading, often producing the ludicrous effect of the prologue to the mechanics' play in *A Midsummer Night's Dream*. There are even some passages where the punctuation is metrical rather than grammatical. I have in general punctuated the plays according to modern standards, except that I have added extra punctuation wherever the complexities of the word order obscure the syntax.

If it had been possible, I would have eliminated footnotes altogether, since their presence cannot help but distract the reader and interrupt the flow of the dramas; but three things have made them necessary. The first is the comparatively untamed syntax of Tudor times, the frequent lack of agreement of subject and verb or of noun and pronoun, the inconsistency of tense or mood, and so on, as well as the freedom of word order in those times, the subject very often (for example) following its verb, and the object preceding. When I have not been able to make the meaning of some of the more contorted clauses immediately clear by means of punctuation, I have provided an interpretation in a footnote.

I have felt impelled to include other footnotes out of loyalty to Seneca himself. The Tudor translators, working from a corrupt text, without the aid of comprehensive Latin dictionaries, and (in the case of Studley, at least) with an uncertain grasp of Latin grammar, have often mistaken Seneca's meaning completely. Occasionally also their own taste has led them to expand or add to certain passages or to eliminate some parts of their author. In order, then, to make these plays useful translations of Seneca (and not merely examples of Tudor verse) I have pointed out in the notes significant variations from the original.

The third class of notes refers to the plays themselves rather than to the translations. Seneca's casual references to ancient customs and to beliefs no longer held have made some explanation necessary; and his copious and often obscure allusions to classical myths and legends in some cases would be meaningless or would pass unnoticed without notes. I hope that not too many of the footnotes will be of the annoying kind that tell the reader only what he already knew or guessed.

The glossary has been added to keep such notes to a minimum. Of the obsolete words and obsolete meanings of surviving words, some at least will be familiar to any reader, while the meanings of others will be made sufficiently clear by the context. Only if a word seems inappropriate or a passage meaningless need the reader seek an explanation; the glossary is provided for such occasions. The index of proper names has been included on the same principle.

The translators appear to have worked from the Florentine edition of Seneca's tragedies printed in 1513 (a very poor text, of course, by modern standards), and many of their apparent mistranslations would have been quite incomprehensible had I not had at hand a copy of this edition. For lending me his copy I should like to thank Mr. Rogers V. Scudder. My thanks are also due to Mr. Dudley Fitts, Mr. G. Chychele Waterston, Mr. Richard N. Walker, and Mr. Lawrence Richardson, Jr., for their sensible and helpful advice.

E. C. B.

INTRODUCTION

Suspice, etiam si decidunt, magna conantes.

Lucius Annaeus Seneca was born *ca.* 5 b.c. in Corduba in what is now Spain, into a wealthy and distinguished family: his father was a well-known lawyer and rhetorician; one of his brothers (the Gallio mentioned in Acts 18:12-15) became governor of Achaea, and the poet Lucan was his nephew. In early childhood he was brought to Rome, where he was educated in the rhetoric which was prerequisite to a political career; he also studied philosophy, which absorbed more and more of his interest as he grew older. In his thirties he entered politics with his election to the quaestorship, and within five years he had become well enough known as an orator to excite the literary jealousy of the Emperor Caligula. In a.d. 41, through the machinations of Messalina, wife of the Emperor Claudius, he was banished to Corsica by Claudius on a charge of adultery with a lady of the imperial family. In 49, he was recalled through the influence of Claudius' third wife Agrippina, and was appointed tutor to her twelve-year-old son Lucius Domitius Ahenobarbus, who was in 50 adopted by Claudius under the name of Nero. When in 54 Nero succeeded to the throne, Seneca became, with Nero's other tutor, Burrus, a sort of unofficial prime minister, for a time holding the official position of Consul Suffect. The first five years of Nero's reign, while he was under Seneca's influence, were long remembered as a kind of miniature Golden Age. But by the time he was twenty-two the young emperor had begun to resent the control of his mother and his tutors, and Seneca's influence waned rapidly. In 59, Nero made an unsuccessful attempt on his mother's life; in fear of her retaliation he turned to his tutors, and

Seneca was forced to become an accomplice to her murder (successful this time). Were the chronology of the tragedies better known, it might be tempting to read into some of the epigrams in them the effect of Agrippina's murder on Seneca's conscience: e.g. (from the *Troas*), "Of hurt constrained the fault return'th to th'author of the ill" ("Ad auctorem redit sceleris coacti culpa"); or conversely, "Who, when he may, forbiddeth not offence doth will the same" ("Qui non vetat peccare cum possit, iubet"), both spoken by unwilling accomplices to murder. In any case the uselessness of trying to oppose Nero's willfulness must have been obvious thereafter; Seneca nevertheless continued to try to influence the Emperor for three years more, and then, on the death of Burrus, asked permission to retire from public life. He was then in his late sixties. He lived in retirement until the year 65, when he was implicated in a conspiracy against Nero's life and forced to commit suicide. It is most unlikely that he was actually involved; Nero probably wanted him dead in order to get his hands on his large fortune (Seneca was one of the wealthiest men of his day) in order to repair the shaky imperial finances.

Of Seneca's prose writings all the orations and some of the philosophical works are lost. Preserved are three letters of condolence and Stoic consolation, nine treatises on Stoic philosophy and ethics, and a series of 124 letters of ethical and philosophical advice to a younger friend, as well as a dissertation on meteorology. He also wrote, in a mixture of prose and verse, a highly amusing satire on the deification, or, as he called it, the "pumpkinification" (*Apocolocyntosis,* a coinage from *apotheosis*) of the Emperor Claudius, which (though as an attack on a dead man it seems in poor taste by modern standards) may be justified by Seneca's eight years of suffering in Corsica under that Emperor. Besides a small collection of epigrams, his preserved poetic works consist of the ten tragedies (or nine, since the authenticity of the *Octavia* is now questioned).

It is difficult to reconcile the literary personality of Seneca with his life as we know it from history: we see a wealthy magnate who insists on the unimportance of riches, a political jackal who preaches incorruptibility, a coward who advocates courage, an adulterer who deplores the rule of the passions. The answer is simply that, as is the case with so many figures of the time, our impression of him is tainted with the gall of Tacitus, our chief source for his life and an author who is notorious for his diabolic cleverness in imputing to historical figures motives which he could not possibly have known. Stripped of Tacitus' interpretations, the bare facts of Seneca's career suggest the picture of a good and courageous man trying, with many false steps, to tread an extremely difficult path. The continual moral dilemmas involved in his position as adviser to an intelligent, vicious, headstrong, and all but omnipotent young monarch must have been almost insoluble.

Certainly the personality which emerges from his letters and essays is not that of a pompous hypocrite. They are full of wit and of compassion; and, what is perhaps more significant, they demonstrate their author's readiness to laugh at himself. Furthermore, they suggest a world-view so close to that of Christianity that for centuries it was assumed that Seneca must have been in touch with Christian thought, perhaps through St. Paul, who had met Seneca's brother in Greece; there seems to be, in fact, some slight evidence that in his youth Seneca was interested in the Hebrew religion. In any case, the deity of his modified Roman stoicism appears to be a benevolent being who works somehow in human life and history; men can be sure that their sufferings are meaningful events in some larger story.

Although it is not stressed, this quasi-Christian conception of the universe forms the background to the tragedies as well, and it is probably this philosophic element which explains much of their popularity of the Renaissance; for, in spite of their pagan trappings, their view of man's relation to the universe is much more congenial to the Western mind than is that of Greek tragedy. This is no doubt why Seneca's influence remained dominant in Western tragedy even after Greek models had become available.

In literary quality, it is true, Seneca's tragedies will not bear comparison with Greek tragedy, but this is partly because such a comparison leads us to look for virtues in Seneca which are not, and could not be, there. He is not writing that kind of tragedy. Seneca is not imitating the Greek tragedians any more than Virgil is imitating Homer. In the case of Virgil and Homer modern literary criticism has awakened to the fact that identity of genre does not justify approaching one literary work completely in terms of another; but the right to be criticized on his own merits has not yet been extended to Seneca. It is true that he, like Virgil, invites comparison with his Greek predecessors, but only to throw his own philosophy into relief by telling the same stories within a totally different moral framework. His method of telling the stories is too different to allow any valid comparison on the strictly literary level.

The most paradoxical result of viewing Seneca in terms of Greek tragedy is that his greatest successes are commonly considered his worst faults. The charges leveled against Senecan tragedy are that there is little or no development of character, and that they are overly rhetorical and epigrammatic; but if we abandon for the moment our notion that such characteristics are inappropriate to tragedy we find that his use of them, on his own terms, is often highly effective.

It seems unlikely that Seneca was at all concerned with character development in his plays; in fact, it would be irrelevant to, or in actual conflict with, the emotional unity, or unity of mood, which he was attempting to achieve. His tragedies sustain the feelings of compassion and terror, of impending doom, at a high level throughout, so that the mood at the opening of a play is not really different in quality from that at the close. There is no room for any real development, any more than in a short story of Poe. It may almost be said that the cause-and-effect relationship of the episodes is not really important; they are connected by the prevailing mood of the play more truly than by motivation or plot development. Instead of the Greek depiction of characters caught in, and twisted by, inflexible circumstances and inexorable events, Seneca gives us unchanging characters who by their very inflexibility bring about a series of dreadful events in their world. Oversimplification is dangerous, but one might say that in Seneca circumstances do not mold, but are molded by, characters. The ever-present mood of each play is the coloring which the persons of the play give to their world. In Seneca the interplay of necessity and responsibility is seen more clearly than in Greek tragedy, and it is seen in essentially moral terms. Seneca conforms more closely to Aristotelian canons, on the whole, than do the Greeks.

The rhetorical and epigrammatic nature of Seneca's style may be designed to protect the unity of mood from the intrusion of too much individuality in his characters. It is odd, in a way, that his style needs defending; he is no more epigrammatic than Corneille and no more rhetorical than Shakespeare. It is perhaps the combination, with its overtones of the debating society, which we find distasteful; for our ears have not been trained, as were the Romans', to the alternation of *oratio* and *altercatio* in forensic and political oratory. Seneca frequently punctuates long passages of high-flown language with succinct expressions of bitter, ironic wit, providing a kind of dramatic relief amid the sustained emotional tension of the plays. He may use both rhetoric and epigram to excess, but (leaving aside the arguable question of the psychological validity of putting this kind of speech into the mouths of people under emotional stress) he often manipulates them to good effect. When, in the *Thyestes,* after a passage in which rhetoric has been pushed to, if not beyond, the point of absurdity, Atreus shows his brother the heads of his children and asks, "Do you by any chance recognize your sons?", Thyestes, instead of embarking on the expected series of clever and contorted conceits, replies merely, "I recognize my brother" ("Gnatos ecquid agnoscis tuos?" "Agnosco fratrem."). Or, to cite a play in this collection, what could be more effective in context than Hecuba's ironic remark at the end of the *Troas,* "The child and virgin both be slain: your battles finished are," or more accurately, "The girl has fallen, and the boy: now the war is really over" ("Concidit virgo, ac puer: bellum peractum est")?

Even when Seneca is carried away by his own rhetoric, the resulting absurdity seems more often the failure of a daring attempt than a mere display of cleverness. He falls into absurdity by attempting flights beyond the range of his talents; and though we may laugh, yet we must admit that the attempt was worth making. He had sufficient talent to have produced mediocrity in perfect safety; his faults arise from his courage in trying to do more. A ludicrous example, from the *Troas,* of his unwillingness to descend even for a moment from the level of heightened emotion, is his making Polyxena show her defiance of the Greeks by falling especially heavily on Achilles' tomb in her death: "She fell, as th'earth should her revenge, with ireful rage to ground" (more literally, "She fell flat, and with an angry force, as if intending to make the earth heavy on Achilles," "Cecidit ut Achilli gravem factura terram, prona et irato impetu"). Seneca's characters refuse to relax their emotional tension even in death.

Oddly enough, Senecan tragedy is often criticized on the unwarranted assumption that the plays were literary exercises, not intended for production. If they had been meant only for private reading we could consider them badly written indeed. A passage which would be at worst melodramatic when delivered from the stage by an actor made to seem larger than life by his built-up buskins and high mask would seem ridiculously bombastic at a private recitation. But there is in fact no evidence at all to suggest that the tragedies were not written for the stage (the question of whether they actually reached the stage is after all irrelevant). The usual argument is that they contain scenes which simply could not be staged, but this is to underestimate the ingenuity of Julio-Claudian stage mechanics. As early as Cicero's day, productions could attain a degree of lavishness unheard of today; and we know from Suetonius that in Nero's time no expense was spared to make the realistic staging of difficult scenes possible. One need only cite a play called *The Fire* (*Incendium*) for which a house was constructed on the stage, furnished, and actually set on fire, the actors (to insure realistic acting) even being allowed to keep whatever they could salvage from it. The same author makes it clear that, in the mimes at least, actors playing characters who were supposed to die were actually put to death on the stage. Seneca himself writes of the extraordinary effects achieved by stage mechanicians, who could cause tall buildings to appear and disappear in a moment. Whether such elaborate effects are in good or bad dramatic taste need not concern us here; they were among the stage conventions of Seneca's day and would be expected by the public. Any author writing for the stage would have to take them into account.

The necessity of making concessions to popular taste is perhaps the real explanation of another flaw often pointed out by Seneca's critics— the incongruous coupling of scenes of blood and horror with Stoic moralizing in the choruses. The seeming irrelevancy of many of the choruses is a real problem, as when at the end of the second act of the *Troas* the chorus, having just heard of the appearance of Achilles' ghost, voices Stoic doubts of the existence of an afterlife, but it may well be that such choruses are actually the essential part of the tragedies, and that the action is primarily meant to attract an audience and to put its members into a frame of mind in which the philosophic principles introduced in the choruses will have some point and importance. In his prose writings Seneca is an enthusiastic proselytizer for the Stoic beliefs, and there is no reason not to suppose that his tragedies sprang from the same enthusiasm, that they are vehicles for Stoic teaching, an attempt to bring philosophy to a larger audience.*

* In this connection it is interesting that each tragedy contains one difficult stage effect, of the sort that would attract the sensation-loving Romans. In the three plays presented here, there are the supernatural behavior of the fire and the victims in the second act of the *Oedipus,* in the *Troas* the huge tomb of

The choruses are not invariably, of course, philosophic disquisitions; and when they are, the coupling of the sensational with the didactic is not always clumsy. Like some of the similes in the *Iliad,* the choruses, with their Stoic calm, often have the effect of removing us for a moment from scenes of blood and horror and giving us a new perspective. We glimpse an ordered universe, the ongoing cosmos whose laws have been violated but whose serenity is undisturbed. The conflict in Senecan tragedy is not a clash of character, but a rebellion of chaos against order; and in the resolution the forces of destruction destroy themselves.

Whatever its merits, the importance of Senecan tragedy in literary history is beyond question. Leaving aside Seneca's effect on the drama of other nations, we may safely say that his was the most important influence on Elizabethan tragedy, through which it has affected English drama in general. Most of the Elizabethan writers of tragedy are purely Senecan in their use of rhetoric, of violent action, and of horror; and even the works of Shakespeare, which transcend all influences, show strong Senecan elements. It was from Seneca that English tragedy borrowed the division into five acts, the introduction of ghosts and other supernatural elements, the importance of revenge as a motivating element, and the scenes of horror, as well as the use of stichomythy, moralizing soliloquy, and long passages of description. Although the historical development of dramatic technique and the genius of its author make it so much more brilliant than any of the plays in this collection, even *Hamlet* is basically Senecan.

Yet the influence on Elizabethan tragedy, at least for such dramatists as had small Latin and less Greek, is not that of Seneca himself, but of Seneca as interpreted by the varying talents of his translators; hence these five men, whose names are scarcely known today, also have their place in the history of English drama.

Jasper Heywood was born in 1535 into a literary family: his father was the epigrammatist John Heywood, his mother was descended from a sister of Sir Thomas More, and the brilliant John Donne was his nephew. He entered Oxford at the age of twelve, and later became a fellow of All Souls'; while at All Souls' he published his three translations— the *Troas* in 1559, the *Thyestes* in 1560, and

---

Hector, solid enough to withstand the attacks of Ulysses' men in the third act, and the vast riches of Troy carried onto the stage in the third and fourth acts of the *Agamemnon.*

the *Hercules Furens* in 1561. The schism of the English Church forced him, as a Roman Catholic, to retire to Rome, where he taught philosophy and theology, later becoming a professor at a Jesuit college in Bavaria. In 1581 he was appointed Superior of the English Jesuit Mission; arrested in 1583, he spent a year in the Tower of London, and was then exiled from England. He died in Naples in 1597.

Alexander Neville was born in 1544 and entered Cambridge, likewise at the age of twelve; he translated the *Oedipus* in 1560, although it was not published until 1563. Unlike Heywood, he remained loyal to the English Church, and was in fact secretary to Archbishop Parker and to two of his successors. He may also have been a member of Parliament. He died in 1614 and was buried in Canterbury Cathedral, of which his brother was dean.

John Studley entered Cambridge in 1563; he published his four translations, *Hippolytus, Medea, Agamemnon* and *Hercules Oetaeus,* while an undergraduate there. He became a fellow of Trinity in 1567, but in 1573 was forced to resign, because of his Puritan convictions, after considerable party strife within the college. He may have become a lawyer afterwards; there was a literary member of the Inns of Court named Studley. The date of his death is not known; he may have been killed at the siege of Breda in 1590.

Little is known of the career of Thomas Nuce. He was graduated from Cambridge in 1561 and was for some time a fellow of Pembroke. He seems to have published his translation of the *Octavia* in 1566, while serving as rector of a village in Norfolk. He died in 1617, having spent the latter part of his life as a prebend of Ely Cathedral.

Thomas Newton was born *ca.* 1542 and studied at both Oxford and Cambridge. In 1581 he collected the translations of the other four translators (who in some cases revised them for republication) and published them under the title *Seneca, His Tenne Tragedies,* translating the *Thebais* himself in order to complete the edition. (It had not been translated before because of its fragmentary nature.) Nothing more is known of him except that he was rector of a village in Essex in 1583.

The striking thing about all the translators (except Newton) is their youth at the time of their translations. None of them was out of his twenties, and Neville (and perhaps Studley as well) was only sixteen. In appraising the quality of their work we must remember that their translations were at the beginning little more than schoolboy exercises which (if we may trust the authors' prefaces) were probably not originally intended for publication. When we keep in mind that English dramatic verse was in its infancy, and that our translators were struggling painfully toward a technique which by Shakespeare's time was canonical, we can more easily overlook their missteps. Much as these translations were admired in their own day, by modern standards they are occasionally quite ludicrous. Their prosody is for the most part jingling, their rhetoric degenerates into bombast, and their most high-flown passages often plunge into bathos, while their renderings of the original Latin are often erroneous or obscure.*

Seneca's meters are extremely varied: he uses iambic trimeter for the bulk of his plays, but many scenes are in other meters, and the choric passages are usually in a wide variety of lyric meters. This variation of rhythm is not echoed to any degree in the translations: except for Nuce's *Octavia* (which uses decasyllabic couplets and octosyllables rhyming alternately) they are written for the most part in fourteeners, although Heywood and Studley often use other meters for their choric passages and occasionally vary their meters even in the non-choric sections of the plays. The fourteeners, used as they are with little enjambment and frequent syntactic pauses at the metrical caesura after the eighth syllable, become almost unbearably monotonous, and often seem comic to an ear tuned to the pentameters of later tragedy. The jingling effect is heightened by the couplet-rhyming, especially since the rhyme often seems even more insistent because of the padding or the syntactic contortion required to make it possible.

Of the translators in this collection, Studley is the worst offender in the monotony of his meters: many of his couplets in the *Agamemnon* are complete sentences or clauses, and there is in general almost no enjambment, while the metrical caesura is usually marked by a syntactic pause. Even in the choral odes at the ends of the first two acts,

* Viewed simply as renderings of Seneca's meaning, without regard to their poetic qualities, the three translations in this collection vary widely. As the footnotes to the text point out, Studley is careless and perhaps ignorant, and Neville on the whole a competent Latinist, whereas Heywood, dealing with a text which was at many points hopelessly corrupt, shows real genius in his bold efforts to make sense of the garbled Latin. His English makes sense throughout, even though it is sometimes the wrong sense; the other two, and especially Studley, are too often willing to translate Latin which they do not understand into nonsense in English.

when he offers the relief of alexandrines, the constant end-stopping and the well-marked caesura after the third foot produce the effect of long series of false starts.

In Neville's *Oedipus* there is no variation at all from the fourteeners, even in the choral passages, except that occasionally a line is lengthened by one or more feet. Neville may have considered even this variation a flaw, since it occurs more frequently in his original publication of the *Oedipus* than in the revision he made for the *Tenne Tragedies*; but this extension of some lines, together with his greater use of enjambment and his frequent elimination of the caesura by allowing a phrase, a closely knit clause, or sometimes even a single word* to run over the normal position of the caesura after the eighth syllable, makes his verse on the whole less monotonous than Studley's. He also on occasion breaks the monotony of the fourteeners by allowing final unaccented syllables to stand as rhymes,** by arranging rhyming lines in triplets instead of couplets, or by inserting an unrhymed line.

Heywood, in the *Troas,* also varies his fourteeners by the use of enjambment and by obscuring the metrical caesura,*** and he provides relief, too, by the introduction of other meters. Even in the non-choric parts of the play he twice abandons his basic meter, once (in the speech of Achilles' ghost at the beginning of the second act) for rime royal, once (in the second scene of the third act) for decasyllables rhyming alternately. This latter example is especially effective, marking as it does Andromache's recognition of the hopelessness of trying to save Astyanax. The change of tone as she turns from the hated Ulysses to address her son so tenderly is made genuinely pathetic by the change of movement in meter and rhyme-scheme. Rime royal and alternate-rhyming decasyllables appear also in the choral odes, as do alternate-rhyming octosyllables; Heywood uses no fourteeners at all for his choric passages in the *Troas.*

In poetic diction as well, the *Agamemnon* must be ranked lowest of the three translations. Almost any passage picked at random will demonstrate its inflated rhetoric, its overuse of alliteration, its frequent bathos. A passage like

* "By these relics of my dismembered body I thee pray."
** "Be sure his life and death and all be quite exempt from misery,/Ere thou do once presume to say, 'This man is blest and happy.'"
*** "The cruel beast, when once removèd is the dam away."

The flashing flames and furious force of fiery fervent heat,
Out-raging in my boiling breast, my burning bones do beat;
It sucks the sappy marrow out, the juice it doth convey,
It frets, it tears, it rends, it gnaws my guts and gall away.
Now feeble fear still eggs me on, with dolor being pressed;
And cankered hate with thwacking thumps doth bounce upon my
    breast

is not far enough for comfort from Peter Quince:

Whereat with blade, with bloody blameful blade,
He bravely broach'd his boiling bloody breast.

Studley's habit of introducing homely words into his most high-flown
passages contributes greatly to the bathetic effect,* as does his delight
in piling up multiple translations for a single Latin word: the first
four lines cited above are a rendering of one line in the Latin, *"Flammae medullas et cor exurant meum,"* so that *"exurunt"* ("burn") is
rendered "do beat . . . sucks . . . doth convey . . . frets . . . tears
. . . rends . . . gnaws," while the whole first line, with its heavy-
handed alliterative effects, translates only the word *"flammae."*
Here the expansion is probably deliberate: Studley presumably felt
that Seneca had not gone far enough; but sometimes it appears to be
mere padding, as when *"pugnat"* is rendered "wrestleth, striveth, struggleth hard, and fighteth." All the translators are guilty of a certain
amount of padding, usually in order to fill out a line or achieve a
rhyme, but Studley does more than the others to dilute the original
in this way. And while the other two translators in this collection also
felt it necessary to augment the plays with passages of their own
composition, Studley's additions seem in much more questionable taste
than theirs. The *Agamemnon* is not one of Seneca's better plays, but

---

* *E.g.,* Lo, nature, chang'd upside-down and out of order turned,
    This mingle-mangle hath she made. O fact to be forlorned!
or
    Whom with the dint of glitt'ring sword Achilles durst not harm,
        Although his rash and desperate dicks the froward knight did arm,
or, again,
    But valiant Agamemnon, he, grand captain of the host
    Who bore the sway among the kings, and rul'd all the roost.

like most of them it has an extremely effective ending—Cassandra's going to her death with a prophecy of Clytemnestra's fate on her lips. Studley manages to destroy its effect with an anticlimactic epilogue spoken by Eurybates.

While the versification of the *Oedipus* is at worst respectable, and that of the *Troas* occasionally reaches a level of poetic skill in translation which it would be hard to match, nevertheless these plays, too, suffer from many of the same faults as the *Agamemnon,* if to a lesser degree. Yet in spite of their flaws, these translations have more than mere antiquarian or historical interest to recommend them. Even at their poorest they have an exuberance, a youthful vigor, almost a violence of expression, which make even Marlowe seem tame by contrast. Their enthusiasm is somehow infectious, and gives them a directness which cuts through all the quaintness and clumsiness, bringing to them a liveliness which is not to be found in their Latin originals.

OEDIPUS

The Fifth Tragedy of Seneca.
Englished the Year of Our Lord
MDLX
by Alexander Neville

The Preface to the Reader

BEHOLD HERE before thy face, good reader, the most lamentable tragedy of that most unfortunate prince, Oedipus, for thy profit rudely translated. Wonder not at the grossness of the style, neither yet account the inventor's diligence disgraced by the translator's negligence, who though that he hath sometimes boldly presumed to err from his author, roving at random where he list, adding and subtracting at pleasure, yet let not that engender disdainful suspicion within thy learned breast. Mark thou rather what is meant by the whole course of the history, and frame thy life free from such mischiefs wherewith the world at this present is universally overwhelmed: the wrathful vengeance of God provoked, the body plagued, the mind and conscience in midst of deep devouring dangers most terribly assaulted, in such sort that I abhor to write; and even at the thought thereof I tremble and quake for very inward grief and fear of mind, assuredly persuading myself that the right high and immortal God will never leave such horrible and detestable crimes unpunished—as in this present tragedy, and so forth in the process of the whole history, thou mayst right well perceive. Wherein thou shalt see a very express and lively image of the inconstant change of fickle fortune in the person of a prince of passing fame and renown, midst whole floods of earthly bliss, by mere misfortune (nay, rather by the deep-hidden secret judgements of God) piteously plunged in most extreme miseries—the whole realm for his sake in strangest guise grievously plagued, besides the apparent destruction of the nobility, the general death and spoil of the commonalty, the miserable transformed face of the city, with an infinite number of mischiefs more which I pass over unrehearsed. Only wish I all men by this tragical history (for to that intent was it written) to beware of sin, the end whereof is shameful and miserable, as in the most unfortunate fall of this unhappy prince right plainly appeareth. Who by inward gripe of fearful consuming conscience wretchedly tormented, beholding the lamentable state of his vile infected realms wasted by the burning rage of privy spoiling pestilence, finds himself in tract of time to be the only plague and misery of the almost quite destroyed city. Whereupon calling together his priests and prophets, and asking counsel of the gods by them for present remedy in those evils wherewith the realm was then universally overflowed, answer was made that the plague should never cease till King Laius' death were thoroughly revenged, and the bloody murderer driven into perpetual exile. Which answer received, Oedipus, far more curious in bolting out the truth than careful of his own state, suddenly slides into an innumerable company of dreadful miseries. For as soon as he had once the perfect view of his own detestable deeds and wicked misdemeanor cast before his eyes, together with the unnatural killing of his father Laius, the incestuous marriage of his mother Jocasta, the preposterous order of his ill misguided life, with a hundred more like mischiefs which chaste and undefiled ears abhor to hear—fretting fury, common enemy and tormentor to corrupted consciences, pricking him forward—all inflamed with frenzy and boiling in inward heat of vile infected mind, he rooteth out his wretched eyes unnaturally, bereaveth his mother her life (though earnestly requested thereto) bestially, and in the end, in most basest kind of slavery banished, dieth miserably, leaving behind him unto all posterity a dreadful example of God's horrible vengeance for sin. Such like terrors as these requireth this our present age, wherein Vice hath chiefest place and Virtue, put to flight, lies as an abject, languishing in great extremity. For the which cause, so much the rather have I suffered this my base-translated tragedy to be published, from its author in word and verse somewhat transformed, though in sense little altered, and yet oftentimes rudely increased with mine own simple invention (more rashly, I confess, than wisely wishing to please all, to offend none). But whereas no man lives so uprightly whom slandering tongues leave undefamed, I refer myself to the judgment of the wisest, little esteeming the prejudicial mouths of such carping merchants who suffer no men's doings, almost, to escape undefiled. In fine, I beseech all together (if so it might be) to bear with my rudeness and consider the grossness of our own country's language, which can by no means aspire to the high lofty Latinist's style. Mine only intent was to exhort men to embrace virtue and shun vice, according to that of the right famous and excellent poet Virgil:

Discite justitiam moniti, et non temnere divos.[1]

This obtained, I hold myself thoroughly contented; in the mean season I end, wishing all men to shun sin, the plain (but most perilous) pathway to perfect infelicity.

A. NEVILLE

[1] "Warned (by me), learn justice, and not to despise the gods," (*Aeneid* vi. 620).

The Speakers' Names

Oedipus [King of Thebes, thought to be the son of the King of Corinth, Polybus, and his wife Merope, but actually the son of Laius and Jocasta]

Jocasta [widow of Laius, former King of Thebes, now the wife of Oedipus]

Chorus [of Theban elders]

Creon [brother of Jocasta]

Tiresias [a blind prophet of Thebes]

Manto [his daughter]

Senex[2] [a messenger sent from Corinth to announce the death of Polybus]

Phorbas [the royal shepherd of Thebes]

Nuntius[3]

[Thebes, before the royal palace]

[2, 3] Neville leaves these words, which mean "old man" and "messenger" respectively, in the original Latin.

THE FIRST ACT

Oedipus the King, Jocasta the Queen

Oed. The night is gone, and dreadful day begins at length t'appear;
And Phoebus, all bedimmed with clouds, himself aloft doth rear,
And, gliding forth with deadly hue, a doleful blaze in skies
Doth bear, great terror and dismay to the beholder's eyes.
Now shall the houses void be seen, with plague devourèd quite;
And slaughter that the night hath made shall day bring forth to light.
Doth any man in princely throne rejoice? O brittle Joy,
How many ills, how fair a face, and yet how much annoy
In thee doth lurk, and hidden lies! what heaps of endless strife!
They judge amiss, that deem the prince to have the happy life!
For as the mountains huge and high the blust'ring winds withstand,
And craggy rocks the belching floods do bash, and drive from land,
Though that the seas in quiet are, and calm on every side:
So kingdoms great all winds and waves of fortune must abide.
How well shunned I my father dear Polybus' sceptre, late!
Exiled, bereft of careful fear, in pilgrim's happy state,
I call the gods to witness this, and stars that glide in skies.
A kingdom is befall'n to me—I fear lest thereof rise
A mischief, mighty Jove, too great; I fear, alas! I fear
Lest these my hands have reft the life of thee, my father dear!
Apollo bids me this beware, and yet a mischief more
Foretells.

Joc. Can any greater be than that you told before,
Of father slain by son's own hand?[4]

Oed. O thrice unhappy state!
With horror all dismayed I stand in dread of threatened fate.
I am ashamed my dest'nies foul, O Queen, to thunder out,
And openly to blaze my fear my trembling mind doth doubt—

---

[4] Most editors make this sentence in the Latin text a part of Oedipus' opening soliloquy, and assume that Jocasta does not enter until her next speech. Neville has considerably expanded and rearranged the passage which follows.

Yet out it goes: Phoebus me bids my mother's bed to fly,
As though that I her son with her incestuously should lie.
This fear, and only this, me caused my father's kingdom great
For to forsake; I fled not thence. When fear the mind doth beat,
The restless thought still dreads the thing it knows can never chance;
Such fancies now torment my heart. My safety to advance,
And eke thine ever sacred laws, O Nature, for to keep,
A stately sceptre I forsook; yet secret fear doth creep
Within my breast, and frets it still with doubt and discontent,
And inward pangs which secretly my thoughts asunder rent.
So, though no cause of dread I see, yet fear and dread I all;
And, scant in credit with myself, my thoughts my mind appall
That I cannot persuaded be (though reason tell me no)
But that the web is weaving still of my decreèd woe.
For what should I suppose the cause: a plague that is so general,
And Cadmus' country wholly spoils, and spreads itself through all,
Should me, amongst so huge a heap of plaguèd bodies, spare?
And we alone amongst the rest reserved to mischiefs are?
O heavy hap! And bide I still alone the spoil to see
Of cities great, of men, of beasts, by plague that wasted be?
And thou, amongst so many ills, a happy life to lead
Couldst once persuade thyself, O wretch, without all fear or dread
Of Phoebus' secret judgements, too—and that in King's estate?
Thou, thou infected hast the air in such a filthy rate;
Thou art the only cause of woe; by thee these evils rise;
By thee to grave, on such a sort, this wretched people plies.
The fiery flaming frying heat, afflicted hearts that wastes,
Is not relieved as wont it was by cold and pleasant blasts.
The gentle western winds have left with healthful puffs to blow,
And now the fiery Dog[5] with blaze of boiling heat doth glow.
The sun in Leo burns so hot, and so the earth doth broil,
That floods and herbs are dryèd up, and nought remains but soil
So throughly scorched and stewed with heat that moisture all is gone,
And now amongst so many floods remains, alas! not one.
The places dry are only seen, the streams are drunken up;
And water that doth yet remain the soaking earth doth sup.
The moon with clouds quite overcast, all sadly forth she glides;

---

[5] Sirius, the dog star. See *Index of Proper Names.*

And doleful darksome shade of night the whole world overhides.
No star on high at all doth shine, but black and hell-like hue
Hath overshaded all the skies, whence deadly mists ensue.
The corn that wonted was to grow and fruitfully to spring
Now to the voided barns nought else but empty stalks doth bring.
No part of all our kingdom is free from destruction,
But all together run and rush to utter confusion.
The old men with the young, alas! the father with the child
The plague consumes. Both man and wife, all beasts, both tame and
    wild,
Are spoilèd by the pestilence. No pomp at all remains,
That wonted was in funerals, to ease the mourners' pains.
Alas! this spoil of people, made by plague, hath dried mine eyes,
And secretly within my breast the grief it boiling fries.
And, that that wonted is to hap in most extremest ills:
My tears are dry, and glutting grief my wretchèd breast it fills.
The crazèd father bears the sons unto their dampish graves;
And after him, with burden like, the mother comes and raves.
And even lamenting as they stand, stark dead down both they fall;
And mourners new in like estate for them and theirs they call,
Who likewise in the midst of all their toil and painful pain
Do drop into the grave they digged, and so the place do gain
That was prepared for others erst. A hell it were to hear
The horror and the miseries that everywhere appear.
A tomb is made for noblemen—fast on the people hie
And in their burdens fling: great Peers all unregarded lie.
For lack of graves, to ashes clean their bodies some do waste,
And some half-burnt do leave them there, and home away for haste
They run, and more they fetch; and then wood, fire, grave, and all
Doth want. And down for very grief the wretched misers fall.
No prayers avail. No art can help this raging plague t'appease,
For none almost is left alive each other's woe to ease.
Before thine altars here, O God, my feeble hands I hold,
Requiring all my destinies, at once with courage bold.
And that by death I may prevent my country pressed to fall,
For this, and only this, O God, upon thy name I call.
Let me not be the last that dies, the last that goes to grave;
Grant this, and then, O mighty Jove, my full request I have.
O cruel gods unkind, O more than thrice unhappy fates,

That only me denièd is that lights on all estates:
I mean a speedy death (alas!) these evils to prevent,
And deadly woes that do my heart with restless rage torment.
Leave off thy blubbering tears, O fool, and fly these kingdoms, foiled
With rotten plagues and botches vile, and graves eachwhere despoiled.
All which diseases thou, unhappy guest, didst bring with thee.
Dispatch, away, go hence! At least unto thy parents flee.

    Joc. What boots it, Sire, these mischiefs great with piteous plaints to
        aggravate?
Stoutly to bear adversity is fitt'st for king's estate.
When dread and danger most assail, when cruel cares do crush
Thy princely breast, then oughtst thou most to bear and bide the push.
It is no point of courage stout to yield to Fortune's frown.

    Oed. Nay, fear could never cause me stoop nor fortune cast me down:
My manly mind was never thrall to vain and peevish fears,
But evermore in each assault it princely courage bears.
No, not a thousand glistering swords, nor Mars himself in field,
Can once dismay my countenance, or cause my heart to yield;
The very Giants fierce and huge in fight withstand I dare!
That monster, Sphinx, whose riddles through the world renownèd are,
Could not dismay my dreadless heart, nor cause my courage slide;
For all the terrors I beheld, I did that fury bide.
I saw him[6] belching gobs of blood, I viewed full well the field
That all to-spattered lay with blood, and bones quite overhilled.
And when that he on mountain's top, with mouth full huge to see,
Stood gaping all with greedy jaws to feed and prey on me,
Oft fluttering with his fearful wings and shaking oft his tail,
Began, full like a lion fierce, with threats me to assail,
Of whom straightway the riddle in it rushed into mine ears,
With roaring sound his wings he claps, the rock for haste he tears,
Desiring with my bowels still his greedy jaws to glut—
But I full soon assoilèd had the question that he put,
And all the subtle points thereof, and twisted knots, untwined.

    Joc.[7] What makes you wish for death too late, and waste your words
        in wind?
You might have dièd then, you know. For Sphinx so noble slain

    [6] Neville inexplicably mistakes the gender; the Sphinx was thought to be a
female monster. See *Index of Proper Names.*
    [7] Most editors of Seneca assign this speech to Oedipus, addressing himself.

This kingdom unto you and yours forever shall remain.

Oed. The ashes of that monster vile against us do rebel:
That vile, misshapen, loathsome beast, that raging fiend of Hell
Is cause of all the plague that does this mournful city smite!
Now only this remains alone: if Phoebus' heavenly might
Can any means invent for us, or way of mercy make
Whereby these burning plagues at length may haply chance to slake.

Chorus[8]

O more than thrice renownèd stock of ancient Cadmus' race,
O mighty Thebès city great—O heavy ruthful case!—
Lo, now you lie all desolate, with plague devourèd quite,
Both you and all your husbandmen—O miserable sight!
O foul and fearful fate! Alas, what causeth all this woe?
O God, whence springs this pestilence that us tormenteth so?
No age, no shape, no form is spared, but all confounded lie.
Thus happiest now the man I count whose chance was first to die,
For he hath shunned a thousand ills which wretched eyes have seen,
And mischiefs great that us do press from him are taken clean.
O God, withhold thy fury great, thy plagues from us remove,
Cease of afflicted souls to scourge, who thee both serve and love.
Pour down on *them* diseases foul that them deservèd have:
A guerdon just for sin, O God, this, this of thee we crave,
And only this. We ask no more; the cause and all is thine.
A thing not used of gods it is, from pity to decline.
My heart doth pant, and trembling cold through all my limbs doth run,
As oft as I, rememb'ring, count the noble stocks undone,
By death and doleful destinies that overwhelmèd lie—
And yet, alas! the people still to grave do faster hie:
In long array, all in a rank by thousands on a row,
On every side, in every street to burial fast they go.
The seven broad wide-open gates are not enough for way;
But thronged the people pestered stand, still in a fearful stay,
And in the midst of all their toil with corpses on their backs,
The number that before doth post the hinder number slacks.
The corpses in the streets do lie and grave on grave is made;

---

[8] Neville has omitted a good deal of mythological embellishment and has expanded considerably (his parode is about a third again as long as the original) the graphic description of the plague and the prayers for relief from it.

But all in vain, for nought it boots: the plague cannot be stayed.
The sacrifices done to gods have too, too ill success;
And such strange sights and signs do rise that nought else I can guess
But that at hand, with ghastly paws, is utter destruction,
With thousand ills accompanied and extreme confusion.
The sheep of rot, by heaps as thick, as dogs do fall and die,
And, belching out their wasted lungs, on ground do sprawling lie.
And I myself of late did see—a sight unseen before!—
As our High Priest stood sacrificing at the temple door
And struck with grievous bloody wound the golden-hornèd bull,
When down with lifeless lump he drops, and members made full dull,
And all the wound wide bleeding gapes, and black-gored blood out-
    spews—
And yet the blade unsprinkled was! The blood it boiling stews
And bubbles on the ground. Alas, what do these things portend?
O mighty Jove, at length vouchsafe some good and happy end;
At length withhold thy hand, O God, and health unto us send!
Nothing, alas! remains at all in wonted old estate,
But all are turnèd topside-down, quite void and desolate.
The fainting horse for sudden pain from back his burden lets,
And after on his master's breast his lifeless limbs he squats,
Who cries for help, but all in vain. The beasts, in field that bide
Unkept, unknowen ways and paths do range and overstride.
The bull for lack of food and meat in field all fainting lies;
And, all his flock dispersèd quite, the silly shepherd dies.
The herdsman eke amongst his beasts his fatal breath expires
And to the heavens, with piteous cries, commends his last desires.
The harts without all fear of wolves do live in wretched peace,
The rage and wrathful roaring sounds of ramping lions cease,
The vengeance-willed outrageous bears are now as tame as sheep;
The ugly serpent that was wont the rocky dens to keep,
Oft quaffing poisoned venom-sips, in inward heat she boils,
And all inflamed and scorched, in vain for longer life she toils.
The woods are not adornèd now with fresh and lively hue;
The wonted shades are gone. All things are quite out of their cue:
No greenish grass on ground doth grow, the earth no moisture sups,
The vine withouten any sap his drowsy head down droops.
What shall I say? All things, alas! are writhen out of course,
And, as they seem to me, are like to fare still worse and worse.

O mighty God above, when end these everduring ills?
When cease this plague that guiltless blood thus fierce and raging spills?
I think but we, almost, alive there do no men remain
Whom doleful darts of destiny on earth have left unslain.
I think the darksome shades of Hell (where filthy floods do flow,
Where plagues and vile diseases, too, where dreadful horrors grow)
And all the Furies, bursten loose, do mischiefs on us throw,
With botch and blain of sundry kinds which southern blasts do blow
And wreckful vexèd hags of Hell do breathe and on us bring.
The angry fiends of Hell, I think, their vengeance on us fling,
And out their mortal poison spew which they against us bear—
Lo, see how greedy Death on us with scowling eyes doth leer!
See, see, oh! Jove how fast he throws his darts! Not one he spares,
But all confounds. His threat'ning force withstand no creature dares.
No doubt the loathsome ferryman,[9] the sinful souls that trains
Through stinking floods, his labor loathes that he for us sustains,
Such press by plumps to him is made, which still renews his pains.
But hark yet monsters more than these: the fame abroad doth fly
That hellish dogs with bawling sound were heard to howl and cry,
And that the ground with trembling shook and under feet did move,
And dreadful blazing comets bright were seen in skies above,
And ghastly shapes of men besides to wander on the ground,
And wood and trees on every side did fearfully resound.
Besides all this, strange ghosts were seen in places where they stood,
And rivers more than one or two that ran all black-gored blood.
O cruel plague, O vile disease, far worse than speedy death!
O we unhappy thrice and more, who do prolong our breath
In these accursèd days and times! But hark to me a while:
When first this loathsome plague begins these misers to defile,
It takes them thus:[10] a fearful cold through all their bones doth run,
And cold and heat, together mixed, their senses all venom;
Then little loathsome marks appear and all their bodies spot,
And all their members flaming glow, and burning fast do rot;
The lights, the lungs, the heart, the guts, and all that inward lie,

[9] Charon. V. Index of Proper Names, s.v. Dis.

[10] Neville's account of the plague is much more circumstantial than the original; the symptoms he describes seem to be those of the bubonic plague, the Black Death which had devastated Europe a century before. Although there were no major epidemics of it in Neville's day, smaller outbreaks were not uncommon.

And all the secret parts, yscorched, with deadly fire fry;
The blood, all clotted in their cheeks, in cluster lies by lumps,
And it and heat together make great strange and ruddy bumps;
The blood and flesh congealèd stand in face as stiff as stake,
And eyes in head fast fixèd sit and often trickling make;
And down apace whole floods they steam, and clots and drops do trill;
And all the skin from off their face by flakes and scales doth peel;
A thousand fearful sounds at once into their ears do rush;
And loathsome blood out of their nose by stilling streams doth gush;
The very anguish of their heart doth cause them for to shake
And, what with pain, and heat, and fear, their worried limbs do quake.
Then some the running rivers haunt, and some on ground do wallow,
And some again, their thirst to slake, cold water gulping swallow.
Thus all our country, tossed with plague, in grief it weltering lies,
And, still desiring for to die, a thousand deaths it dies.
But God to hear them then is pressed, and death to none denies;
Besides all this, the church[11] some do frequent—but not to pray,
But only for to glut the gods with that that they do say . . .
But who is this that comes to court in haste, with posting pace?
What? Is't Creon, that noble prince for deeds and stately race,
Or doth my mind, oppressed with care, things false for true contrive?
Creon it is, long lookèd for! His sight doth me revive.

THE SECOND ACT

The First Scene

Oedipus, Creon

Oed. For fear my body chills, alas! and trembling all I stand
In quaking dread. I seek and toil these mischiefs to withstand.
But all in vain I spend my thoughts: it will not be, I see,
As long as all my senses thus by cares distracted be.
My mind, desirous still, O God, the truth for to unfold,
With doubtful dread is daunted so that it can scarce uphold
Itself. O brother dear, if way or mean of health thou know,
Declare it out, and stick not all the truth to me to show.
Cre. The Oracle, most noble King, is dark, and hidden lies.

---

[11] A quaintly anachronistic translation of *delubra,* "shrines"; needless to say, ancient polytheism had no congregational aspect.

Oed. Who doubtful health to sick men brings, all health to them
    denies.

Cre. Apollo's use it is, the truth in darksome dens to hold.

Oed. And Oedipus of gods it hath, things hidden to unfold.[12]
Speak out, tell all and spare not, man; all doubts I can discuss.

    Cre. Apollo then, most noble King, himself commandeth thus:
"By exile purge the prince's seat, and plague with vengeance due
That hapless wretch whose bloody hands of late King Laius slew.
Before that this performèd be, no hope of milder air.
Wherefore do this, O King, or else all hope of help despair."

    Oed. Dared any man on earth attempt that noble prince to slay?
Show me the man, that I may him dispatch out of the way.

    Cre. God grant I may it safely tell! The hearing was too terrible,
My senses all amazèd are; it is a thing so horrible
That I abhor to utter it. O God, for fear I quake;
And even at the very thought my limbs begin to shake.
As soon as I Apollo's church had entered in afraid,
Upon my face flat down I fell; and thus to him I prayed:[13]
"O God, if ever thou didst rue on wretched misers' state,
If ever men oppressed thou eased, or didst their cares abate,
If ever thou in present need didst present help declare,
If ever thou afflicted hearts with cares consumed didst spare,
Show now thy wonted clemency and pity known of yore!"
Scant had I said; resounding, all the mountains thund'ring roar,[14]
And filthy fiends spout out their flames out of their darksome caves,
And woods do quake, and hills do move, and up the surging waves
Do mount into the skies aloft; and I amazèd stand,
Still looking for an answer at Apollo's sacred hand—
When out with ruffled hair disguised the prophet[15] comes at last;
And when that she had felt the heat of mighty Phoebus' blast,
All puffing out she swells in rage, and patt'ring still she raves;
And scant she entered had into Apollo's shining caves,
When out a thund'ring voice doth burst that's far above man's reach—
So dreadful seemèd then to me the mighty Phoebus' speech.

[12] *I.e.,* "Oedipus has from the gods the gift of unfolding hidden things."

[13] The following prayer is an interpolation of the translator's.

[14] Neville here provides a much more sensational list of portents than does the
original.

[15] See *Index of Proper Names, s.v. Pythia.*

Then thus he spake, and thus at length into mine ears he rushed,
While, sprawling, still the prophet lay before the doors in dust:
"The Theban city never shall be free from plagues," quoth he,
"Except from thence the king-killer forthwith expellèd be
(Unto Apollo known he was ere ever he was born):
Do this, or else no hope of health. To this the gods have sworn.
And as for thee, thou shalt not long in quiet state endure,
But with thyself wage war thou shalt, and war thou shalt procure
Unto thy children dear, and creep again thou shalt into thy mother's
    womb."
  Oed. Look, what the gods commanded have accomplishèd shall be;
Nor never shall these eyes of mine abide the day to see
A king of kingdom spoiled by force, by guile or craft suppressed.
A king to kings the prop ought be, and chiefest cause of rest.
No man regards his death at all whom living he did fear.
  Cre. Great cause made me my prince's death conceal and closely bear.
  Oed. Ought any cause of fear or grief thy duty for to let?
  Cre. The threat'ning of the prophecies do still my breast beset.
  Oed. Let us, since God commands, forthwith some good atonement
    make,
If any way or means there be their wrathful rage to slake.
Thou, God, that sits on seat on high, and all the world dost guide,
And thou by whose commandèment the stars in skies do glide,
Thou, thou that only ruler art of seas, of floods, and all,
On thee and on thy godhead great for these requests I call:
Whoso hath slain King Laius—O Jove, I do thee pray!—
Let thousand ills upon him fall before his dying day.
Let him no health nor comfort have, but all to-crushed with cares
Consume his wretched years in grief; and, though that death him spares
Awhile, yet mischiefs all at length upon him light.
With all the evils under sun that ugly monster smite!
In exile let him live, a slave, the rated course of life,
In shame, in care, in penury, in danger, and in strife.
Let no man on him pity take; let all men him revile.
Let him his mother's sacred bed incestuously defile;
Let him his father kill. And yet let him do mischiefs more—
What thing more heinous can I wish than that I wished before?—
Let him do all those ills, I say, that I have shunned and passed;

All those and more—if more may be—O God, upon him cast.[16]
Let him no hope of pardon have, but sue and all in vain;
All hellish Furies on him light for to increase his pain.
O Jove, pour down thy fury great, thy thund'ring thumps outthrow;
Let Boreas' boisterous blasts and stormy plagues upon him blow.
Consume him quite, fret out his guts with pocks and botches vile;
Let all diseases on him light that wretched bodies file.
Let these and more—if more may be—upon that monster fall.
Let Harpies' paws and greedy paunch devour his members all!
Let no man him regard, or seek his limbs in grave to lay;
But let him die ten thousand deaths before his dying day.
By this my kingdom I do swear, and kingdom that I left,
By all my country's gods that be in temples closely kept,
I swear, I vow, I do protest and thereto witness take
The stars, the seas, the earth, and all that e'er thy hand did make.
Except that I myself forthwith this bloody monster find,
To wreak the wrath of God some way with solemn oath I bind.
And so my father Polybus his happy days outlive,
And so my mother Merope no marriage new contrive,
As he shall die that did this deed, and none shall him excuse.
Whoso he be, here I protest for that he shortly rues!
But where this wicked deed was done, Creon, now tell me plain,
Both by what means, and where, and how King Laius was slain.
  Cre. Passing through Castalia's woods and mountains heaped with
    snow,
Where groves, and shrubs, and bushes thick, and brambles sharp do
    grow,
A three-pathed crooked way there is that diversely doth go:
One unto Bacchus' city bends, that Phocis doth hight;
The other to Olenia forth stretcheth out aright;
The third, that reacheth through the vales and by the rivers lies,
Tends down unto the banks whereby Elean water plies.
There, unawares—O piteous chance!—a troop of thieves entraps
The noble prince, and murders him. Hence spring these great mishaps
Which heap your realms with hideous woes and plagues on every side,
By just decree of heavenly powers which can no murder bide.

---

[16] The next ten lines of the curse are added by Neville.

But see Tiresias where he comes with old and trembling pace;
I think Apollo's heavenly might has brought him to this place.
See where he comes, and Manto, too, his steps directing stays;
'Tis he who for your grace, O King, and for your country prays.

The Second Scene

Oedipus, Tiresias, Manto

Oed. Come, holy priest, to Phoebus next, these doubtful answers
  loose;
And whom that dest'nies will to die straightway to me disclose.
  Tir. Renownèd Prince, though still I stand in silence dumb dismayed,
And though by inward fear of mind my ling'ring tongue is stayed,
Yet pardon me, O noble Prince, and give me leave a while.
From lack of sight springs ignorance, which pow'r hath to exile
Unspotted truth from doubtful breasts. This thing full well you know;
But whither God and country call with willing mind I go.
Let deadly fatal destinies be bolted out at length.
O King, if I of greener years had now my wonted strength,
This matter soon discussed should be, and I would take in hand
Myself, in presence of the gods, in temple for to stand.
A mighty ox, all colored white, upon the altars rear,
Which never yet on wearied neck the crooked yoke did bear;
And Manto, thou, O daughter mine, mine only prop and stay,
The secret hidden mysteries and sacred signs out say.
  Man. The beast before the altar stands.
  Tir. To gods a prayer make,
And on the holy altars eke some pleasant odors shake.
  Man. 'Tis done, and all the fires fierce with incense bright do flame.
  Oed. O Manto, now what signs seest thou? How do thy matters
  frame?
What? doth the fire the sacrifice encompass round about?
  Man. Not so, but first it mounts aloft, and straight it flasheth out.
  Tir. Well yet, how? doth the sacred flame, all shining bright and
  clear,
Itself on high unto the skies with sparkling flakes uprear?
Or doth it, oft rebounding back, itself from skies unfold?
Or all, with rumbling roaring noise, about the place is't rolled?

Or, dimmed with smoke, is't tossed from place to place, now here, now
    there?

Man. Not one, but divers colors mixed the flame doth with it bear,
Much like unto the rainbow, which with sundry painted hues
Foreshows unto the husbandmen the weather that ensues.
What color it wants, or what it hath, to me is like uncertain;
Now is it black, now blue, now red, and even now again
Quite out it is. Yet once again all fierce it flashing flames—
But lo! yet mischiefs more than this unluckily it frames.
The fire quite asunder parts, and flame with flame doth fight!
O father, I abhor to see this ugly loathsome sight!
The wine to blood is turnèd quite, and all the Prince's head
With thick black clouds encompassed is, with smoke all overspread!
O father, tell what this portends.

Tir. What should I tell, alas?
My mind for fear astonished stands, and trembling cold doth pass
Through all my limbs. What shall I say, or where shall I begin?
O cruel plagues, O wreckful gods, O vengeance due for sin!
Some dire and bloody deed, alas! these hideous signs declare;
What's that the gods would have revealed, and yet do bid beware
To utter it? By certain signs their wrath is oft descried;
Such signs appear, and yet they seem their fury great to hide.
They are ashamed, I wot ne'er what. Come hither, quickly bring
Some salt with thee, and it upon the sacrifice go fling.
What? are their looks pleasant and mild, and do they gently bide
The touching of thy sacred hands?

Man. What may this thing betide?
The bull—a wonder great to see!—his head on high he lifts;
And, turnèd still unto the east, from thence it always shifts
Still loathing, as he seems to me, of heaven to see the light,
Oft scowling with his blearing eyes, with ghastly ruthful sight.

Tir. But doth one blow drive them to ground, or more than one they
    have?

Man. The heifer, as it seemed, inflamed with courage stout and brave
Upon the mortal blade did rush, and there herself destroys,
When out the blood it foaming spouts, and mounts unto the skies.
The brawny bull, twice struck or thrice, with groveling groaning tires;
And, toiling up and down, he moils, and still to live desires,

And yet at length with much ado his brutish breath expires.

Tir. What, doth the wound wide open gape, or is it closèd up,
Or doth the deepness of the hole the blood in-soaking sup?

Man. Out of the wounded heifer's breast black-bluish waters rush.
As for the bull, but little blood out of his wounds doth gush;
It back rebounds, and from his mouth and eyes by streams doth flow.
But what these dreadful signs portend the gods alone do know.

Tir. By this unhappy sacrifice great fears within me rise.
But tell me now, in the inner parts what secret hidden lies?

Man. O father, what means this, alas! that more than wonted guise
The inwards stir, and shake my hands, and heaving oft arise?
The blood by streams out of the veins full strangely skips aloft,
The heart all scorched and hidden lies, and streaks are seen full oft
Of color very wan and pale; the chiefest parts do want.
The liver blackish gall outspurts, and, somewhat rising, pants;
And that that mischiefs great to kingdoms doth foreshow:
Two heads[17] are seen, and yet both heads one skin doth overgrow
And overhills them quite; but yet the skin it is so thin
That easily one may discern with lieth hid therein.
And, that which horror doth increase, a man may plainly see
How both the heart, the lights, the lungs, and all, disturbèd be.[18]
The fearful noise and sound you hear is not of beasts, but fire
That roaring on the altars makes, presaging wreckful ire
Of angry gods, who do foretell some purpose that they have
For to revenge some foul misdeed that vengeance just doth crave.
No part his proper place observes, nor keeps his order due,
But altogether quite disguised, with an unwonted hue,
Misshapen, out of frame, transformed, displacèd quite, alas!
What thing is that the gods intend ere long to bring to pass?

Oed. Why, then, declare from whence and why these deadly signs
   arise.
With courage stout I will it hear; it shall not once agrise

---

[17] Of the liver; *i.e.*, lobes. The two lobes, like the division of the sacrificial
flame above, probably prophesy the strife of Eteocles and Polynices (see *Index
of Proper Names, s.v. Creon 1*).

[18] The rest of this description seems to have been based on a corrupt text:
the next four verses should come at the end; and two of the portents, the finding
of a foetus in the unmated heifer and the reanimation of the animals' corpses,
are omitted.

My valiant mind. Extremest ills have pow'r to banish fear.

Tir. You will wish that unheard which you so much desire to hear.

Oed. Yet since the gods will have him known, tell me, I say, his name
That slew your king.

Tir. Nor wing nor womb of bird or beast the same
Can tell, O King. New sacrifice, new means we must invent.
From dreadful dark infernal damps some Fury must be sent[19]
These mischiefs great for to unfold. Or else King Ditis, he
That empire keeps on grisly ghosts, entreated needs must be
These things forthwith for to disclose. Tell who shall have the charge;
A king thou art, then mayst not thou go through those kingdoms large.

Oed. Then, noble Creon, thou shalt go; this pain is first for thee,
Who must this crown and kingdom great enjoy after me.

The Third Act

Oedipus, Creon[20]

Oed. Though that thy face where sadness sits in heavy mourning
 guise
Nought else portend but deadly griefs, and mischiefs still to rise,
Yet tell some means whereby at length the gods we may appease,
And purchase to our kingdom's waste some hope of health and ease.

Cre. Alas, you bid me that disclose which fear doth bid me hide.

Oed. If that the Theban cities great, by doleful plagues destroyed,
Pierce not thy heart, yet oughtest thou these kingdoms for to rue,
Which were unto thy brother's house of ancient title[21] due.

[19] The preceding lines refer to divination by observation of the flight of birds
(augury) or by the inspection of the entrails of sacrificed animals (extispicy). In
the original, the ghost of King Laius is to be summoned from the Lower World,
rather than some Fury.

[20] In the original, the interval between the acts, the time taken by Creon for
his necromancy, is filled by a chorus, introduced by Tiresias, in praise of Bacchus,
patron god of Thebes.

[21] The verse rendered by "yet . . . due," "at sceptra moveant lapsa cognatae
domus," "yet let the tottering sceptre of a house related to you move you," seems
to refer only to the fact that Oedipus is Creon's brother-in-law. If "brother" in
Neville refers to Oedipus, it is hard to justify "of ancient title due," since
Oedipus, so far as he now knows, has no other claim to the throne than his
killing of the Sphinx. Creon himself had a claim to the throne as the descendant
of Pentheus, but he had no brother.

Cre. You wish the thing to know which you will wish unknown at
  length.

Oed. Why so? A simple remedy, of little force and strength,
Is ignorance of our estate when dangers us betide.
But what? wilt thou so great a good for common safety hide?

Cre. Irksome med'cines and perilous in sickness I abhor.

Oed. And I likewise at subjects' hands disdain to take a dor.
Speak out with speed, or else by proof of torment thou shalt find
How dangerous a case it is to gall a prince's mind.

Cre. Kings often use to wish untold what they had tell before.

Oed. Go to, dispatch, and cease in time to vex me any more!
Except that thou forthwith to me this heinous deed disclose,
The gods I do protest, to death for all thou only goes.

Cre. O pardon me, most noble King; O let me hold my peace!
Of all the graces princes grant what favor may be less?

Oed. As though the silence hurts not more both king and country's
  weal
Than speech, oft-times, which subjects' thoughts to princes doth reveal!
Dispatch at once, stir me no more; thou know'st my guise of old.

Cre. Silence denied, what privilege may silly subject hold?

Oed. A traitor he is who silence keeps when king commands to speak.

Cre. Then pardon my constrainèd speech, since silence for to break
You me compel. A doleful tale, O King, my tongue must tell,
And which I fear your majesty will not interpret well.

Oed. Was ever man rebuked for that that he was bid to say?

Cre. Well, then, since needs I must, I am contented to obey.
A wood there is, from city far, enhanced with stately trees,
Where many a plant and herb doth grow which Phoebus never sees.
With everduring bushes green the cypress there doth rise
And puts his old and lofty head within the cloudy skies,
The ancient time-eaten oak with crooked bended limbs,
The teil-tree fine, the alder which in Neptune's kingdoms swims,[22]
The bays with bitter berries eke, the elms, dear friends to vines,
And many a noble tree besides, as myrtles, firs, and pines.
Amidst them all one tree there is with large outstretchèd arms,
Whose roaring sound and creaking noise the lesser woods ycharms,
And overshades them all, a tree of monstrous huge estate

[22] The alder was much used in ship-building in ancient times; elms were
planted as vine props.

Beset with fearful woods. There is that dire and dreadful gate
That leads to loathsome Limbo lake, and pits that ever flow,
Where chokèd miry mud doth stream with slimy course full slow.
Here when the priest was entered in, with comely aged pace,
He stayèd not; no need there was, for night was still in place.[23]
Then all the ground wide open gapes, and smothering vapors rise,
And fire and smoke, and stifling stink, mounts up into the skies.
The priest, with wailing weed yclad, his fatal rod out took;
And, entering in in black array, full often times it shook,
With heavy cheer and doleful pace. His hoary hair was twined
With boughs of mortal yew, a tree wherewith the mourners wind
Their mourning heads, and garlands make. In this guise all arrayed,
The sacred priest doth enter in, with trembling limbs dismayed.
Then in the sheep and oxen black by backward course are drawn;
And odors sweet, and frankincense, on flaming fires are thrown.
The beasts, on burning altars cast, do quake with scorchèd limbs,
And bloody streams, with fire mixed, about the altars swims.
Then on the dark infernal gods and him that rules them all,
With deadly shrieking voice, aloud the prophet gins to call,
And rolls the magic verse in mouth, and hidden arts doth prove
Which either power have to appease or else the gods to move.
Then bloody streaming liquors black with broiling heat do boil,
And all the beasts consume and burn. The prophet then to toil
Begins, and mixèd wine and milk upon the altars throws;
And all the dungeon dark and wide, with streaming blood it flows.
Then out with thund'ring voice again the prophet calls and cries,
And straight as much with mumbling mouth he champs in secret wise.
The trees do turn, the rivers stand, the ground with roaring shakes,
And all the world, as seems to me, with fearful trembling quakes.
"I am heard, I am heard!" then out aloud the priest began to cry,
When all the damnèd souls by heaps abroad outrushing fly.
Then woods, with rumbling noise, do oft resounding make,
And heaven and earth together go, and boughs and trees do creak,
And thunders roar, and lightnings flash, and waves aloft do fly,
And ground retires, and dogs do bawl. And beasts are heard to cry,
An whether long of Acheron, that loathsome flood that flows
All stinking streams, or of the earth, that out her bowels throws,

---

[23] *I.e.,* night was always there. Ordinarily necromancy could be practiced only at night, but these woods were always dark as night.

Free place to sprites to give, or of that fierce infernal hound[24]
That at such times doth bustling make with chains and rattling sound.
The earth all wide it open gapes, and I did see on ground
The gods, with color pale and wan, that those dark kingdoms keep;
And very Night I saw indeed, and thousand shapes, to creep
From out those filthy stinking lakes and loathsome pits of Hell,
Where all the evils under sun in darksome shades do dwell.
So quaking all for fear, I stood with mind right sore appalled,
Whilst on those gods with trembling mouth the priest full often called,
Who all at once out of their dens did skip with grisly face;
And monsters grim and stinging snakes seemed t'wander in that place,
And all the foulest fiends of Hell and Furies all were there,
And all transformèd ghosts and sprites that ever Hell did bear,
With Cares, and all Diseases vile, that mortal minds do crush.
All those, and more, I saw out of those dungeons deep to rush;
And Age I saw, with shriveled face, and Need, and Fear, and Death,
And fire and flames and thousand ills out from those pits to breathe.
Then was I gone, and quite amazed—the wench in worser case;
And yet of old acquainted with her father's art she was.
The priest himself unmovèd stood, and boldly cited out
Whole armies of King Ditis' men, who, clust'ring in a rout,
All flutt'ring thin like clouds, dispersed abroad in air do fly,
And, bearing sundry shapes and forms, do scud about in sky.
A thousand woods, I think, have not so many leaves on trees,
Ten thousand meadows fresh have not so many flowers for bees,
Ten hundred thousand rivers not so many fowls can show,
Nor all the drops and streams and gulfs that in the seas do flow,
If that they might be weighed, can sure so great a number make,
As could those shapes and forms that flew from out of Limbo lake:
Both Tantalis, and Zethus too, and pale Amphion's ghost,
And Agave, and after her ten thousand sprites do post.
Then Pentheus, and more and more, in like estate ensue,
Till out at length comes Laius, with foul and grisly hue,
Uncomely dressed, in wretched plight, with filth all overgrown,
All pierced with wounds—I loath to speak!—with blood quite
overflown,
A miser right as seemed to me, and most of misers all.

[24] Cerberus, *q.v.* in *Index of Proper Names*.

Thus, in this case, at length he spake, and thus began to call:
"O Cadmus' cruel city vile, that still delights in blood,
O Cadmus, thou which kinsmen's death account'st as chiefest good,[25]
Tear out the bloody bowels of your children! Learn of me:
Do that and more, rather than you would bide the day to see
Like ills as late on me are lit. Lo, mother's love, alas,
Hath caused the greatest misery that e'er in Thebe was.
The country with the wrath of gods at this time is not tossed,
Nor earth nor air infected's not the cause that all be lost,
No, no! A bloody king is cause of all these mischiefs great,
A bloody wretch, a wretched child that sits in father's seat
And mother's bed defiles, O wretch, and enters in again
In places whence he came from once, and doubleth so her pain,
Whilst that he fills the hapless womb wherein himself did lie
With graceless seed, and causeth her twice childbirth's pangs to try.
Unhappy son! but father worse and most unhappy, he
By whom the laws of sacred shame so sore confounded be;
For that that very beasts, almost, do all abhor to do,
Even of his mother's body he hath gotten brothers two.
O mischief great! O dreadful deed! Than Sphinx O monster more!
Example unto ages all, of gods foretold before.
But I thee, thee that sceptre holdst, thy father, will pursue
And wreak myself on thee and thine with plagues and vengeance due;
All restless rage of spite and pain I will upon thee blow,
And all the Furies foul of Hell upon thee I will throw.
I will subvert thy houses clean for this, thy loathsome lust;
I will do this, thou wretch, and thee and thine consume to dust.
Wherefore dispatch; at once, I say, into exile drive your king!
That ground that first of all he leaves with fresh green grass shall spring,
And sweet and pleasant air and healthful blasts shall rise;
And all the evils under sun that mortal men surprise,
The pocks, the piles, the botch, the blain, and death, with him shall fly,
And with him mischiefs all shall pass, and monsters under sky.
And as for him, I know he would depart with willing mind,
But I will clog his feet and hands. His way he shall not find,
But, groping with his aged staff, shall pass from place to place.
This shall he do; and none shall rue upon his ruthful case.

[25] A reference to the mutual slaughter of the sons of the dragon's teeth (see
Index of Proper Names, s.v. Cadmus).

Rid you the monster from the earth; for heaven let me alone."[26]
No sooner said but straight away his dreadful ghost was gone,
And fast, by thousands, after him th' other sprites in-hide.
Then cold and trembling fear began through all my bones to glide.

   Oed. The thing I always feared, I see, upon me now is laid;
But slender props they are, God wot! whereby your treason is stayed:
Merope, my mother dear, shall me from this defend;
Polybus eke shall purge me quite; from actions all that tend
To murder or to incest vile they both shall me excuse.
In such a case, no means at all of trial I refuse.
Lay what you can unto my charge, no fault in me remained:
The Thebans, long ere I came here, of Laius' death complained;
My mother yet alive, my father still in like estate—
No, no! this is some doltish drift of yon false prophet's pate!
Or else some mighty god above doth bear me no good will
And seeks by plagues on me to wreak his wrathful vengeance still.
Ah, sir, I am glad at length I smell your drifts and fetches fine;
I know the whole confederacy, your sleights I can untwine!
That beastly priest, that blear-eyed wretch, belies the gods and me;
And thee, thou traitor, in my place hath promised king to be.

   Cre. Alas, would I my sister of her lawful kingdom spoil?
Think you such treason may have place in brother's breast to boil?
If that mine oath could me not keep content with my degree
But that, contemning mean estate, I would climb, aloft to be,
Yet should ill fortune me deter from such attempts, I trow,
Whose guise it is on princes' heads huge heaps of cares to throw.
I would advise your grace betimes this charge from you to cast
Lest, ling'ring long all unawares, you be oppressed at last.
Assure yourself, in baser state more safer you may live,
And shun a thousand cares and griefs which princes' hearts do rive.

   Oed. And dost thou me exhort, thou slave, my kingdom for to leave?
O faithless head, O shameless heart that could such treasons weave!
Dar'st thou attempt, thou villain vile, this thing to me to break,
And fear'st not thou in such a case so boldly for to speak?

   Cre. I would persuade them so, O King, who freely might possess
Their realms, such piteous cares, I see, do princes' hearts oppress;

[26] *I.e.,* "As for heaven, let me alone rid him of that," referring to the blindness which his curse will bring upon Oedipus.

But as for you, of force you must your fortune's change abide.

Oed. The surest way for them that gape for kingdoms large and wide
Is, first, things mean, and rest, and peace, and base estate to praise,
And yet with tooth and nail to toil to mount aloft all ways.
So, often times, most restless breasts do chiefly rest commend.

Cre. Shall not my service long suffice my truth for to defend?

Oed. Time is the only means for such as thou to work their will.

Cre. It is so, Sire, but as for me, of goods I have my fill:
A great resort, a pleasant life from princely cares exempt—
All these might surely me dissuade from such a foul attempt.
There is no day, almost, O King, the whole year thoroughout
Wherein some royal gifts are not from countries round about
Unto me sent, both gold and pearls, and things of greater cost
Which I let pass, lest I should seem but vainly for to boast.
Besides, the life of many a man hath been preserved by me.
In such a blissful state, O King, what can there wanting be?

Oed. Good Fortune can no mean observe, but still she presseth higher.

Cre. Shall I then guileless die, alas! my cause and all untried?

Oed. Were unto you at any time my life, my deeds descried?
Did any man defend me yet, or else my causes plead?
And guiltless yet I am condemned. To this you do me lead,
And me express example give, which I intend to take:
What measure you do mete to me, like measure must I make.[27]

Cre. The mind which causeless dread appalls true cause of fear
        betrays:
That conscience is not guiltless, sure, which every blast dismays.

Oed. He that in midst of perils deep and dangers hath been cast
Doth seek all means to shun like ills as he hath overpassed.

Cre. So hatreds rise.

Oed. He that too much doth use ill-will to fear
Unskillful is, and knows not how he ought himself to bear
In king's estate; for fear alone doth kingdoms chiefly keep.
Then he that thus doth arm himself from fear all free may sleep.

Cre. Whoso the cruel tyrant plays, and guiltless men doth smite,
He dreadeth them that do him dread, so fear doth chiefly light
On causers chief—a just revenge for bloody minds at last!

[27] Here Creon should ask, "But what if I am innocent?" and Oedipus reply,
"Kings usually have as much fear of uncertain as of certain dangers."

Oed. Come take this traitor vile away! In dungeon deep him fast
Enclose. There for his due deserts let him abide such pain
And scourge of mind as meet it is false traitors to sustain.

Chorus[28]

See, see the miserable state of princes' careful life!
What raging storms, what bloody broils, what toil, what endless strife
Do they endure! O God, what plagues, what grief do they sustain!
A princely life? No, no! No doubt an everduring pain,
A state e'en fit for men on whom Fortune would wreak her will,
A place for cares to couch them in, a door wide open still
For griefs and dangers, all that be, to enter when they list.
A king these mates must ever have; it boots not to resist.
Whole floods of privy pinching fear, great anguish of the mind,
Apparent plagues, and daily griefs, these playferes princes find,
And other none, with whom they spend and pass their wretched days.
Thus, he that princes' lives and base estate together weighs
Shall find the one a very hell, a perfect infelicity,
The other eke a heaven right, exempted quite from misery.
Let Oedipus example be of this unto you all,
A mirror meet, a pattern plain of princes' care-full thrall.
Who late in perfect joy (as seemed) and everlasting bliss
Triumphantly his life out led, a miser now he is,
And most of wretched misers all, even at this present time
With doubtful waves of fear ytossed, subject to such a crime
Whereat my tongue amazèd stays. God grant that at the last
It fall not out as Creon told! Not yet the worst is past.

THE FOURTH ACT

The First Scene

Oedipus, Jocasta

Oed. My mind with doubtful waves of dread is tossèd to and fro.
I wot not what to say, alas! I am tormented so.
For all the gods on me do cry for pains and vengeance due:
They say that these my guiltless hands King Laius lately slew.

---

[28] This is an addition of Neville's. The original choral ode at this point tells
of the curses which have dogged Thebes and the House of Cadmus.

But this my conscience, void of crime, and mind, from mischief free,
(To gods untried, to me well known) deny it so to be.
Full well I do remember, once by chance I did dispatch
A man who sought by force with me presumptuously to match.
His purpose was—a fond attempt!—my chariot for to stay.
This I remember well enough, the strife was in the way,
And he a man well steeped in years, and I a lusty blood,
And yet of mere disdain and pride in vain he me withstood.
But this from Thebès far was done—a crooked three-pathed way,
That was the place in which we fought; it hard by Phocis lay.
Dear wife, resolve my doubts at once, and me expressly tell
How old was Laius the King when this mischance befell.
Was he of fresh and lusty years, or stricken well in age,
When he was killed? Oh, ease my thoughts of this tormenting rage!
   Joc. Betwixt an old man and a young, but nearer to an old.
   Oed. Were there great bands of men with him his person to uphold?
   Joc. Some by the way deceivèd were, and some deterred by pain;
A few, by toil and labor long, did with their prince remain.
   Oed. Were any slain in his defense?
   Joc. Of one report is rife
Who, constant in his prince's cause, full stoutly lost his life.
   Oed. It is enough. I know the man that hath this mischief done.
The number and the place agree; the time untried alone
Remains—then tell what time he died, and when that he was slain.
   Joc. 'Tis ten years since. You now revive my chiefest cares again.

The Second Scene

Senex, Oedipus

   Sen. The Corinth people all, O King, in father's place to reign
Do call your Grace. Polybus doth eternal rest obtain.
   Oed. O God, what fortune vile doth me oppress on every side!
How do my sorrows still increase! Tell how my father died.
   Sen. No sickness, Sire, but very age did of his life him reave.
   Oed. And is he dead indeed, not slain? What joy may I conceive!
How may I now triumph! The gods to witness I do call,
To whom are known my hidden thoughts and secret workings all,
Now may I lift to skies my hands, my hands from mischief free—
But yet the chiefest cause of fear remaineth still to me.

Sen. Your father's kingdom ought all dread out of your mind to drive.

Oed. That I confess; but secret thoughts my trembling heart do rive
With inward doubt of deep distress: my mother I do fear.
This grudge is that continually my heart doth rend and tear.

Sen. Do you your mother fear, on your return that only stays?

Oed. I fear not her, but from her sight a godly zeal me frays.

Sen. What? will you her a widow leave?

Oed. Now, now thou wound'st my heart!
This, this and only this, alas! is cause of all my smart.

Sen. Tell me, O King, what doubtful fear doth press thy princely
breast;
Kings' counsels I can well conceal, that be with cares oppressed.

Oed. Lest, as Apollo hath foretold, I should a marriage make
With mine own mother. Only this foul fear doth make me quake.

Sen. Such vain and peevish fears at length from out your breast exile:
Merope your mother is not in deed. You do yourself beguile.

Oed. What vantage should it be to her, adopted sons to have?

Sen. A kingdom she shall gain thereby. Her husband laid in grave,
The chiefest prop to stay her realms from present confusion
Is children for to have, and hope of lawful succession.

Oed. What are the means whereby thou dost these secrets
understand?

Sen. Myself your Grace, an infant, gave into your father's hand.

Oed. Didst thou me to my father give? Who then gave me to thee?

Sen. A shepherd, Sire, that wonted on Cithaeron's hills to be.

Oed. What made thee in those woods to range? What hadst thou
there to do?

Sen. Upon those hills my beasts I kept, sometime a shepherd too.

Oed. What knots, what privy marks hast thou whereby thou dost me
know?

Sen. The holes that through your feet are bored, from whence your
name did grow.[29]

Oed. Declare forthwith what was his name that gave me unto thee.

Sen. The King's chief shepherd, then that was, delivered you to me.

Oed. What was his name?

Sen. O King, old men's remembrance soon doth fail;
Oblivion, for the chiefest part, doth hoary heads assail

---

[29] Oedi-pus: swollen foot; *v. Index of Proper Names.*

And drowns their former memory of things long out of mind.

   Oed. What, canst thou know the man by sight?

   Sen. Perhaps I should him find

And know by face. Things overwhelmed by time, and quite oppressed,

A small mark oft to mind revokes, and fresh renews in breast.

   Oed. Sirs, bid the herdsmen forthwith drive their beasts to altars all;

Away with speed, make haste, the master shepherds to me call.

   Sen. Since that your dest'ny this doth hide, and fortune it detain

And closely keep, let it be so. From opening that refrain

That long concealed hath hidden lain; that seek not to disclose.

Such thing, outsearched and found, ofttimes against the searcher goes.

   Oed. Can any mischief greater be than this that now I fear?

   Sen. Advise you well; remember first what weight this thing doth

     bear

That thus you go about to search and sift with tooth and nail.

Observe the golden mean, beware, bear still an equal sail.

Your country's wealth, O King, your life and all upon this lies.

Though you stir not, be sure at length your fortune you descries.

   Oed. A happy state for to disturb doth not at all behoove;[30]

When things be at the worst, of them a man may safely move.

   Sen. Can you have aught more excellent than is a prince's state?

Beware lest of your parents found it you repent too late.[31]

   Oed. No, father, no, I warrant that: repent not I, I trow.

I seek it not to that intent: I have decreed to know

The matter at the full, wherefore I will it now pursue.

Lo, Phorbas where he trembling comes, with comely agèd hue,

To whom of all the King's flock, then, the care and charge was due.

Dost thou his name, his speech, his face, or yet his person know?

   Sen. Methinks I should have seen his face; and yet I cannot show

The places where I have him seen. Small time brings such a change

As well-acquainted faces oft to us appear full strange.

This look is neither throughly known nor yet unknown to me.

I cannot tell. I doubt it much, and yet it may be he.

In Laius' time, long since, when he these kingdoms great did keep,

Wast thou not on Cithaeron hills chief shepherd to his sheep?

---

[30] Neville, with the old editions, assigns this verse somewhat inappropriately to Senex.

[31] It repent you of: you repent.

The Third Scene

Phorbas, Senex, Oedipus

Pho. Sometime a charge of sheep I had, unworthy though I were,
And did upon those hills chief rule on other shepherds bear.

Sen. Know'st thou not me?

Pho. I cannot tell.

Oed. Didst thou once give this man
A child? Speak out! Why dost thou stay? If so, declare it then;
Why dost thou blush, and doubting stand? Truth seeketh no delay.

Pho. Things out of mind you call again, almost quite worn away.

Oed. Confess, thou slave! or else, I swear, thou shalt constrainèd be.

Pho. Indeed I do remember, once an infant young by me
Delivered was unto this man, but, well I wot, in vain:
I know he could not long endure nor yet alive remain.
Long since he is dead, I know it well; he lives not at this day.

Sen. No? God forbid! He lives no doubt, and long may live, I pray.

Oed. Why dost thou say the child is dead that thou this man did give?

Pho. With irons sharp his feet were bored; I know he could not live,
For of the sore a swelling rose. I saw the blood to gush
From out of both the wounds, and down by pouring streams to flush.

Sen. Now stay, O King! No farther now! You know almost the
    truth.[32]

Oed. Whose child was it? Tell me forthwith!

Pho. I dare not, for mine oath.[33]

Oed. Thine oath, thou slave? Some fire here! I'll charm thine oath
    and thee
With fire and flames, except forthwith thou tell the truth to me.

Pho. Oh pardon me![34] Though rude I seem, I seek not to withstand
Your Grace's mind, most noble King; my life is in your hand.

Oed. Tell me the truth! What child? and whose? What was his
    mother's name?

Pho. Born of—*your wife.*

---

[32] Modern editors of Seneca assign this verse to Oedipus, addressing himself.

[33] *I.e.*, of loyalty to Oedipus as King.

[34] The rest of this speech should be Oedipus': "If I seem to thee cruel or headstrong, thou hast thy vengeance in thine hand: tell me the truth."

Oed. O gaping earth, devour my body quite![35]
Or else thou god that ruler art of houses void of light,
To Hell my soul with thunderbolts, to Hell my soul down drive
Where grisly ghosts in darkness weep, and endless pain do live.
For thee alone these plagues do rage, for thee these mischiefs rise,
For thee the earth lies desolate, for thee, thou wretch, the skies
Infected are, for thee, for thee, and for thy filthy lust,
A hundred thousand guiltless men consumèd are to dust.
O people, throw, cast heaps of stones upon this hateful head!
Bathe all your swords within my breast! You Furies, overshed
My restless thoughts with raging woes; and plunged in seas of pain
Let me those horrors still endure which damnèd souls sustain.
You citizens of stately Thebes, vex me with torments due:
Let father, son, and wife, and all, with vengeance me pursue.
Let those that for my sake alone with plagues tormented be
Throw darts, cast stones, fling fire and flames and tortures all on me.
O shame! O slander of the world! O hate of gods above!
Confounder, oh! of nature! Thou to laws of sacred love
Even from thy birth an open foe! Thou didst deserve to die
As soon as thou wast born. Go, go, unto the court thee hie;
There with thy mother, slave, triumph! Rejoice, as thou may'st do
Who hast thy house increasèd with unhappy children so.
Make haste! with speed away! something thy mischiefs worthy find,
And on thyself wreak all the spite of thy revenging mind!

Chorus[36]

Fortune, the guide of human life, doth all things change at will,
And stirring still, with restless thoughts our wretched minds doth fill.
In vain men strive their stars to keep when hideous tempests rise
And blust'ring wind of dangers deep set death before their eyes.
Who saith he doth her fawning feel, and changeth not his mind
When fickle fit of Fortune's wheel doth turn by course of kind?
These grievous plagues from private house to princely thrones do flow,

[35] The following speech, although true to the original in spirit, is considerably expanded in the translation.

[36] This ode, although similar in theme to the original, is not a translation or paraphrase. Seneca's ode at this point is a short piece praising moderation in all things, and illustrating the point with the story of Icarus and Daedalus.

And oft their minds with cares they souse, and thick upon them strew
Whole heaps of grief and dire debate. A woeful thing to see
A princely life to miser's state converted for to be!
O Oedipus, thy fatal fall, thy dreadful mischiefs right,
Thy doleful state, thy misery, thy thrice unhappy plight,
These things shall blaze through all the world. What heart may then
 rejoice
At thy distress? I can no more. My tears do stop my voice.
But what is he that yonder stamps and raging puffs and blows,
And often shakes his vexèd head? Some mischief great he knows.
Good sir, your count'nance doth import some great and fearful thing;
Tell us therefore, if that you may, what news from court you bring.

The Fifth Act

The First Scene

Nuntius[37]

Nun. When Oedipus, accursed wretch! his fatal falls had spied,
To Hell he damned his wretched soul, and on the gods he cried
For vengeance due; and posting fast with frantic mood and grisly hue,
Unto his doleful court he went, his thoughts for to pursue.
Much like a lion, ramping wild, his furious head that shakes
And roars with thund'ring mouth aloud and often gnashing makes,
None otherwise this miser fared, a loathsome sight to see.
Beside himself for very rage, he still desires to die;
And rolling round his wretched eyes, with visage pale and wan,
Ten thousand curses out he pours. Himself the unhappiest man
Of all that live he doth account, as justly he may do,
A wretch, a slave, a caitiff vile, the cause of all our woe;
And in this case, inflamed with spite, he cries, he stamps, he raves,
And, boiling in his secret thoughts, he still desires to have
All torments under sun that may his cares conceived increase.
Oh wretched wight, what should he do? What man may him release?
Thus foaming all for rage at mouth, with sighs and sobs and groans,
His damnèd head ten thousand times, as oft his wearied bones

[37] The following account of the Messenger follows in general the development
of the original, but Neville has expanded it by the addition of much rhetorical
embroidery of the details.

He beats, and often puffing makes, and roars and swells and sweats,
And on the gods for death he calls, for death he still entreats.
Three times he did begin to speak, and thrice his tongue did stay;
At length he crièd out aloud, "O wretch, away, away!
Away, thou monstrous beast!" he said, "Wilt thou prolong thy life?
Nay, rather some man strike this breast with stroke of bloody knife;
Or all you gods above on me your flaming fires outcast
And dints of thunderbolts down throw. This is my prayer last.
What greedy vile devouring gripe upon my guts will gnaw?
What tiger fierce my hateful limbs will quite asunder draw?
Lo, here I am, you gods, lo, here! Wreak now on me your will.
Now, now, you fiery fiends of Hell, of vengeance take your fill;
Send out some wild outrageous beast, send dogs me to devour,
Or else all ills you can devise at once upon me pour.
O woeful soul, O sinful wretch, why dost thou fear to die?
Death only rids from woes thou know'st; then stoutly death defy!"
With that his bloody fatal blade from out his sheath he draws;
And loud he roars with thund'ring voice, "Thou beast, why dost thou
      pause?
Thy father, cursèd caitiff thou, thy father thou hast slain,
And in thy mother's bed hast left an everduring stain;
And brothers thou hast got—nay, sons (thou liest) thy brothers all
They are. Thus for thy monstrous lust thy country down doth fall.
And think'st thou, then, for all these ills enough so short a pain?
Think'st thou the gods will be appeased if thou forthwith be slain?
So many mischiefs done, and is't enough one stroke to bide?
Account'st thou it sufficient pains, that once thy sword should glide
Quite through thy guilty breast for all? Why, then, dispatch and die;
So may'st thou recompense thy father's death sufficiently—
Let it be so; what mends unto thy mother wilt thou make?
Unto thy children what? These plagues, O wretch, how wilt thou slake
That thus for thee thy country waste? One push shall end them all?
A proper fetch, a fine device! For thee a worthy fall!
Invent, thou monstrous beast, forthwith a fall even worthy for
Thyself invent, whom all men hate and loath, and do abhor;
And as Dame Nature's lawful course is broke, O wretch, by thee,
So let to such a mischief great thy death agreeing be.
Oh, that I might a thousand times my wretched life renew!
Oh, that I might revive and die by course, in order due,

Ten hundred thousand times and more! then should I vengeance take
Upon this wretched head, then I perhaps in part should make
A meet amends indeed for this my foul and loathsome sin,
Then should the proof of pain reprove the life that I live in.
The choice is in thy hand, thou wretch; then use thine own discretion
And find a means whereby thou may'st come to extreme confusion,
And that that oft thou may'st not do, let it prolongèd be.
Thus, thus may'st thou procure at length an endless death to thee.
Search out a death whereby thou may'st perpetual shame obtain,
And yet not die, but still to live in everlasting pain.
Why stay'st thou, man? Go to, I say, what mean these blubb'ring tears?
Why weep'st thou thus, alas! too late? Leave off thy foolish fears.
And is't enough to weep, think'st thou? Shall tears and wailing serve?
No, wretch, it shall not be! Thou dost ten thousand deaths deserve.
Mine eyes do dally with me, I see, and tears do still outpour;
Shall tears suffice? No, no, not so! I shall them better score.
Out with thine eyes!" he said; and then, with fury fierce inflamed,
Like to a bloody raging fiend and monstrous beast untamed,
With fiery flaming spotted cheeks, his breast he often beats,
And scratch and tear his face he doth, and skin asunder treats,
That scarce his eyes in head could stand, so sore he them besets.
With furious fierce outrageous mind he stamps and cries aloud,
And roars and rails with ramping rage. Thus, in this case he stood
Perplexed and vexèd sore in mind, with deadly sighs and tears—
When suddenly all frantically himself from ground he tears,
And rooteth out his wretched eyes, and sight asunder tears.
Then gnasheth he his bloody teeth, and bites, and gnaws, and champs,
His eyes all bathed and brued in blood, for fury fierce he stamps;
And, raging more than needs, alas! his eyes quite rooted out,
The very holes in vain he scrapes, so sore the wretch doth doubt
Lest sight should chance for to remain, he rends and mangles quite
His face, his nose, his mouth; and all whereon his hands do light
He rigs and rives. Thus foully rayed, alas, in piteous plight
At length his head aloft he lifts, and therewith gives a shright;
And when he sees that all is gone, both light, and sight, and all,
Then screeching out he thus begins upon the gods to call:
"Now spare you, Gods, now spare at length my country pressed to fall!
I have done that you did command; your wraths revengèd be.
This wretched look, this mangled face is fittest now for me."

Thus speaking, down the blackish blood by streams doth gushing flow
Into his mouth; and clotted lumps of flesh the place do strew
Wherein he stands. Beware betimes, by him beware, I speak unto you all;
Learn justice, truth, and fear of God by his unhappy fall.

Chorus[38]

Man's life with tumbling fatal course of fortune's wheel is rolled.
To it give place, for it doth run all swiftly, uncontrolled;
And cares and tears are spent in vain, for it cannot be stayed,
Since high decree of heavenly powers perforce must be obeyed.
What mankind bides or does on earth it cometh from above;
Then wailing groans poured out in grief do nought at all behoove.
Our life must have her pointed course—alas, what shall I say?—
As fates decree, so things do run. No man can make them stay;
For at our birth to gods is known our latter dying day.
No prayer, no art, not God himself may fatal fates resist;
But fastened all in fixèd course, unchangèd they persist.
Such end them still ensues as they appointed were to have.
Then fly all fear of fortune's change, seek not to live a slave
Enthralled in bondage vile to fear; for fear doth often bring
Dest'nies that dreaded be, and mischiefs feared upon us fling.
Yea, many a man hath come unto his fatal end by fear;
Wherefore set peevish fear aside, and worthy courage bear.
And, thou that subject art to death, regard thy latter day,[39]
Think no man blest before his end. Advise thee well and stay:
Be sure his life and death and all be quite exempt from misery,
Ere thou do once presume to say, "This man is blest and happy."
But thou, alas! see where he comes, a wretch without a guide,
Bereft of sight, half spoiled of life, without all pomp and pride.

The Second Scene

Oedipus, Chorus, Jocasta

Oed. Well, well, 'tis done. More yet? No, no, no mischief more
remains.

[38] Neville's ode here differs from Seneca's chiefly in its lack of mythological reference and in its somewhat expanded development of the ideas.

[39] The idea expressed in this and the following three verses, though a commonplace in antiquity, is not brought into this ode by Seneca.

My father's rites performèd are. What god, on miser's pains
That rues, within this cloud hath rolled and wrapped my wretched
    pate?
Ah, sirs, this is a life alone, this is a happy state,
This is a case e'en fit for thee, for thee, thou wretch! for thee
From whose accursed sight the sun, the stars and all do flee.
Yet mischiefs more who gives to do? The dreadful day I have
Escaped. Thou filthy parricide, thou vile mischievous slave,
Unto thy right hand nought thou ow'st: all things performèd be—
Oh, woe is me that ever I lived this luckless day to see![40]
Where am I now? Alas, alas, the light and all doth me
Abhor. O wretched Oedipus, this look is first for thee!

    Cho. See, see, where Jocasta comes, with fierce and furious mood
Quite past herself. For very rage she frets and waxeth wood,
Much like to Cadmus' daughter[41] mad who late her son did kill.
Fain would she speak her mind; for fear, alas! she dares not. Still
She stays; and yet from out her breast these ills have quite exiled
All shamefacedness. See how she looks, with count'nance fierce and
    wild.

    Joc. Fain would I speak—I am afraid. For what should I thee call?
My son? Doubt not, thou art my son. My son thou art, for all
These mischiefs great—alas, alas, I shame my son to see!
O cruel son, where dost thou turn thy face?[42] Why dost thou flee
From me, from me, thy mother dear? Why dost thou shun my sight,
And leave me thus in misery, with cares consumèd quite?

    Oed. Who troubles me? Let me alone; I thought not to be found.
Who now restores mine eyes to me? Mother—or mother's sound:
Our labor all is spent in vain. Now may we meet no more;
The seas divide those meetings vile that we have had before;
The gaping earth divide us both, the one from th' other quite,
Still let our feet repugnant be: so shall I shun the light
That most of all me grieves, so shall I space obtain to wail
These bleeding woes, on every side that do my thoughts assail.

    Joc. The destinies are in fault—blame them—alas, alas, not we!

    Oed. Spare now, leave off to speak in vain; spare now, O mother, me,

[40] This verse and the following, and hence the inappropriate change of mood
which they introduce, are an addition of Neville's.

[41] Agave, *q.v.* in *Index of Proper Names.*

[42] The rest of this speech of Jocasta's has been added by Neville.

By these relics of my dismembered body I thee pray,
By mine unhappy children, pledges left—what shall I say?—
By all the gods I thee beseech, by all that in my name
Is good or bad,[43] let me alone! Alas, you are to blame
To trouble me! You see what hell my hapless heart doth pain;
You see that in my conscience ten thousand horrors reign.

    Joc. O dying heart, O sin-drowned soul, why dost thou faint, alas,
Why dost thou seek and toil in vain these ills to overpass?
What mean these sighs and scalding tears? Why dost thou death refuse,
Thou mate of all his mischiefs, thou by whose means only rues
The law of nature all, by whom, ah, ah! confounded lie
Both god, and man, and beast, and all that either live or die?
Die thou! dispatch, at once thrust through thy vile incestuous breast;
Thou hast none other means, alas! to set thine heart at rest.
Not thou, if God himself, if he his flaming fires should throw
On thee, or mischiefs all by heaps upon thy body strew,
Couldst once for thy deservèd ills due pains or vengeance pay;
Some means, therefore, to wreak God's wrath upon thyself assay.
Death, death now best contenteth me. Then seek a way to die:
So may'st thou yet at length find end for all thy misery.
O son, lend me thy hand! Since that thou art a parricide,
This labor last of all remains, this labor doth thee bide:
Dispatch, rid me, thy mother dear, from all my deadly woe.
It will not be. No prayers avail. Thyself this deed must do;
Take up this sword—go to, with this thy husband late was slain—
Husband? Thou term'st him false; he was thy sire.[44] Oh, deadly pain!
Shall I quite through my breast it drive, or through my throat it thrust?
Canst thou not choose thy wound? Away! die, die, alas! thou must—
This hateful womb then wound, O wretch, this, this with thine own
    hand
Strike, strike it hard, oh, spare it not, since both a husband and
The same a son it bare.

    Cho. Alas, alas, she is slain, she is slain, dispatchèd with a push!
Who ever saw the like to this? See how the blood doth gush![45]
O heavy doleful case! Who can this direful sight endure,
Which for the hideousness thereof might tears of stones procure?

---

[43] The rest of this speech has been added by Neville.

[44] *I.e.*, father-in-law.

[45] The rest of this speech has been added by Neville.

Oed. Thou god, thou teller-out of fates,[46] on thee, on thee I call:
My father only I did owe unto the destinies all.
Now twice a parricide, and worse than I did fear to be,
My mother I have slain, alas! The fault is all in me.[47]
O Oedipus, accursèd wretch, lament thine own calamity,
Lament thy state, thy grief lament, thou caitiff born to misery!
Where wilt thou now become, alas! thy face where wilt thou hide?
O miserable slave, canst thou such shameful torments bide?
Canst thou, which hast thy parents slain, canst thou prolong thy life?
Wilt thou not die, deserving death, thou cause of all the grief
And plagues and dreadful mischiefs all that Theban city press?
Why dost thou seek by longer life thy sorrows to increase?
Why dost thou toil and labor thus in vain? It will not be—
Both God and man, and beast and all, abhor thy face to see.
O earth, why gap'st thou not for me? Why do you not unfold,
You gates of Hell, me to receive? Why do you hence withhold
The fierce infernal fiends from me, from me, so wretched wight?
Why break not all the Furies loose, this hateful head to smite
With plagues, which them deservèd hath? Alas, I am left alone:
Both light and sight and comfort all from me, O wretch! is gone.
O cursed head! O wicked wight whom all men deadly hate,
O beast, what mean'st thou still to live in this unhappy state?
The skies do blush, and are ashamed at these thy mischiefs great;
The earth laments, the heavens weep, the seas for rage do fret
And blustering rise, and storms do stir—and all, thou wretch, for thee
By whose incest and bloody deeds all things disturbèd be
Quite out of course, displacèd quite. O cursèd fatal day!
O mischiefs great! O dreadful times! O wretch, away, away!
Exile thyself from all men's sight. Thy life half spent in misery
Go, end, consume it now outright in thrice as great calamity.
O lying Phoebe, thy oracles my sin and shame surmount:
My mother's death amongst my deeds thou never didst recount,
A meet exploit for me that am to nature deadly foe!
With trembling fearful pace go forth, thou wretched monster, go,
Grope out thy ways on knees in dark, thou miserable slave;
So may'st thou yet in tract of time due pains and vengeance have
For thy mischievous life. Thus, thus the gods themselves decree,

[46] Apollo, *q.v.* in *Index of Proper Names.*
[47] The next twenty-six verses are an interpolation by Neville.

Thus, thus thy fates, thus the skies appoint it for to be.

Then headlong hence, with a mischief hence, thou caitiff vile, away!

Away, away, thou monstrous beast! Go, run—stand, stay,

Lest on thy mother thou do fall. All you that wearied bodies have, with
    sickness overpressed.

Lo, now I fly, I fly away, the cause of your unrest.

Lift up your heads; a better state of air shall straight ensue

When I am gone, from whom alone these dreadful mischiefs grew.

And you that now half dead yet live in wretched miser's case,

Help those whom present torments press. Forth, hie you on apace!

For lo, with me I carry hence all mischiefs under skies,

All cruel fates, diseases all that for my sake did rise;

With me they go, with me both grief, plague, pocks, botch, and all

The ills that either now you press or ever after shall,

With me they go, with me. These mates be meet'st of all for me,

Who am the most unhappiest wretch that ever sun did see.

FINIS

TROAS

The Sixth Tragedy of the Most Grave
and Prudent Author Lucius Annaeus Seneca,
Entitled Troas, with divers and sundry additions
to the same, by Jasper Heywood

To the Reader

ALTHOUGH, GENTLE READER, thou mayst perhaps think me arrogant for that I only, among so many fine wits and towardly youth (with which England this day flourisheth), have enterprised to set forth in English this present piece of the flower of all writers, Seneca, as who say, not fearing what graver heads might judge of me in attempting so hard a thing, yet upon well pondering what next ensueth, I trust both thyself shalt clear thine own suspicion, and thy changed opinion shall judge of me more rightful sentence. For neither have I taken this work first in hand as once intending it should come to light—of well doing whereof I utterly despaired—and being done but for mine own private exercise, I am in mine opinion herein blameless, though I have, to prove myself, privately taken the part which pleased me best of so excellent an author; for better is time spent in the best than other, and at first to attempt the hardest writers shall make a man more prompt to translate the easier with more facility. But now, since by request and friendship of those to whom I could deny nothing this work against my will extorted is out of my hands, I needs must crave thy patience in reading and facility of judgement: when thou shalt apparently see my witless lack of learning, praying thee to consider how hard a thing it is for me to touch at full in all points the author's mind, being in many places very hard and doubtful, and the work much corrupt by the default of evil-printed books; and also how far above my power to keep that grace and majesty of style that Seneca doth, when both so excellent a writer hath passed the reach of all limitation and also this our English tongue, as many think and I here find, is far unable to compare with the Latin. But thou, good reader, if I in any place have swerved from the true sense, or not kept the royalty of speech meet for a tragedy, impute the one to my youth and lack of judgement, the other to my lack of eloquence.

Now, as concerning sundry places augmented and some altered in this my translation: first, forasmuch as this work seemed unto me in some places imperfect—whether left so of the author, or part of it lost, as time devoureth all things, I wot not—I have, where I thought good, with addition of mine own pen supplied the want of some things, as the first Chorus after the First Act, beginning thus: "O ye to whom, etc." Also in the Second Act I have added the speech of Achilles' sprite, rising from Hell to require the sacrifice of Plyxena, beginning in this wise: "Forsaking now, etc." Again, the three last staves of the Chorus after the same act. And as for the third Chorus, which in Seneca beginneth thus: "Quae vocat sedes?," forasmuch as nothing is therein but a heaped number of far and strange countries, considering with myself that the names of so many unknown countries, mountains, deserts, and woods should have no grace in the English tongue, but be a strange and unpleasant thing to the readers (except I should expound the histories of each one, which would be far too tedious), I have in the place thereof made another beginning in this wise: "O Jove that lead'st, etc." Which alteration may be borne withal, seeing that chorus is no part of the substance of the matter. In the rest I have for my slender learning endeavored to keep touch with the Latin, not word for word or verse for verse as to expound it, but, neglecting the placing of the words, observed their sense. Take, gentle reader, this in good worth with all its faults, favor my first beginnings, and amend rather, with good will, such things as herein are amiss, than to deprave or discommend my labor and pains for the faults, seeing that I have herein but only made way to other that can far better do this or like, desiring them that as they can, so they would. Farewell, gentle reader, accept my good will.

THE ARGUMENT

(added to the tragedy by the translator)

The ten years' siege of Troy who list to hear,
And of th'affairs that there befell in fight,
Read ye the works that long since written were
Of all th'assaults, and of that latest night
When turrets' tops in Troy they blazèd bright.
Good clerks they were that have it written well.
As for this work, no word thereof doth tell.

But Dares Phrygian well can all report,
With Dictys eke of Crete, in Greekish tongue,
And Homer tells, to Troy the Greeks resort,
In scannèd verse, and Maro hath it sung;
Each one in writ hath penned a story long.
Who doubts of aught, and casteth care to know,
These antique authors shall the story show.

The ruins twain[48] of Troy, the cause of each,
The glittering helms, in fields the banners spread,
Achilles' ires, and Hector's fights they teach.
There may the gests of many a knight be read,
Patroclus, Pyrrhus, Ajax, Diomed,
With Troilus, Paris, many other more
That day by day there fought in field full sore.

And how the Greeks at end an engine made,
A hugy horse, where many a warlike knight
Enclosèd was, the Trojans to invade,
With Sinon's craft, when Greeks had feignèd flight,
While close they lay at Tenedos from sight,
Or how Aeneas else (as others say)
And false Antenor did the town betray.

[48] For the first ruin of Troy, *v. Hercules* in the *Index of Proper Names.*

But as for me, I naught thereof indite;
Mine author hath not all that story penned.
My pen his words in English must recite
Of latest woes that fell on Troy at end,
What final fates the cruel god could send,
And how the Greeks, when Troy was burnt, gan wreak
Their ire on Trojans; thereof shall I speak.

Not I, with spear who piercèd was in field,
Whose throat there cut or head ycarvèd was,
Nor bloodshed blows that rent both targe and shield
Shall I recite; all that I overpass.
The work I write more woeful is, alas!
For I the mothers' tears must here complain,
And blood of babes that guiltless have been slain.

And such as yet could never weapon wrest,
But on the lap are wont to dandled be,
Nor yet forgotten had the mother's breast,
How Greeks them slew, alas! here shall ye see.
To make report thereof, ay! woe is me;
My song is mischief, murder, misery.
And hereof speaks this doleful tragedy.

Thou Fury fell that from the deepest den
Couldst cause this wrath of Hell on Troy to light,
That workest woe, guide thou my hand and pen
In weeping verse of sobs and sighs to write
As doth mine author them bewail aright.
Help, woeful Muse! for me beseemeth well
Of others' tears with weeping eye to tell.

When battered were to ground the tow'rs of Troy,
In writ as ancient authors do recite,
And Greeks again repaired to seas with joy,
Up riseth here from Hell Achilles' sprite.
Vengeance he craves, with blood his death to quite,
Whom Paris had in Phoebus' temple slain,
With guile betrapped for love of Polyxene.

And wrath of Hell there is none other price
That may assuage; but blood of her alone,
Polyxena, he craves for sacrifice,
With threat'nings on the Grecians many one
Except they shed her blood before they gone.
The sprites, the Hell and deepest pits beneath,
O virgin dear, alas! do thrust thy death.

And Hector's son, Astyanax, alas,
Poor silly fool, his mother's only joy,
Is judged to die by sentence of Calchas.
Alas the while, to death is led the boy,
And tumbled down from turret's tops in Troy.
What ruthful tears may serve to wail the woe
Of Hector's wife, that doth her child forego?

Her pinching pang of heart who may express
But such as of like woes have borne a part?
Or who bewail her ruthful heaviness
That never yet have felt thereof the smart?
Full well they wot the woes of heavy heart;
What is to lose a babe from mother's breast
They know that are in such a case distressed.

First, how the Queen laments the fall of Troy,
As hath mine author done, I shall it write;
Next, how from Hector's wife they led the boy
To die, and her complaints, I shall recite;
The maiden's death then I must last indite.
Now, who that list the Queen's complaint to hear,
In following verse it shall forthwith appear.

The Speakers' Names

Hecuba, Queen of Troy [widow of Priam and now a captive]

A Company of Women [Trojan captives, forming the Chorus]

Talthybius, a Grecian [herald]

Agamemnon, King of Greeks [in the Trojan War]

Astyanax [young son of Hector and Andromache]

Nuntius[49]

Calchas [a Greek priest and prophet]

Pyrrhus [son of Achilles]

Chorus[50]

Andromache [widow of Hector and now a captive]

An Old Man, Trojan [devoted to Andromache]

Ulysses [King of Ithaca, a leader of the Greeks]

Helena [wife of Menelaus, King of Sparta, later of Paris, a prince of Troy; her abduction by Paris was the cause of the war]

The Sprite of Achilles[51] [the most valiant of the Greek leaders, killed by Paris]

[*The shore near the ruins of Troy*]

[49] "Messenger" (Latin word).

[50] In the original the chorus is the group of captive women; but Heywood may suppose that the choral interludes between the acts are to be sung, as in some of Seneca's tragedies, by a chorus which does not participate in the action of the play.

[51] A character added by Heywood. Polyxena also appears in the play, but does not speak.

THE FIRST ACT

The First Scene

Hecuba

Hec. Whoso in pomp of proud estate or kingdom sets delight,
Or who that joys in prince's court to bear the sway of might,
Nor dreads the Fates,[52] which from above the wavering gods down
    flings,
But fast affiance fixèd hath in frail and fickle things,
Let him in me both see the face of Fortune's flattering joy
And eke respect the ruthful end of thee, O ruinous Troy.
For never gave she[53] plainer proof than this ye present see
How frail and brittle is the state of pride and high degree.
The flow'r of flow'ring Asia, lo! whose fame the heavens resound,
The worthy work of gods above,[54] is battered down to ground,
And whose assaults they sought afar from west, with banners spread,
Where Tanais[55] cold her branches seven abroad the world doth shed,
With hugy host, and from the east,[56] where springs the newest day,
Where lukewarm Tigris' channel runs and meets the ruddy sea,
And which from wandering-land of Scyth the band of widows[57] sought,
With fire and sword thus battered be her turrets down to nought.
The walls, but late of high renown, lo, here their ruinous fall;
The buildings burn, and flashing flame sweeps through the palace all.
Thus every house full high it smokes of old Assarac's land,
Nor yet the flames withhold from spoil the greedy victor's hand.
The surging smoke the azure sky and light hath hid away,

[52] The relation here implied between the Fates and the gods is not in the original, which says merely, "He who dreads not the fickle gods."

[53] Fortune.

[54] Neptune and Apollo, the builders of Troy, *v. Laomedon* in *Index of Proper Names*.

[55] The home of Rhesus, *q.v.* in *Index of Proper Names*.

[56] The home of Memnon, *q.v.* in *Index of Proper Names*.

[57] The Amazons under Penthesilea's leadership; for this use of *"widow" v.* Glossary.

And, as with cloud beset, Troy's ashes stain the dusky day.
Though pierced with ire and greedy of heart, the victor from afar
Doth view the long-assaulted Troy, the gain of ten years' war,
And eke the miseries thereof abhors to look upon,
And though he see it, yet scant himself believes might be won.
The spoils thereof with greedy hand they snatch and bear away;
A thousand ships would not receive aboard so huge a prey.
The ireful might I do protest of gods adverse to me,
My country's dust, and Trojan King, I call to witness thee
Whom Troy now hides, and underneath the stones art overtrod,
With all the gods that guide the ghost,[58] and Troy that lately stood,
And you also, you flocking ghosts of all my children dear,
Ye lesser sprites! Whatever ill hath happened to us here,
Whatever Phoebus'[59] wat'rish[60] face in fury hath foresaid
At raging rise from seas, when erst the monsters had him frayed,
In childbed bands I saw it yore,[61] and wist it should be so;
And I in vain before Cassandra told it long ago.
Not false Ulysses kindled hath these fires, nor none of his,
Nor yet deceitful Sinon's craft that hath been cause of this;
My fire it is wherewith ye burn, and Paris is the brand
That smoketh in thy tow'rs, O Troy, the flow'r of Phrygian land.
But ay! alas, unhappy age,[62] why dost thou yet so sore
Bewail thy country's fatal fall? Thou knewest it long before.
Behold thy last calamities, and *them* bewail with tears;
Account as old Troy's overturn, and past by many years.
I saw the slaughter of the King, and how he lost his life
By th' altar side, more mischief was, with stroke of Pyrrhus' knife,
When in his hand he wound his locks and drew the King to ground,
And hid to hilts his wicked sword in deep and deadly wound.
Which when the gorèd King had took, as willing to be slain,

[58] This verse should refer to "the shades of thee in whose lifetime Troy stood," *i.e.,* Hector.

[59] An error for "Phoebas," "bride of Phoebus," *i.e.,* Cassandra.

[60] A mistranslation of *"lymphato,"* "maddened"; the mistake gives rise to Heywood's odd misinterpretation of the next verse, which should be something like "although the god forebade that she be believed"; *v.* Cassandra in *Index of Proper Names.*

[61] When, pregnant with Paris, she dreamed that she would give birth to a firebrand.

[62] *I.e.,* her own old age.

Out of the old man's throat he drew his bloody[63] blade again.
Not pity of his years, alas! in man's extremest age,
From slaughter might his hand withhold, nor yet his ire assuage.
The gods are witness of the same, and eke the sacrifice
That in his kingdom holden was, that flat on ground now lies.
The father of so many kings, Priam of ancient name,
Untombèd lieth, and wants, in blaze of Troy, his funeral flame.
Nor yet the gods are wreaked; but lo, his sons[64] and daughters all,
Such lords they serve as doth by chance of lot to them befall.
Whom shall *I* follow now for prey? or where shall I be led?
There is perhaps among the Greeks that Hector's wife will wed;
Some man desires Helenus' spouse; some would Antenor's have;
And in the Greeks there wants not some that would Cassandra crave;
But I, alas! most woeful wight, whom no man seeks to choose,
I am the only refuse left; and me they clean refuse.
Ye careful captive company, why stints your woeful cry?
Beat on your breasts, and piteously complain with voice so high
As meet may be for Troy's estate. Let your complaints rebound
In tops of trees, and cause the hills to ring with terrible sound!

The Second Scene

The Women, Hecuba

Wom. Not folk unapt or new to weep, O Queen,
Thou will'st to wail. By practice are we taught:
For all these years in such case have we been
Since first the Trojan guest[65] Amyclae sought
And sailed the seas that led him on his way,
With sacred ship to Cybel dedicate,
From whence he brought his unrepining prey,[66]
The cause, alas! of all this dire debate.
Ten times now hid the hills of Ida be
With snow of silver hue all overlaid,
And bared is, for Trojan roges, each tree;

[63] "Bloodless" in the original; Priam was so pitiably old that his blood was dried up.
[64] An error for "daughters-in-law."
[65] Paris.
[66] Helen.

Ten times in field the harvestman afraid
The spikes of corn hath reaped, since never day
Its wailing wants. New cause renews our woe;
Lift up thy hand, O Queen, cry "Wellaway!"
We follow thee. We are well taught thereto.
　Hec. Ye faithful fellows of our casualty,
Untie th'attire that on your heads ye wear
And, as behoveth state of misery,
Let fall about your woeful necks your hair.
In dust of Troy rub all your arms about.
In slacker weed and let your breasts be tied:
Down to your bellies let your limbs lie out—
For what wedlock should you your bosoms hide?
Your garments loose; and have in readiness
Your furious hands upon your breast to knock.
This habit well beseemeth our distress;
Its pleaseth me, I know the Trojan flock.
Renew again your long-accustomed cries,
And more than erst lament your miseries,
We bewail Hector!
　Wom. Our hair we have untied now, every each one;
All rent for sorrow of our cursèd case
Our locks outspread. The knots we have undone,
And in these ashes stainèd is our face.
　Hec. Fill up your hands, and make thereof no spare;
For this[67] yet lawful is from Troy to take.
Let down your garments from your shoulders bare,
And suffer not your clamor so to slake.
Your naked breasts wait for your hands to smite.
Now, dolor deep, now, sorrow, show thy might,
Make all the coasts that compass Troy about
Witness the sound of all your careful cry!
Cause from the caves the echo to cast out
Rebounding voice of all your misery,
Not, as she wonts, the latter word to sound,
But all your woe; from far let it rebound,
Let all the seas it hear, and eke the land.

[67] The ashes.

Spare not your breasts with heavy stroke to strike,
Beat ye yourselves each one, with cruel hand;
For yet your wonted cry doth me not like,
We bewail Hector!

Wom. Our naked arms thus here we rend for thee,
And bloody shoulders, Hector, thus we tear,
Thus with our fists our heads, lo! beaten be,
And all for thee, behold, we hale our hair.
Our dugs, alas! with mothers' hands be torn;
And where the flesh is wounded round about
Which for thy sake we rend, thy death to mourn,
The flowing streams of blood, they spring thereout.
Thy country's shore,[68] and destiny's delay,
And thou to weary Trojans wast an aid,
A wall thou wast, and on thy shoulders Troy
Ten years it stood, on thee alone it stayed;
With thee it fell, and fatal day, alas,
Of Hector both and Troy, but one there was.

Hec. Enough hath Hector. Turn your plaint, and moan
And shed your tears for Priam, every each one.

Wom. Receive our plaints, O lord of Phrygian land,
And old twice captive king, receive our tear!
While thou wert king, Troy hurtless then could stand,
Though shaken twice with Grecian sword it were,
And twice did shot of Herc'les' quiver bear.[69]
At latter loss of Hecuba's sons all
And roges for kings that high on piles we rear,
Thou, father, shut'st our latest funeral;
And beaten down, to Jove for sacrifice
Like lifeless block in Troy thy carcass lies.

Hec. Yet turn ye once your tears another way;
My Priam's death should not lamented be.
O Trojans all, "Full happy is Priam!" say;
For free from bondage down descended he
To the lowest ghost, and never shall sustain
His captive neck with Greeks to yokèd be.
He never shall behold the Atrids twain,

[68] *I.e.,* her prop.
[69] *V. Index of Proper Names, s.vv. Hercules* and *Philoctetes.*

Nor false Ulysses ever shall he see;
Not he, a prey for Greeks to triumph at,
His neck shall subject to their conquests bear,
Nor give his hands to tie behind his back
That to the rule of sceptres wonted were,
Nor following Agamemnon's car in band
Shall he be pomp to proud Mycenae's land.
   Wom. "Full happy Priam is!" each one we say,
That took with him his kingdom then that stood.
Now, safe in shade, he seeks the wand'ring way
And treads the paths of all Elysium's wood,
And, in the blessed sprites full happy he,
Again there seeks to meet with Hector's ghost.
Happy Priam! Happy whoso may see
His kingdom all at once with him be lost.

Chorus

(added to the tragedy by the translator)

O ye to whom the Lord of land and seas,
Of life and death, hath granted here the pow'r,
Lay down your lofty looks, your pride appease;
The crownèd king flee'th not his fatal hour.
Whoso thou be that lead'st thy land alone,
Thy life was limit from thy mother's womb;
Not purple robe, not glorious glittering throne,
Nor crown of gold, redeems thee from the tomb.
A king he[70] was, that, waiting for the vail
Of him that slew the Minotaur in fight,
Beguil'd with blackness of the wonted sail,
In seas him sunk, and of his name they hight.
So he[71] that willed to win the golden spoil
And first with ship by seas to seek renown,
In lesser wave at length to death gan boil,
And thus the daughters brought their father down.
Whose[72] songs the woods hath drawn, and rivers held,

[70] Aegeus, *q.v.* in *Index of Proper Names.*
[71] Pelias, *q.v.* in *Index of Proper Names.*
[72] Orpheus, *q.v.* in *Index of Proper Names.*

And birds, to hear his notes, did theirs forsake,
In piecemeal thrown amid the Thracian field,
Without return hath sought the Stygian lake.
They[73] sit above that hold our life in line,
And what we suffer down they fling from high;
No cark, no care, that ever may untwine
The threads that woven are above the sky.
As witness he[74] that, sometime king of Greece,
Had Jason thought in drenching seas to drown,
Who scaped both death and gained the Golden Fleece.
Whom Fates advance there may no pow'r pluck down;
The highest god sometime, that Saturn hight,
His fall taught him to credit their decrees;
The rule of heavens, he lost it by their might,
And Jove, his son, now turns the rolling skies.
Who weeneth here to win eternal wealth,
Let him behold this present perfect proof
And learn the secret step of chance's stealth,
Most near, alas! when most it seems aloof.
In slipp'ry joy let no man put his trust,
Let none despair that heavy haps hath passed;
The sweet with sour she mingleth as she lust
Whose doubtful web pretendeth nought to last.
Frailty is the thread that Clotho's rock hath spun,
Now from the distaff drawn, now knapped in twain.
With all the world at length his end he won
Whose works have wrought his name should great remain;
And he[75] whose travails twelve his name display,
That fearèd nought the force of worldly hurt,
In fine, alas! hath found his fatal day
And died with smart of Deianira's shirt.
If prowess might eternity procure,
Then Priam yet should live in liking lust.
Aye, portly pomp of pride, thou art unsure!
Lo, learn by him, O kings, ye are but dust.
And Hecuba, that waileth now in care,

[73] The Fates, *q.v.* in *Index of Proper Names.*
[74] Pelias, *q.v.* in *Index of Proper Names.*
[75] Hercules, *q.v.* in *Index of Proper Names.*

That was so late of high estate a queen,
A mirror is to teach you what you are:
Your wavering wealth, O princes, here is seen.
Whom dawn of day hath seen in high estate,
Before sun's set, alas! hath had his fall;
The cradle's rock appoints the life its date
From settled joy to sudden funeral.

THE SECOND ACT

The First Scene

The Sprite of Achilles

(added to the tragedy by the translator)

Spr. Forsaking now the places tenebrous
And deep dens of th' infernal region,
From all the shadows of illusions
That wander there the paths, full many one,
Lo, here am I returnèd all alone,
The same Achill whose fierce and heavy hand
Of all the world no wight might yet withstand.

What man so stout, of all the Grecians' host,
That hath not sometime craved Achilles' aid?
And, in the Trojans, who of prowess most
That hath not feared to see my banner splayed?
Achilles, lo, hath made them all afraid,
And in the Greeks hath been a pillar-post
That sturdy stood against their Trojan host.

Where I have lacked, the Grecians went to wrack.
Troy provèd hath what Achill's sword could do;
Where I have come, the Trojans fled aback,
Retiring fast from field their walls unto.
No man that might Achilles' stroke fordo!
I dealt such stripes amid the Trojan rout
That with their blood I stained the fields about.

Mighty Memnon, that with his Persian band
Would Priam's part with all might maintain,
Lo, now he lieth and knoweth Achilles' hand.
Amid the field is Troilus also slain.
Yea, Hector great, whom Troy accounted plain
The flow'r of chivalry that might be found—
All of Achilles had their mortal wound.

But Paris, lo, such was his false deceit,
Pretending marriage of Polyxene,
Behind the altar lay for me in wait,
Where I un'wares have fall'n into the train,
And in Apollo's church he hath me slain.
Whereof the Hell will now just vengeance have;
And here again I come, my right to crave.

The deep Avern my rage may not sustain
Nor bear the angers of Achilles' sprite:
From Acheron I rent the spoil in twain,
And through the ground I grate again to sight.
Hell could not hide Achilles from the light!
Vengeance and blood doth Orcus' pit require
To quench the furies of Achilles' ire.

The hateful land that worse than Tartar is,
And burning thirst exceeds of Tantalus,
I here behold again, and Troy is this.
Oh, travail worse than stone of Sisyphus,
And pains that pass the pangs of Tityus!
To light more loathsome Fury hath me sent
Than hookèd wheel that Ixion's flesh doth rent.

Remembered is a-low, where sprites do dwell,
The wicked slaughter wrought by wily way;
Not yet revengèd hath the deepest Hell
Achilles' blood on them that did him slay.
But now of vengeance comes the ireful day;
And darkest dens of Tartar from beneath
Conspire the fates of them that wrought my death.

Now mischief, murder, wrath of Hell draweth near,
And dire Phlegethon's flood doth blood require.
Achilles' death shall be revengèd here
With slaughter such as Stygian lakes desire:
Her[76] daughter's blood shall slake the spirit's ire
Whose son[77] we slew; whereof doth yet remain
The wrath beneath, and Hell shall be their pain.

From burning lakes the Furies' wrath I threat
And fire that nought but streams of blood may slake.
The range of wind and seas their ships shall beat,
And Ditis deep on you shall vengeance take.
The sprites cry out, the earth and seas do quake;
The pool of Styx, "Ungrateful Greeks," it saith,
"With slaughtered blood revenge Achilles' death!"

The soil doth shake to bear my heavy foot
And fear'th again the sceptres of my hand,
The pools with stroke of thunderclap ring out,
The doubtful stars amid their course do stand,
And fearful Phoebus hides his blazing brand,
The trembling lakes against their course do flite,
For dread and terror of Achilles' sprite.

Great is the ransom owed of due to me
Wherewith ye must the sprites and Hell appease:
Polyxena shall sacrificèd be
Upon my tomb, their ireful wrath to please;
And with her blood ye shall assuage the seas.
Your ships may not return to Greece again
Till on my tomb Polyxena be slain.

And, for that she should then have been my wife,
I will that Pyrrhus render her to me,
And in such solemn sort bereave her life
As ye are wont the weddings for to see.

[76] Hecuba.
[77] Hector.

So shall the wrath of Hell appeasèd be.
Nought else but this may satisfy our ire;
Her will I have, and her I you require.

The Second Scene

Talthybius, Chorus

Tal. Alas, how long the ling'ring Greeks in haven do make delay
When either war by seas they seek,[78] or home to pass their way!
  Cho. Why, show what cause doth hold your ships and Grecian
    navy stays;
Declare if any of the gods have stopped your homeward ways.
  Tal. My mind is maz'd, my trembling sinews quake and are
    afeared;
For stranger news, of truth, than these, I think, were never heard.
Lo, I myself have plainly seen, in dawning of the day
When Phoebus first gan to approach and drive the stars away,
The earth all shaken suddenly; and from the hollow ground
Methought I heard, with roaring cry, a deep and dreadful sound
That shook the woods, and all the trees rang out with thunder-stroke.
From Ida's hills down fell the stones; the mountain tops were broke.
And not the earth hath only quaked; but all the sea likewise
Achilles' presence felt and knew, and high the surges rise.
The cloven ground Erebus' pits then showed, and deepest dens,
That down to gods that guide beneath the way appeared from hence.
Then shook the tomb, from whence anon, in flame of fiery light,
Appeareth from the hollow caves Achilles' noble sprite.
As wonted he his Thracian[79] arms and banners to deploy
And wield his weighty weapons well against th' assaults of Troy,
The same Achilles seemed he then that he was wont to be
Amid the hosts; and eas'ly could I know that this was he
With carcass slain in furious fight that stopped and filled each flood,
And who with slaughter of his hand made Xanthus run with blood,
As when in chariot high he sat with lofty stomach stout,

[78] A reference to the delay at Aulis (*q.v.* in *Index of Proper Names*) when the Greek fleet set out for Troy.

[79] An error; the original mentions that Achilles defeated Thracian arms (those of Cisseus, a hero of Thrace). Achilles himself was not connected with Thrace.

While Hector both and Troy at once[80] he drew the walls about.
Aloud he cried, and every coast rang with Achilles' sound;
And thus with hollow voice he spoke, from bottom of the ground:
"The Greeks shall not with little price redeem Achilles' ire!
A princely ransom must they give; for so the Fates require:
Unto my ashes Polyxena spoused shall here be slain
By Pyrrhus' hand, and all my tomb her blood shall overstain!"
This said, he straight sank down again to Pluto's deep region.
The earth then closed, the hollow caves were vanishèd and gone;
Therewith the weather waxèd clear, the raging winds did slake,
The tumbling seas began to rest, and all the tempest brake.

The Third Scene

Pyrrhus, Agamemnon, Calchas

Pyr. What time our sails we should have spread upon Sigean seas
With swift return from long delay to seek our homeward ways,
Achilles rose, whose only hand hath given Greeks the spoil
Of Troia, sore annoyed by him and leveled with the soil,
With speed requiting his abode and former long delay
At Scyros' isle and Lesbos, both amid the Aegean Sea.
Till he came here, in doubt it stood, of fall or sure estate.
Then, though ye haste to grant his will, ye shall it give too late;
Now have the other captains all the price of their manhood.
What else reward for his prowess than her all only blood?
Are his deserts, think you, but light, that when he might have fled
And, passing Pylius' years in peace, a quiet life have led,
Detected yet his mother's crafts, forsook his woman's weed,
And with his weapons proved himself a manly man indeed?
The King of Mysia, Telephus, that would the Greeks withstand
Coming to Troy, forbidding us the passage of his land,
Too late repenting to have felt Achilles' heavy stroke,
Was glad to crave his health again where he his hurt had took;
For when his sore might not be salved, as told Apollo plain,
Except the spear that gave the hurt restorèd help again,
Achilles' plasters cured his cuts, and saved the king alive.
His hand both might and mercy knew, to slay and then revive.

---

[80] Because Troy's fate was bound up with that of Hector.

When Thebes fell, Eetion saw it and might it not withstand;
The captive king could nought redress the ruin of his land.
Lyrnesos, little, likewise felt his hand, and down it fell,
With ruin overturnèd like[81] from top of haughty hill.
And taken Briseis' land it is, and prisoner is she caught.
The cause of strife between the kings,[82] is Chryse come to nought.
Tenedos' isle, well known by fame and fertile soil, he took,
That fost'reth fat the Thracian flocks; and sacred Cilla shook.
What boots to blaze the bruit of him whom trump of fame doth show
Through all the coasts where Caicus' flood with swelling stream doth
flow?
The ruthful ruin of these realms, so many towns beat down,
Another man would glory count, and worthy great renown;
But thus my father made his way, and these his *journeys* are,
And battles many one he fought while war he doth *prepare*.
As whisht I may his merits more, yet shall not this remain
Well-known and counted praise enough, that he hath Hector slain,
During whose life the Grecians all might never take the town?
My father only vanquished Troy; and you have plucked it down.
Rejoice I may you, parent, praise,[83] and bruit abroad his acts;
It seemeth the son to follow well his father's noble facts.
In sight of Priam Hector slain, and Memnon, both they lay.
With heavy cheer his[84] parent wailed to mourn his dying day;
Himself abhorred his handiwork in sight, that had them slain:
The sons of gods, Achilles knew, were born to die again.[85]
The woman,[86] Queen of Amazons, that grieved the Greeks full sore,
Is turned to flight. Then ceased our fear; we dread their bows no more.
If ye well weigh his worthiness, Achilles ought to have,
Though he from Argos or Mycenae[87] would a virgin crave.

---

[81] *I.e.,* overturned with like ruin.

[82] As the birthplace of Chryseis, *q.v.* in *Index of Proper Names.*

[83] The translation reads, "Rejoice I may your parents prayse," this emendation brings it nearer the meaning of the text ("It pleases me to recount my father's illustrious praise") but leaves a too abrupt change of persons in the pronouns.

[84] Memnon's; his mother Aurora (*q.v.* in *Index of Proper Names*) dawned pale at his death.

[85] Achilles, like Memnon, is the son of a goddess.

[86] Penthesilea, *q.v.* in *Index of Proper Names.*

[87] Even a daughter of Agamemnon, like Iphigenia.

Doubt ye herein? Allow you not that straight his will be done?
And count ye cruel Priam's blood to give to Peleus' son?
For Helen's sake your own child's[88] blood appeased Diana's ire;
A wonted thing, and done ere this, it is that I require.

Aga. The only fault of youth it is, not to refrain its rage.
The father's blood already stirs in Pyrrhus'[89] wanton age.
Sometime Achilles' grievous checks I bore with patient heart;
The more thou may'st,[90] the more thou ought'st to suffer in good part.
Whereto would ye with slaughtered blood a noble spirit stain?
Think what is meet the Greeks to do, and Trojans to sustain.
The proud estate of tyranny may never long endure;
The king that rules with modest mean of safety may be sure.
The higher step of princely state that Fortune hath us signed,
The more behov'th a happy man humility of mind
And dread the change that chance may bring, whose gifts so soon be
    lost,
And chiefly then to fear the gods, while they thee favor most.
In beating down what war hath won, by proof I have been taught
What pomp and pride in twink of eye may fall and come to nought.
Troy made me fierce and proud of mind; Troy makes me frayed
    withal.
The Greeks now stand where Troy late fell—each thing may have its
    fall.
Sometime, I grant, I did myself, and sceptres, proudly bear;
The thing that might advance my heart makes me the more to fear.
Thou, Priam, perfect proof present'st. Thou art to me eftsoons
A cause of pride, a glass of fear, a mirror for the nonce.
Should I account the sceptres aught but glorious vanity,
Much like the borrowed braided hair, the face to beautify?
One sudden chance may turn to nought and maim the might of men
With fewer than a thousand ships, and years in less than ten;
Not she that guides the slipp'ry wheel of Fate doth so delay
That she to all possession grants of ten years' settled stay.
With leave of Greece, I will confess I would have won the town,
But not with ruin thus extreme to see it beaten down—
But lo, the battle made by night, and rage of fervent mind,

---

[88] Iphigenia, *q.v.* in *Index of Proper Names.*
[89] The translation reads "Priams," apparently a *lapsus calami.*
[90] *I.e.,* the more powerful thou art.

Could not abide the bridling bit that reason had assigned.
The happy sword, once stained with blood, insatiable is;
And in the dark the fervent rage doth strike the more amiss.
Now are we wreaked on Troy so much, let all that may remain.
A virgin born of princes' blood for offering to be slain,
And given be to stain the tomb and ashes of the dead,
And under name of wedlock see the guiltless blood be shed,
I will not grant; for mine should be thereof both fault and blame.
Who, when he may, forbiddeth not offence doth will the same.

   Pyr. And shall his sprites have no reward their angers to appease?
   Aga. Yes, very great: for all the world shall celebrate his praise;
And lands unknown, that never saw the man so praised by fame,
Shall hear and keep for many years the glory of his name.
If bloodshed vail his ashes aught, strike off an ox's head,
And let no blood that may be cause of mother's tears be shed.
What furious frenzy may this be that doth your will so lead
This earnest careful suit to make, in travail, for the dead?
Let not such envy toward your father in your heart remain
That for his sacrifice ye would procure another's pain!

   Pyr. Proud tyrant while prosperity thy stomach doth advance!
And cowardly wretch that shrinks for fear in case of fearful chance!
Is yet again thy breast inflamed with brand of Venus' might?[91]
Wilt thou alone so oft deprive Achilles of his right?
This hand shall give the sacrifice, the which if thou withstand
A greater slaughter shall I make, and worthy Pyrrhus' hand.[92]
And now too long from Prince's slaughter doth my hand abide;
And meet it were that Polyxene[93] were laid by Priam's side.

   Aga. I not deny but Pyrrhus' chief renown in war is this,
That Priam, slain with cruel sword, to your father humbled is.[94]

   Pyr. My father's foes, we have them known submit themselves
     humbly,
And Priam *presently,* yet wot, was glad to crave mercy;

---

[91] This and the following verse are a reference to the incident of Briseis (*q.v.* in *Index of Proper Names*).

[92] *I.e.,* he threatens to kill Agamemnon himself.

[93] Heywood has mistaken the sense. The original makes its clear that it is Agamemnon who is to join Priam in death.

[94] The translation misses the point, which is that Pyrrhus has slain a man who was suppliant to his father (in the claiming of Hector's corpse).

But thou, for fear not stout to rule, liest close from foes up shut
While thou to Ajax and Ulysses dost thy will commit.[95]

   Aga. But needs I must, and will, confess, your father did not fear
When burnt our fleet with Hector's brands, and Greeks they
    slaughtered were;
While loit'ring then aloof he lay, unmindful of the fight,
Instead of arms with scratch of quill his sounding harp to smite.

   Pyr. Great Hector then, despising thee, Achilles' songs did fear;
And Thessal ships in greatest dread in quiet peace yet were.

   Aga. For why aloof the Thessal fleet they lay from Trojan hands;
And well your father might have rest: he felt not Hector's brands.[96]

   Pyr. Well seems a noble king to give another king relief.

   Aga. Why hast thou then a worthy king bereavèd of his life?

   Pyr. A point of mercy sometimes is what lives in care to kill.

   Aga. But now your mercy moveth you a virgin's death to will.

   Pyr. Account ye cruel *now* her death whose sacrifice I crave?
Your own dear daughter once, ye know, yourself to th' altars gave.

   Aga. Nought else could save the Greeks from seas but th' only blood
    of her;
A king before his children ought his country to prefer.

   Pyr. The law doth spare no captives' blood, nor will'th their death
    to stay.

   Aga. That which the law doth not forbid yet shame doth oft say nay.

   Pyr. The conqueror what thing he list may lawfully fulfill.

   Aga. So much the less he ought to list that may do what he will.

   Pyr. Thus boast ye these, as though in all ye only bore the stroke,
When Pyrrhus loosèd hath the Greeks from bond of ten years' yoke?

   Aga. Hath Scyros' isle such stomachs bred?

   Pyr. No brethren's wrath it knows.[97]

   Aga. Beset about it is with wave.

   Pyr. The seas it do enclose.[98]

---

[95] In the embassy to Achilles (*q.v.* in *Index of Proper Names*).

[96] The sense of this verse should be: "Hector's father had deep peace there,"
a reference to Priam's claiming of Hector's corpse.

[97] A reference to the feud of Atreus and Thyestes (*v.* Atreus in *Index of
Proper Names*).

[98] This should be: "Yes, the waves of a kindred sea," a reference to Thetis
(*q.v.* in *Index of Proper Names*).

Thyestes' noble stock I know, and Atreus' eke, full well;
And of the brothers' dire debate perpetual fame doth tell.
    Aga. And thou a bastard of a maid[99] deflowered privily
Whom, then a boy, Achilles got in filthy lechery!
    Pyr. The same Achill that doth possess the reign of gods above:
With Thetis, seas; with Aeacus, sprites; the starrèd heaven with Jove.
    Aga. The same Achilles that was slain by stroke of Paris' hand.
    Pyr. The same Achilles whom no god durst ever yet withstand!
    Aga. The stoutest man I rather would his checks he should refrain.
I could them tame, but all your brags I can full well sustain;
For even the captives spares my sword. Let Calchas callèd be;
If destinies require her blood, I will thereto agree.
Calchas, whose counsel ruled our ships and navy hither brought,
Unlock'st the pole, and hast by art the secrets thereof sought,
To whom the bowels of the beast,[100] to whom the thunderclap
And blazing star with flaming train betokeneth what shall hap,
Whose words with dearest price I brought,[101] now tell us by what
    mean
The will of gods agreeth that we repair to Greece again.
    Cal. The Fates appoint the Greeks to buy their ways with wonted
    price;
And with what cost ye came to Troy ye shall return to Greece:
With blood ye came, with blood ye must from hence return again
And where Achilles' ashes lie the virgin shall be slain.
In seemly sort of habit, such as maidens wont ye see
Of Thessaly, or Mycenae else, what time they wedded be,
With Pyrrhus' hand she shall be slain. Of right it shall be so;
And meet it is that he, the son, his father's rite should do.
But not this only stayeth our ships: our sails may not be spread
Before a worthier blood than thine, Polyxena, be shed
Which thirst the Fates for. Priam's nephew, Hector's little boy,
The Greeks shall tumble headlong down from highest tower in Troy.
There let him die. This only way ye shall the gods appease;
Then spread your thousand sails with joy. Ye need not fear the seas.

[99] Deidamia, *q.v.* in *Index of Proper Names.*
[100] A reference to the practice of divination by inspection of the inner organs
of sacrificed animals (extispicy).
[101] By the sacrifice of Iphigenia.

Chorus

May this be true, or doth the fable feign,
When corpse is dead, the sprite to live as yet?
When Death our eyes with heavy hand doth strain
And fatal day our leams of light hath shet
And in the tomb our ashes once be set,
Hath not the soul likewise its funeral
But still, alas! do wretches live, in thrall?

Or else doth all at once together die?
And may no part its fatal hour delay,
But with the breath the soul from hence doth fly
And, like the clouds, to vanish quite away,
As danky shade flee'th from the pole by day?
And may no jot escape from destiny
When once the brand hath burnèd the body?

Whatever, then, the rise of sun may see,
And what the west, that sets the sun, doth know,
In all Neptunus' reign whatever be
That restless seas do wash and overflow
With purple waves still tumbling to and fro,
Age shall consume. Each thing that liv'th shall die
With swifter race than Pegasus doth fly.

And with what whirl the twice six signs[102] do fly,
With course as swift as rector[103] of the spheres
Doth guide those glistering globes eternally,
And Hecate her changèd horns repairs,
So draw'th on death, and life of each thing wears,
And never may the man return to sight
That once hath felt the stroke of Parcae's might.

For as the fume that from the fire doth pass
With turn of hand doth vanish out of sight,
And swifter than the northern Boreas

---

[102] Of the Zodiac.
[103] The sun.

With whirling blast and storm of raging might
Driv'th far away and puts the clouds to flight,
So flee'th the sprite that rules our life away;
And nothing tarryeth after dying-day.

Swift is the race we run, at hand the mark.
Lay down your hope, that wait here aught to win;
And who dreads aught, cast off thy careful cark.
Wilt thou it wot, what state thou shalt be in
When dead? Thou art as thou hadst never been.
For greedy time, it doth devour us all;
The world, it sways to chaos' heap to fall.

Death hurts the corpse and spareth not the sprite.
And, as for all the dens of Taenar deep,
With Cerberus' kingdom dark, that knows no light,
And straitest gates that he there sits to keep,
They fancies are, that follow folk by sleep.
Such rumors vain, but feignèd lies they are,
And fables, like the dreams in heavy care.

Oh, dreadful day! Alas, the sorry time[104]
Is come of all the mother's ruthful woe.
Astyanax, alas! thy fatal line
Of life is worn; to death straight shalt thou go.
The sisters[105] have decreed it should be so.
There may no force, alas! escape their hand;
There mighty Jove their will may not withstand.

To see the mother her tender child forsake
What gentle heart that may from tears refrain?
Or who so fierce that would no pity take
To see, alas! this guiltless infant slain?
For sorry heart the tears mine eyes do stain
To think what sorrow shall her heart oppress
Her little child to lose remediless.

[104] The last three staves are added by the translator.
[105] The Fates.

The double cares of Hector's wife to wail,
Good ladies, have your tears in readiness;
And you, with whom should pity most prevail,
Rue on her grief, bewail her heaviness.
With sobbing heart lament her deep distress
When she with tears shall take leave of her son.
And now, good ladies, hear what shall be done.

The Third Act

The First Scene

Andromache, Senex,[106] *Ulysses*

And. Alas, ye careful company, why hale ye thus your hairs?
Why beat you so your boiling breasts and stain your eyes with tears?
The fall of Troy is new to you; but unto me not so:
I have foreseen this careful case ere this time long ago.
When fierce Achilles Hector slew and drew the corpse about,
Then, then methought I wist it well that Troy should come to nought.
In sorrows sunk I senseless am, and wrapped, alas! in woe.
But soon, except this babe me held, to Hector would I go—
This silly fool my stomach tames amid my misery
And in the hour of heaviest haps permits me not to die;
This only cause constrains me yet the gods for him to pray,
With tract of time prolongs my pain, delays my dying day.
He takes from me the lack of fear, the only fruit of ill;
For, while he lives yet, have I left whereof to fear me still.
No place is left for better chance; with worst we are oppressed.
To fear, alas! and see no hope is worst of all the rest.
  Sen. What sudden fear thus moves your mind and vexeth you so
    sore?
  And. Still, still, alas, of one mishap there riseth more and more;
Nor yet the doleful destinies of Troy be come to end.
  Sen. And what more grievous chances yet prepare the gods to send?
  And. The caves and dens of Hell be rent for Trojans' greater fear,
And from the bottoms of their tombs the hidden sprites appear.
May none but Greeks alone from Hell return to life again?

---

[106] Latin for "old man."

Would god the Fates would finish soon the sorrows I sustain!
Death thankful were. A common care the Trojans all oppress,
But me, alas! amazeth most the fearful heaviness
That all astounded am, for dread and horror of the sight
That in my sleep appeared to me, by dream this latter night.

    Sen. Declare what sights your dream hath showed, and tell what
      doth you fear.

    And. Two parts of all the silent night almost then passèd were,
And then the clear seven clustered beams of stars were fallen to rest,
And first the sleep so long unknown my wearied eyes oppressed
(If this be sleep, the astounded maze of mind in heavy mood),
When suddenly before mine eyes the sprite of Hector stood,
Not like as he the Greeks was wont to battle to require,
Or when amid the Grecian ships he threw the brands of fire,
Nor such as, raging on the Greeks, with slaught'ring stroke had slain
And bore indeed the spoils of him[107] that did Achilles feign,
His countenance not now so bright, nor of so lively cheer,
But sad and heavy, like to ours, and clad with ugly hair.
It did me good to see him, though, when shaking then his head,
"Shake off thy sleep in haste," he said, "and quickly leave thy bed!
Convey into some secret place our son, O faithful wife,
This only hope there is to help find mean to save his life.
Leave off thy piteous tears," he said, "dost thou yet wail for Troy?
Would god it lay on ground full flat, so ye might save the boy!
Up stir" he said "thyself! In haste convey him privily;
Save, if ye may, the tender blood of Hector's progeny!"
Then straight in trembling fear I woke, and rolled mine eyes about,
Forgetting long my child, poor wretch, and after Hector sought;
But straight—alas, I wist not how—the sprite away did pass
And me forsook before I could my husband once embrace.
O child, O noble father's brood and Trojans' only joy,
O worthy seed of th' ancient blood and beaten House of Troy,
O image of thy father, lo, thou lively bear'st his face:
This count'nance, lo, my Hector had, and even such was his pace,
The pitch of all his body such; his hands thus would he bear;
His shoulders high, his threat'ning brows, even such as thine they
    were.

---

[107] Patroclus, *q.v.* in *Index of Proper Names.*

O son, begot too late for Troy, but born too soon for me,
Shall ever time yet come again, and happy day may be
That thou may'st once revenge and build again the tow'rs of Troy
And to the town and Trojans both restore their name with joy?
But why do I, forgetting state of present destiny,
So great things wish? Enough for captives is to live only.
Alas! what privy place is left my little child to hide?
What seat so secret may be found where thou may'st safely hide?
The tower that with the walls of gods[108] so valiant was of might,
Through all the world so notable, so flourishing to sight,
Is turned to dust; and fire hath all consumed that was in Troy.
Of all the town not so much now is left to hide the boy.
What place were best to choose for guile? The holy tomb is here,
That th' en'mies' sword will spare to spoil, where lie'th my husband
  dear,
Which costly work his father built, King Priam, liberal,
And it up raised with charges great, for Hector's funeral.
Herein the bones and ashes both of Hector, lo, they lie—
Best is that I commit the son to his father's custody.
A cold and fearful sweat doth run throughout my members all.
Alas! I, careful wretch, do fear what chance may thee befall.
  Sen. Hide him away. This only way hath savèd many more:[109]
To make the en'mies to believe that they were dead before.
He will be sought. Scant any hope remaineth of safeness,
The payse of his nobility doth him so sore oppress.
  And. What way were best to work, that none our doings might
    bewray?
  Sen. Let none bear witness what ye do; remove them all away.
  And. What if the en'mies ask me where Astyanax doth remain?
  Sen. Then shall ye boldly answer make that he in Troy was slain.
  And. What shall it help to have him hid? At length they will him
    find.

---

108 Neptune and Apollo, *q.v.* in *Index of Proper Names.*
109 In this and the next twelve verses, Heywood performs in masterly fashion
the task of making sense of an almost hopelessly corrupt passage in the text
merely by the insertion of a few words here and there. Modern editors have
restored what was probably the original reading by rearranging the verses; but as
the sense of the conversation is roughly the same as in Heywood's version it
does not seem worthwhile to supply a translation of the emended text.

Sen. At first the en'my's rage is fierce; delay doth slake his mind.

And. But what prevails, since free from fear we may him never
hide?

Sen. Yet let the wretch take his defense, me careless there to bide.

And. What land unknown, out of the way, what unfrequented place
May keep thee safe? Who aids our fear? Who shall defend our case?
Hector! Hector, that evermore thy friends did well defend,
Now chiefly aid thy wife and child, and us some succor send;
Take charge to keep and cover close the treasures of thy wife,
And in thy ashes hide thy son. Preserve in tomb his life.
Draw near, my child, unto the tomb. Why flyest thou backward so?
Thou tak'st great scorn to lurk in dens; thy noble heart I know:
I see thou art ashamed to fear. Shake off thy princely mind
And bear thy breast as thee behooves, as chance hath thee assigned.
Behold our case, and see what flock remaineth now of Troy:
The tomb, I, woeful captive wretch, and thou, a silly boy.
But yield we must to sorry fates; thy chance must break thy breast.
Go to, creep underneath thy father's holy seats to rest.
If aught the Fates may wretches help, thou hast thy safeguard there;
If not, already then, poor fool, thou hast thy sepulcher.

Sen. The tomb him closely hides. But lest your fear should him
betray,
Let him here lie and far from hence go ye some other way.

And. The less he fears that fears at hand. And yet, if need be so,
If ye think meet, a little hence for safety let us go.

Sen. A little while keep silence now; refrain your plaint and cry.
His cursèd foot now hither moves the lord of Cephally.

And. Now open, earth; and thou, my spouse, from Styx rend up the
ground;
Deep in thy bosom hide thy son, that he may not be found.
Ulysses comes with doubtful pace and changèd countenance;
He knits in heart deceitful craft for some more grievous chance.

Uly. Though I be made the messenger of heavy news to you,
This one thing first shall I desire, that ye take this for true:
That though the words come from my mouth and I my message tell.
Of truth yet are they none of mine. Ye may believe me well,
It is the word of all the Greeks, and they the authors be
Whom Hector's blood doth yet forbid their countries for to see.
Our careful trust of peace unsure doth still the Greeks detain,

And evermore our doubtful fear yet draw'th us back again
And suff'reth not our wearied hands our weapons to forsake,
In child yet of Andromache while Trojans comfort take.

   And. And saith your augur Calchas so?

   Uly. Though Calchas nothing said,
Yet Hector tells it us himself, of whose seed are we frayed.
The worthy blood of noble men (ofttimes we see it plain)
Doth after in their heirs succeed, and quickly springs again.
For so the hornless youngling yet of high and sturdy beast
With lofty neck and branchèd brow doth shortly rule the rest;
The tender twig that of the loppèd stock doth yet remain
To match the tree that bore the bough in time starts up again
With equal top, to former wood the room it doth supply,
And spreads on soil a-low the shade, to heaven its branches high;
Thus of one spark, by chance yet left, it happ'neth so full oft
The fire hath quickly caught its force and flam'th again aloft.
So fear we yet lest Hector's blood might rise ere it be long.
Fear casts in all th' extremity, and oft interprets wrong.
If ye respect our case, ye may not blame these old soldiers
Though after years and months twice five they fear again the wars
And other travails, dreading Troy not yet to be well won.
A great thing doth the Grecians move: the fear of Hector's son;
Rid us of fear. This stayeth our fleet and plucks us back again;
And in the haven our navy sticks till Hector's blood be slain.
Count me not fierce for that by Fates I Hector's son require,
For I as well, if chance it would, Orestes[110] should desire.
But since that needs it must be so, bear it with patient heart
And suffer that[111] which Agamemnon suffered in good part.

   And. Alas, my child, would God thou wert yet in thy mother's hand,
And that I knew what destinies thee held, or in what land!
For never should the mother's faith her tender child forsake,
Though through my breast the en'mies all their cruel weapons strake,
Nor though the Greeks with pinching bonds of iron my hands had
    bound,
Or else in fervent flame of fire beset my body round.
But now my little child—poor wretch, alas!—where might he be?
Alas, what cruel destiny, what chance hath happed to thee?

---

[110] He would sacrifice even Agamemnon's son if necessary.
[111] In allowing the sacrifice of Iphigenia, *q.v.* in *Index of Proper Names.*

Art thou yet ranging in the fields, and wand'rest there abroad,
Or smothered else in dusty smoke of Troy, or overtrod?
Or have the Greeks thee slain, alas! and laughed to see thy blood?
Or torn art thou with jaws of beasts, or cast to fowls for food?

Uly. Dissemble not. Hard is for thee Ulysses to deceive;
I can full well the mothers'[112] crafts and subtlety perceive,
The policy of goddesses[113] Ulysses hath undone—
Set all these feignèd words aside. Tell me, where is thy son?

And. Where is Hector? Where all the rest that had with Troy their
fall?
Where Priamus? You ask for one; but I require of all.

Uly. Thou shalt constrainèd be to tell the thing thou dost deny!

And. A happy chance were death, to her that doth desire to die.

Uly. Who most desires to die would fainest live, when death draw'th
on;
These noble words, with present fear of death, would soon be gone.

And. Ulysses, if ye will constrain Andromache with fear,
Threaten me life; for now to die my chief desire it were.

Uly. With stripes, with fire, tormenting death, we will the truth
out wrest,
And dolor shall thee force to tell the secrets of thy breast;
And what thy heart hath deepest hid for pain thou shalt express.
Ofttimes th' extremity prevails much more than gentleness.

And. Set me in midst of burning flame, with wounds my body rent,
Use all the means of cruelty that ye may all invent;
Prove me with thirst and hunger both, and every torment try,
Pierce through my sides with burning irons, in prison let me lie.
Spare not the worst ye can devise, if aught be worse than this,
Yet never get ye more of me. I wot not where he is.

Uly. It is but vain to hide the things that straight ye will detect.
No fears may move the mother's heart; she doth them all neglect;[114]
This tender love ye bear your child, wherein ye stand so stout,
So much more circumspectly warn'th the Greeks to look about
Lest, after ten years' tract of time, and battle born so far,
Someone should live that on our children might renew the war.

---

[112] *E.g.*, Clytemnestra's, when he persuaded her to send Iphigenia to the
sacrifice.

[113] Thetis' ruse of hiding her son at Lycomedes' court.

[114] This verse is now usually assigned to Andromache.

As for myself, what Calchas saith I would not fear at all;
But on Telemachus I dread the smart of wars would fall.

And. Now will I make Ulysses glad, and all the Greeks also.
Needs must thou, woeful wretch, confess. Declare thy hidden woe.
Rejoice, ye sons of Atreus, there is no cause of dread.
Be glad, Ulysses, tell the Greeks that Hector's son is dead.

Uly. By what assurance prov'st thou that? How shall we credit thee?

And. Whatever thing the en'mies' hand may threaten hap to me,
Let speedy Fates me slay forthwith, and earth me hide at once,
And after death from tomb again remove yet Hector's bones,
Except my son already now do rest among the dead,
And that except Astyanax into his tomb be led.[115]

Uly. Then fully are the fates fulfilled with Hector's child's decease;
Now shall I bear the Grecians word of sure and certain peace—
Ulysses! Why, what dost thou now? The Greeks will every each one
Believe thy words . . . whom credit'st *thou*? The mother's tale alone?
Think'st thou for safeguard of her child the mother will not lie,
And dread the more the worse mischance, to give her son to die?
Her faith she binds with bond of oath, the truth to verify . . .
What thing is more of weight to fear than so to swear, and lie?
Now call thy crafts together all, bestir thy wits and mind,
And show thyself Ulysses[116] now, the truth herein to find!
Search well the mother's mind. Behold, she weeps and waileth out,
And here and there, with doubtful pace, she rangeth all about;
Her careful ears she doth apply to hearken what I say.
More frayed she seems than sorrowful. Now work some wily way;
For now most need of wit there is and crafty policy.
Yet once again, by other means, I will the mother try.
Thou, wretched woman, may'st rejoice that dead he is. Alas,
More doleful death by destiny for him decreed there was:
From turret's top to have been cast and cruelly been slain,
Which only tow'r of all the rest doth yet in Troy remain.

And. My sprite fail'th me, my limbs do quake, fear doth my wits
confound;
And as the ice congeals with frost, my blood with cold is bound.

Uly. She trembleth; lo, this way, this way I will the truth out wrest!

[115] Under oath Andromache cannot lie; but she tells the truth in such a way as to imply that Astyanax is indeed dead.
[116] *I.e.*, wily; Ulysses' chief fame was in his guile.

The mother's fear detecteth all the secrets of her breast;
I will renew her fear. Go, sirs, bestir you speedily
To seek this en'my of the Greeks, wherever that he lie.
Well done! He will be found at length; go to, still seek him out.[117]
Now shall he die. What dost thou fear? Why dost thou look about?
 And. Would god that any cause there were yet left that might me
   fray!
My heart at last, now all is lost, hath laid all fear away.
 Uly. Since that your child now hath, ye say, already suffered death,
And with his blood we may not purge the hosts, as Calchas saith,
Our fleet pass not (as, well inspired, doth Calchas prophesy)
Till Hector's ashes, cast abroad, the waves may pacify,
And tomb be rent. Now, since the boy hath scaped his destiny,
Needs must we break this holy tomb where Hector's ashes lie.
 And. What shall I do? My mind distracted is with double fear,
On th' one my son, on th' other side my husband's ashes dear.
Alas, which part should move me most? The cruel gods I call
To witness with me in the truth, and ghosts that guide thee all,
Hector, that nothing in my son is else that pleaseth me
But thou alone. God grant him life, he might resemble thee.
Shall Hector's ashes drownèd be? Bide I such cruelty
To see his bones cast in the seas? Yet, let Astyanax die,
And canst thou, wretched mother, bide thine own child's death to see,
And suffer from the high tow'r's top that headlong thrown he be? ...
I can, and will, take in good part his death and cruel pain,
So that my Hector after death be not removed again! ...
The boy, that life and senses hath, may feel his pain and die,
But Hector, lo, his death hath placed at rest in tomb to lie—
What dost thou stay? Determine which thou wilt preserve of twain.
Art thou in doubt? Save this![119] Lo, *here* thy Hector doth remain:
Both Hectors be, th' one quick of sprite and drawing toward his
   strength
And one that may perhaps revenge his father's death at length.
Alas! I cannot save them both. I think that best it were

---

[117] In the original Ulysses in this verse pretends that his men have actually found Astyanax, hoping that if he is not dead Andromache will show some fear, as indeed (we may gather from the next verse) she does.

[118] *I.e.,* in order that he may resemble thee.

[119] *I.e.,* the one who is present, Astyanax.

That of the twain I savèd him that doth the Grecians fear.[120]

Uly. It shall be done, what Calchas' words to us do prophesy,
And now shall all the sumptuous work[121] be thrown down utterly.

And. That once ye sold?[122]

Uly. I will it all from top to bottom rend.

And. The faith of gods I call upon! Achilles, us defend;
And, Pyrrhus, aid thy father's right![123]

Uly. This tomb abroad shall lie.

And. Oh mischief! Never durst the Greeks show yet such cruelty.
Ye stain the temples and the gods that most have favored you;[124]
The dead ye spare. Not on their tombs your fury rageth. Now
I will their weapons all resist myself, with naked hand;
The ire of heart shall give me strength their armor to withstand!
As fierce as did the Amazons beat down the Greeks in fight,
And Maenad, once inspired with god, in sacrifice doth smite
With spear in hand, and while with furious pace she treads the
　　ground
And wood, as one in rage she strikes and feeleth not the wound,
So will I run on midst of them and on their weapons die,
And in defense of Hector's tomb among his ashes lie!

Uly. Cease ye?[125] Doth rage and fury vain of women move ye
　　aught?
Dispatch with speed what I command, and pluck down all to nought!

And. Oh, slay me rather here; with sword rid me out the way!
Break up the deep Avern, and rid my destiny's delay.
Rise, Hector, and beset thy foes! Break thou Ulysses' ire—
A sprite, art good enough for him. Behold, he casteth fire
And weapon shakes with mighty hand! Do ye not, Greeks, him see?
Or else doth Hector's sprite appear but only unto me?

Uly. Down quite with all!

[120] *I.e.,* frighten.
[121] Hector's tomb.
[122] Achilles had sold to Priam Hector's body, and hence the right to entomb him.
[123] *I.e.,* Achilles' duty to his bargain with Priam.
[124] Andromache probably refers in particular to the pollution of the Palladium (*q.v.* in *Index of Proper Names*) by Ulysses and Diomedes.
[125] His men, who have apparently stopped demolishing the tomb at Andromache's onslaught.

And. What, wilt thou suffer both: thy son be slain,
And after death thy husband's bones to be removed again?
Perhaps thou may'st with prayer yet appease the Grecians all.
Else down to ground the holy tomb of Hector straight shall fall—
Let rather die the child, poor wretch, and let the Greeks him kill,
Than father and the son should cause the one the other's ill![126]
Ulysses, at thy knees I fall and humbly ask mercy;
These hands that no man's feet else knew, first at thy feet they lie.
Take pity on the mother's case and sorrows of my breast!
Vouchsafe my prayers to receive and grant me my request;
And by how much the more the gods have thee advancèd high,
More eas'ly strike the poor estate of wretched misery.
God grant the chaste bed of thy godly wife Penelope
May thee receive, and so again Laertes may thee see;
And that thy son Telemachus may meet thee joyfully,
His grandsire's years and father's wit to pass full happily,
Take pity on the mother's tears her little child to save!
He is my only comfort left, and th' only joy I have.
   Uly. Bring forth thy son, and ask.

The Second Scene

Andromache

And. Come hither, child, out of the dens to me,
Thy wretched mother's lamentable store.
This babe, Ulysses, lo, this babe is he
That stayeth your ships and feareth you so sore.
Submit thyself, my son, with humble hand,
And worship, flat on ground, thy master's feet.
Think it no shame, as now the case doth stand;
The thing that Fortune will'th a wretch is meet.
Forget thy worthy stock of kingly kind,
Think not on Priam's great nobility,
And put thy father Hector from thy mind;
Such as thy fortune let thy stomach be.

---

[126] Astyanax would harm Hector in not surrendering himself to save his father's ashes; Hector would kill Astyanax in the collapse of his tomb.

Behave thyself as captive, bend thy knee;
And though thy grief pierce not thy tender years,
Yet learn to wail thy wretched state by me
And take ensample at thy mother's tears.
Once Troy hath seen the weeping of a child,
When little Priam turned Alcides' threats
And he to whom all beasts in strength did yield,
That made his way from Hell, and broke their gates,
His little en'mies tears yet overcame.
"Priam," he said, "receive thy liberty;
In seat of honor keep thy kingly name,
But yet thy sceptres rule more faithfully."[127]
Lo, such the conquest was of Hercules;
Of him yet learn your hearts to mollify.
Do only Herc'les' cruel weapons please?[128]
And may no end be of your cruelty?
No less than Priam, kneels to thee this boy
That lie'th and asketh only life of thee.
As for the rule and governance of Troy,
Wherever Fortune will, there let it be.
Take mercy on the mother's ruthful tears
That with their streams my cheeks do overflow,
And spare this guiltless infant's tender years
That humbly falleth at thy feet so low.

The Third Scene

Ulysses, Andromache, Astyanax

Uly. Of truth the mother's great sorrow doth move my heart full
sore;
But yet the mothers of the Greeks of need must move me more
To whom this boy may cause in time a great calamity.
And. May ever he the burnt ruins of Troy revest, he?
And shall these hands, in time to come, erect the town again?
If this be th' only help we have, there doth no hope remain

[127] Than his father Laomedon (*q.v.* in *Index of Proper Names*).
[128] And not his mercy?

For Troy; we stand not now in case to cause your fear of mind.
Doth aught avail his father's force, or stock of noble kind?
His father's heart abated was, he drawn the walls about.
Thus evil haps, the haughtiest heart at length they bring to nought.
If ye will needs oppress a wretch, what thing more grievous were
Than on his noble neck he should the yoke of bondage bear?
To serve in life, doth any man this to a king deny?

   Uly. Nor Ulysses will'th his death, but Calchas' prophecy.

   And. O false inventor of deceit and heinous cruelty,
By *manhood* of whose hand in war no man did ever die;
But by deceit, and crafty train of mind that mischief seeks,
Before this time full many one dead is—yea, of the Greeks![129]
The prophet's words and guiltless gods, say'st thou, my son require?
Nay, mischief of thy breast it is; thou dost his death desire.
Thou night soldier,[130] and stout of heart a little child to slay!
This enterprise thou tak'st alone and that by open day.

   Uly. Ulysses' manhood well to Greeks, too much to you, is known.
I may not spend the time in words. Our navy will be gone.

   And. A little stay, while I my last farewell give to my child,
And have with oft embracing him my greedy sorrows filled.

   Uly. Thy grievous sorrows to redress would God it lay in me!
But at thy will to take delay of time, I grant it thee.
Now take thy last leave of thy son, and fill thyself with tears;
Ofttimes the weeping of the eyes the inward grief outwears.

   And. O dear, O sweet, thy mother's pledge, farewell, my only joy,
Farewell, the flow'r of honor left of beaten House of Troy,
O Trojans' last calamity, and fear to Grecians' part,
Farewell, thy mother's only hope, and vain comfort of heart!
Oft wished I thee thy father's strength and half thy grandsire's years,
But all for nought—the gods have all dispointed our desires.
Thou never shalt in regal court thy sceptres take in hand,
Nor to thy people give decrees, nor lead with law thy land,
Nor yet thine en'mies overcome by might of handy stroke,
Nor send the conquered nations all under thy servile yoke;

---

[129] *E.g.,* Iphigenia, Palamedes, and Ajax, *q.v.* in *Index of Proper Names.*
[130] Perhaps a reference to the theft of the Palladium (*q.v.* in *Index of Proper Names*).

Thou never shalt beat down in fight and Greeks with sword pursue,
Nor at thy chariot Pyrrhus pluck, as Achill Hector drew,
And never shall these tender hands thy weapons wield and wrest;
Thou never shalt in woods pursue the wild and mighty beast,
Nor, as accustomed is by guise and sacrifice in Troy,
With measures swift between the altars shalt thou dance for joy.
Oh, grievous kind of cruel death that doth remain for thee!
More woeful things than Hector's death the walls of Troy shall see.

Uly. Now break off all thy mother's tears. I may no more time spend.
The grievous sorrows of thy heart will never make an end.

And. Ulysses, spare as yet my tears, and grant a while delay
To close his eyes[131] yet with my hands, ere he depart away.
Thou die'st but young, yet feared thou art. Thy Troy doth wait for
    thee;
Go, noble heart! Thou shalt again the noble Trojans see.

Ast. Help me, mother!

And. Alas, my child, why tak'st thou hold by me?
In vain thou call'st where help none is. I cannot succor thee.
As when the little tender beast that hears the lion cry
Straight for defense he seeks his dam and crouching down doth lie,
The cruel beast, when once removèd is the dam away,
In greedy jaw with ravening bite doth snatch the tender prey,
So straight the en'mies will thee take, and from my side thee bear.
Receive my kiss and tears, poor child, receive my rended hair.
Depart thou hence now, full of me, and to thy father go,
Salute my Hector in my name, and tell him of my woe;
Complain thy mother's grief to him. If former cares may move
The sprites, and that in funeral flame they lose not all their love,
O cruel Hector, suff'rest thou thy wife to be oppressed
With bond of Grecians' heavy yoke, and lie'st thou still at rest?
Achilles rose. Take here again my tears and rended hair
And, all that I have left to send, this kiss t' thy father bear.
Thy coat yet for my comfort leave; the tomb hath touchèd it.
If of his ashes aught here lie I'll seek it every whit.

Uly. There is no measure of thy tears. I may no longer stay.
Defer no further our return; break off our ships' delay.

---

[131] As if he were already dead.

Chorus

(altered by the translator[132])

O Jove, that lead'st the lamps of fire
And deck'st with flaming stars the sky,
Why is it ever thy desire
To care *their* course so orderly
That now the frost the leaves hath worn,
And now the spring doth clothe the tree,
Now fiery Leo[133] ripes the corn,
And still the soil should changèd be?
But why art thou, that all dost guide,
Between whose hands the pole doth sway,
And at whose will the orbs do slide,
Careless of man's estate alway?
Regarding not the good man's case,
Not caring how to hurt the ill,
Chance beareth rule in every place
And turneth man's estate at will.
She gives the wrong the upper hand,
The better part she doth oppress;
She makes the highest low to stand.
Her kingdom all is orderless.
Oh, perfect proof of her frailty:
The princely tow'rs of Troy beat down,
The flow'r of Asia here ye see
With turn of hand quite overthrown,
The ruthful end of Hector's son,
Whom to his death the Greeks have led.
His fatal hour is come and gone

[132] In the chorus which stands here in the original the Trojan women wonder into which lands they will be carried off as booty; they conclude by praying that they may not be taken to Sparta, Mycenae or Ithaca, the homes respectively of Helen, Agamemnon, and Ulysses. The chorus is a fabric of learned geographical and mythological references, not worth giving a version of "except [to quote Heywood] I should expound the Historyes of each one, which would be farre to tedious."

[133] As the Zodiac sign of August.

And by this time the child is dead.
Yet still, alas! more cares increase,
Oh, Trojans' doleful destiny!
Fast doth approach the maid's decease,
And now Polyxena shall die.

THE FOURTH ACT
Helena, Andromache, Hecuba[134]

Hel. Whatever woeful wedding yet were cause of funeral,
Of wailing, tears, blood, slaughter else, or other mischiefs all,
A worthy match for Helena and meet for me it were!
My wedding torch hath been the cause of all the Trojans' care;
I am constrained to hurt them yet after their overthrow.
The false and feignèd marriages[135] of Pyrrhus must I show,
And give the maid her Greek attire;[136] and by my policy
Shall Paris' sister be betrayed, and by deceit shall die. . . .
But let her be beguilèd thus; the less should be her pain
If that unware, without the fear of death, she might be slain.
What ceasest thou the will of Greeks, and message, to fulfill?
Of hurt constrained the fault return'th to th' author of the ill.
O noble virgin of the famous house and stock of Troy,
To thee the Grecians have me sent. I bring thee news of joy.
The gods rue on thy afflicted state; more merciful they be:
A great and happy marriage, lo, they have prepared for thee.
Thou never shouldst, if Troy had stood, so nobly wedded be,
Nor Priam never could prefer thee to so high degree,
Whom flower of all the Grecians' name, the prince of honor high
That bears the sceptres over all the land of Thessaly,
Doth in the law of wedlock choose, and for his wife require:
To sacred rites of lawful bed doth Pyrrhus thee desire.
Lo, Thetis great, with all the rest of gods that guide by sea,
Each one shall thee account as theirs, and joy, by wedding day;
And Peleus shall thee daughter call when thou art Pyrrhus' wife,
And Nereus shall account thee his the space of all thy life.

---

[134] Polyxena is also present, and is addressed by Helen in the thirteenth verse
of her first speech, but does not herself speak.

[135] With Polyxena.

[136] *I.e.,* her bridal clothing.

Put off thy mourning garment now; this regal vesture wear.
Forget henceforth thy captive state, and seemly braid thy hair.
Thy fall hath lift thee higher up and doth thee more advance;
Oft to be taken in the war doth bring the better chance.

And. This ill the Trojans never knew, in all their griefs and pain:
Before this time ye never made us to *rejoice* in vain.
Troy's tow'rs give light; oh, seemly time for marriage to be made!
Who would refuse the wedding day that Helen doth persuade?
The plague and ruin of each part, behold, dost thou not see,
These tombs of noble men, and how their bones here scattered be?
Thy bride-bed hath been cause of this, for thee all these be dead,
For thee the blood of Asia both and Europe hath been shed,
When thou, in joy and pleasure, both the fighting folk from far
Hast viewed, in doubt to whom to wish the glory of the war.
Go to, prepare the marriages. What need the torches light?
Behold, the tow'rs of Troy do shine with brands that blaze full bright!
O Trojans all, set to your hands, this wedlock celebrate:
Lament this day with woeful cry and tears, in seemly rate.

Hel. Though care do cause the want of wit and reason's rule deny,
And heavy hap doth ofttimes hate his mates in misery,
Yet I before most hateful judge dare well defend my part
That I of all your grievous cares sustain the greatest smart.
Andromache for Hector weeps, for Priam Hecuba;
For only Paris privily[137] bewaileth Helena.
A hard and grievous thing it is captivity to bear?
In Troy that yoke I suffered long, a prisoner whole ten year.
Turned are the Fates? Troy beaten down? To *Greece* I must repair.
The native country to have lost is ill—but worse to fear!
For dread thereof you need not care. *Your* evils all be past;
On *me* both parts will vengeance take. All lights on me at last.
Whom each man prisoner takes, god wot, she stands in slipp'ry stay;[138]

---

[137] She cannot, as can the others, lament her husband openly before the Greeks.

[138] In this and the following three verses Heywood has missed the sense, which should go somewhat like this: "It has depended for some time now on the uncertain lot which master each of *you* shall follow as slave; *my* master [Menelaus] dragged me off immediately, with no lot drawn. Was I the cause of wars and so much disaster to the Trojans? Think that true if a *Spartan* ship sailed your seas; but if I was a helpless prey carried off by *Trojan* oarsmen, if the goddess willed it so, . . ."

And me, not captive made by lot, yet Paris led away.
I have been cause of all these wars; and then your woes were wrought
When first your ships the Spartan seas and land of Grecia sought.
But if the goddess[139] willed it so, that I their prey should be,
And for reward to her beauty's judge she had appointed me,
Then pardon Paris.[140] Think this thing in wrathful judge doth lie:
The sentence Menelaus gives, and he this case shall try.
Now turn thy plaints, Andromache, and weep for Polyxene[141]—
Mine eyes for sorrows of my heart their tears may not refrain.

   And. Alas, what care makes *Helen* weep? What grief doth she
     lament?
Declare what crafts Ulysses casts, what mischief hath he sent.
Shall she from height of Ida's hill be headlong tumbled down?
Or else out of the turret's top in Troy shall she be thrown?
Or will they cast her from the cliffs into Sigean seas,
In bottom of the surging waves to end her ruthful days?
Show what thy count'nance hides, and tell the secrets of thy breast.
Some woes in Pyrrhus' wedding are far worse than all the rest.
Go to, give sentence on the maid, pronounce her destiny;
Delude no longer our mishaps. We are prepared to die.

   Hel. Would God th' expounder[142] of the gods would give his doom
     so right
That I, also, on point of sword might lose the loathsome light,
Or at Achilles' tomb with stroke of Pyrrhus' hand be slain
And bear a part of all thy fates, O wretched Polyxene
Whom yet Achilles woo'th to wed, and where his ashes lie
Requireth that thy blood be shed, and at his tomb to die.

   And. Behold, lo! how her noble mind of death doth gladly hear.
She decks herself, her regal weed in seemly wise to wear;
And to her head she sets her hand, the braided hair to lay.
To wed she thought it death; to die she thinks a wedding day.
But help, alas! my mother swoons to hear her daughter's death.

---

[139] Venus, after the judgment of Paris.
[140] The text Heywood followed reads *Paridi* for *praedae*; this should be, "pardon [me] the booty."
[141] By this rendering Heywood loses the effect of Helen's suddenly breaking down; she should say, "Forget your griefs for a little, Andromache, and persuade her, for I—I cannot keep back my tears."
[142] Calchas.

Arise, pluck up your heart, and take again the panting breath.
Alack, good mother, how slender stay that doth thy life sustain!
A little thing shall happy thee;[143] thou art almost past pain.
Her breath returns. She doth revive; her limbs their life do take.
So see, when wretches fain would die, how death doth them forsake.

  Hec. Doth yet Achilles live, alas! to work the Trojans spite?
Doth he rebel against us yet! O hand of Paris light![144]
The very tomb and ashes, lo, yet thirsteth for our blood.
A happy heap of children late on every side me stood;
It wearied me to deal the mother's kiss among them all.
The rest are lost; and this alone now doth me mother call.
Thou only child of Hecuba, a comfort left to me,
A stayer of my sorry state, and shall I now lose thee?
Depart, O wretched soul, and from this careful carcass fly
And ease me of such ruthful fates, to see my daughter die!
My weeping wets, alas, my eyes, and stains them over all,
And down my cheeks the sudden streams and show'rs of tears do fall.
But thou, dear daughter, may'st be glad! Cassandra would rejoice,[145]
Or Hector's wife, thus wed to be, if they might have their choice.

  And. We are the wretches, Hecuba; in cursèd case we stand
Whom straight the ship shall toss by seas into a foreign land.
But as for Helen, griefs be gone and turnèd to the best:[146]
She shall again her native country see, and live at rest.

  Hel. Ye would the more envy my state, if ye might know your own.
  And. And grow'th there yet more grief to me that erst I have not
    known?
  Hel. Such masters must ye serve as doth by chance of lots befall.
  And. Whose servant am I then become? Whom shall I master call?
  Hel. By lot ye fall to Pyrrhus' hands; you are his prisoner.

[143] *I.e.*, her long-desired death is near.

[144] Paris should have struck harder; Achilles is not dead enough.

[145] This verse and the following, though in this position in the manuscripts, so clearly make better sense after Hecuba has learned the fate of Andromache and Cassandra that most editors now transpose them to follow Helen's announcement that Cassandra belongs to Agamemnon and to precede Hecuba's question as to her own fate.

[146] By a mistranslation of one word, Heywood has missed the point: Andromache speaks not of Helen but of Polyxena, "The dear soil of her native land will cover *her*." So in Helen's speech following she would say, "Ye would the more envy *her* state, . . ."

And. Cassandra is happy! Fury saves perhaps,[147] and Phoebus, her.

Hel. Chief king[148] of Greeks Cassandra keeps, and his captive is she.

Hec. Is any one among them all that prisoner would have me?

Hel. You chancèd to Ulysses are; his prey ye are become.

Hec. Alas! what cruel, dire, and ireful dealer of the doom,

What god unjust, doth so divide the captives to their lords?

What grievous arbiter is he that to such choice accords?

What cruel hand to wretched folk so evil fates hath cast?

Who hath among Achilles' armor[149] Hector's mother placed?

Now am I captive, and beset with all calamity;

My bondage grieves me not, but *him* to serve it shameth me.

He that Achilles' spoils hath won shall Hector's also have.

Shall barren land, in closed with seas,[150] receive my bones in grave?

Lead me, Ulysses, where thou wilt, lead me. I make no stay.

My master I, and me my fates, shall follow every way:

Let never calm come to the seas, but let them rage with wind;

Come fire and sword! mine own mischance and Priam's let me find.[151]

In mean time haps this deep distress (my cares can know no calm):

I ran the race with Priamus, but he hath won the palm.[152]

But Pyrrhus comes with swiftened pace, and threat'ning brows doth wrest.

What stay'st thou, Pyrrhus? Strike thy sword now through this woeful breast,

And both at once the parents of thy father's wife[153] now slay.

Murderer of age, likes thee her blood? He draws my daughter away.

---

[147] *Sorte*, which Heywood renders as "perhaps," should be "from the lot": "Her madness and Phoebus [whose priestess she is] save her from the lot."

[148] Agamemnon.

[149] Ulysses had won Achilles' armor in the contest with Ajax.

[150] Ithaca, often described as small and barren.

[151] *I.e.*, "let find me"; Hecuba hopes that the fates that dog her will overtake her and involve Ulysses as well.

[152] *I.e.*, Priam has died first. Heywood most ingeniously makes sense of this verse and the preceding, in spite of a corrupt text. As emended by modern editors, the verses would mean: "Until they [her fates] shall come upon you, meanwhile this takes the place of your punishment: I used up your lot, I have stolen your prize," meaning that in the allotment of one slave-woman each Ulysses has drawn an ugly old woman.

[153] Polyxena; Pyrrhus has already killed her father Priam.

Defile the gods, and stain the sprites of Hell with slaughtered blood!—
To ask your mercy what avails? Our prayers do no good;
The vengeance ask I on your ships: that it the gods may please
According to this sacrifice[154] to guide you on the seas!
This wish I to your thousand sails: gods' wrath light on them all,
Even to the ship that beareth me, whatever may befall.

Chorus

A comfort is to man's calamity
A doleful flock of fellows in distress,
And sweet to him that mourns in misery
To hear them wail whom sorrows like oppress;
In deepest care his grief him bites the less
That his estate bewails not all alone,
But seeth with him the tears of many one.

For still it is the chief delight in woe,
And joy of them that sunk in sorrows are,
To see like fates befall to many moe
That may take part of all their woeful fare,
And not alone to be oppressed with care;
There is no wight of woe that doth complain
When all the rest do like mischance sustain.

In all this world if happy man were none,
None, though he were, would think himself a wretch;
Let once the rich, with heaps of gold, be gone,
Whose hundred head his pastures overreach,
Then would the poor man's heart begin to stretch.
There is no wretch whose life him doth displease
But in respect of those who live at ease.

Sweet is to him that stands in deep distress
To see no man in joyful plight to be.
Whose only vessel wind and wave oppress
Full sore his chance bewails, and weepeth he
That with his own none other's wrack doth see

154 *I.e.*, in a manner suitable to such an impious offering.

When he alone makes shipwreck on the sand
And naked falls to long-desirèd land.

A thousand sail who see'th to drench in seas
With better will the storm hath overpassed;
His heavy hap doth him the less displease
When broken boards abroad be many cast
And shipwrecked ships to shore they flit full fast,
With doubled waves, when stoppèd is the flood
With heaps of them that there have lost their good.

Full sore did Phrixus Helle's[155] loss complain,
What time the leader of his flock of sheep
Upon his back alone he bore them twain
And wet his golden locks amid the deep;
In piteous plaint, alas, he gan to weep.
The death of her it did him deep displease
That shipwreck made amid the drenching seas.

And piteous was the plaint, and heavy mood
Of woeful Pyrrha, and eke Deucalion,
That nought beheld about them but the flood,
When they of all mankind were left alone;
Amid the seas full sore they made their moan
To see themselves thus left alive in woe,
When neither land they saw, nor fellows moe.

Anon these plaints and Trojans' tears shall quail,
And here and there the ships them toss by seas.
When trumpet's sound shall warn to hoist up sail
And through the waves with wind to seek their ways,
Then shall these captives go to end their days
In land unknown, when once with hasty oar
The drenching deep they take, and shun the shore.

[155] Heywood has "Pyrrhus" and "Helen's," though it is clear from the rest of
the passage that the story of Phrixus and Helle (*q.v.* in *Index of Proper Names*).
is intended. It may be that Heywood did not know the myth at all, since his
rendering of the stanza seems a bit eccentric (though perhaps "shipwreck" in
the final verse is intended to be a metaphor).

What state of mind shall then in wretches be
When shore shall sink from sight, and seas arise,
When Ida's hill to lurk aloof they see?
Then point with hand from far where Troia lies
Shall child and mother, talking in this wise,
"Lo, yonder Troy, where smoke it fumeth high."
By this the Trojans shall their country spy.

The Fifth Act

Nuntius, Andromache, Hecuba

Nun. O dire, fierce, wretched, horrible, O cruel Fates accursed,
Of Mars his ten years' bloodshed-blows the woeful'st and the worst!
Alas! which should I first bewail? Thy cares, Andromacha?
Or else lament the wretched age of woeful Hecuba.

Hec. Whatever man's calamity ye wail for, mine it is:
I bear the smart of all their woes; each other feels but his,
Whoever he. I am the wretch; all haps to me at last.

Nun. Slain is the maid, and from the walls of Troy the child is cast;
But both, as them became, they took their death with stomach stout.

And. Declare the double slaughters, then, and tell the whole
    throughout.

Nun. One tow'r of all the rest, ye know, doth yet in Troy remain,
Where Priam wonted was to sit and view the armies twain,
His little nephew[156] eke with him to lead, and from afar
His father's fights with fire and sword to show, on feats of war.
This tow'r, sometime well known by fame, and Trojans' honor most,
Is now with captains of the Greeks beset on every coast:
With swift recourse, and from the ships in clustered heaps anon,
Both tag and rag they run to gaze what thing should there be done.
Some climb the hills to seek a place where they might see it best;
Some ones the rocks a-tiptoe stand to overlook the rest.
Some on their temples wear the pine, some beech, some crowns of
    bay;[157]

[156] Astyanax.
[157] Heywood has inexplicably inverted subjects and objects: "A pine bears
one man, a laurel-tree another, a beech one; the forest shakes with a whole nation
clinging to it."

For garlands torn is every tree that standeth in their way.
Some from the highest mountain's top aloof beholdeth all,
Some scale the buildings half-burnt, and some the ruinous wall;
Yea, some there were—oh, mischief, lo!—that, for the more despite,
The tomb of Hector sit upon, beholders of the sight.
With princely pace Ulysses then passed through the pressèd band
Of Greeks, King Priam's little nephew leading by the hand.
The child with unrepining gait passed through his en'mies' hands
Up toward the walls; and as anon in turret's top he stands,
From thence adown his lofty looks he cast on every part.
The nearer death, more free from care he seemed, and fear of heart.
Amid his foes his stomach swells, and fierce he was to sight,
Like tiger's whelp, that the rats in vain with toothless chap do bite.[158]
Alas! for pity then each one rues on his tender years;
And all the rout that present were, for him they shed their tears.
Yea, not Ulysses them restrained, but trickling down they fall;
And only he wept not, poor fool, whom they bewailèd all.
But while on gods Ulysses called, and Calchas' words expound,
In midst of Priam's land, alas! the child leapt down to ground.
   And. What cruel Colchus[159] could, or Scyth, such slaughter take in
      hand,
Or by the shore of Caspian Sea what barbarous lawless land?
Busiris to the altars yet no infants' blood hath shed,
Nor never yet were children slain for feast of Diomed.[160]
Who shall, alas! in tomb thee lay, or hide thy limbs again?
   Nun. What limbs from such a headlong fall could in a child
      remain?
His body's payse thrown down to ground hath battered all his bones,
His face, his noble father's marks, are spoiled against the stones,
His neck unjointed is, his head so dashed with flint-stone stroke
That scattered is the brain about, the skull is all to-broke.
Thus lie'th he now, dismembered corpse, deformed and all to-rent.
   And. Lo, herein doth he yet likewise his father represent.[161]

---

   [158] The simile is actually of a cub too young to bite, who nevertheless bristles and tries to bite.
   [159] Heywood has "Calchas," probably a misprint.
   [160] *I.e.,* for his famous horses.
   [161] Because Hector's body, too, had been disfigured by being dragged behind Achilles' chariot.

Nun. What time the child hath headlong fall'n thus from the walls
   of Troy
And all the Greeks themselves bewailed the slaughter of the boy,
Yet straight return they back, and at Achilles' tomb again
The second mischief go to work, the death of Polyxene.
This tomb the waves of surging seas beset, the outer side,
The other part the fields enclose about, and pastures wide.
In vale environèd with hills that round about do rise,
Aslope on height erected are the banks, in theatre wise.
By all the shore then swarm the Greeks, and thick on heaps they press;
Some hope that by her death they shall their ships' delay release,
Some others joy their en'mies stock thus beaten down to be,
A great part of the people both the slaughter hate—and see.
The Trojans eke no less frequent their own calamities,
And all afraid beheld the last of all their miseries,
When first proceeded torches bright, as guise of wedlock is,
And, author thereof, led the way the lady Tyndaris.[162]
"Such wedlock," pray the Trojans then, "god send Hermiona!
And would god to her husband so restored were Helena!"
Fear mazed each part. But Polyxene her bashful look down cast;
And more than erst her glittering eyes and beauty shined at last,
As sweetest seems then Phoebus' light when down his beams do sway,
When stars again, with night at hand, oppress the doubtful day.
Astounded much the people were, and all they her commend;
And now much more than ever erst they praised her at her end.
Some with her beauty movèd were, some with her tender years,
Some to behold the turns of chance, and how each thing thus wears.
But most them moves her valiant mind and lofty stomach high,
So strong, so stout, so ready of heart, and well prepared to die.
Thus pass they forth, and bold before King Pyrrhus goeth the maid.
They pity her, they marvel her, their hearts were all afraid.
As soon as then the hard hill-top, where die she should, they trod
And high upon his father's tomb the youthful Pyrrhus stood,
The manly maid she never shrunk one foot, nor backward drew,
But boldly turns to meet the stroke with stout unchangèd hue.
Her courage moves each one; and lo, a strange thing, monstrous-like,
That Pyrrhus even himself stood still for dread, and durst not strike.

[162] Heywood has "Pindaris," probably a typographical error.

But as he had his glitt'ring sword in her to hilts updone,
The purple blood at mortal wound then gushing out it spun;
Nor yet her courage her forsook when dying in that stound:
She fell, as th' earth should her revenge, with ireful rage to ground.
Each people wept, the Trojans first with privy fearful cry,
The Grecians eke, each one bewailed her death apparently.
This order had the sacrifice. Her blood the tomb up drank;
No drop remain'th above the ground, but down forthwith it sank.

   Hec. Now go, now go, ye Greeks, and now repair ye safely home;
With careless ships and hoisted sails now cut the salt sea-foam.
The child and virgin both be slain, your battles finished are.
Alas, where shall I end my age, or whither bear my care?
Shall I my daughter or my nephew or my husband moan?
My country else? or all at once? or else myself alone?
My wish is death, that children both and virgins fiercely takes!
Wherever cruel death doth haste to strike, it me forsakes:
Amid the en'mies weapons all, amid both sword and fire
All night sought for, thou flee'st from me that do thee most desire.
Not flame of fire, not fall of tow'r, not cruel en'my's hand
Hath rid my life. How near, alas! could death to Priam stand?[163]

   Nun. Now, captives all, with swift recourse repair ye to the seas!
Now spread the ships their sails abroad, and forth they seek their ways.

FINIS

---

[163] *I.e.,* "How near could death stand to Priam and not take me also?"
Editors now read *steti* for *stetit*: "And yet how near to Priam I stood [when
he was killed]!"

AGAMEMNON

The Eighth Tragedy of L. Annaeus Seneca,
Entitled Agamemnon.
Translated out of Latin into English
by John Studley

THE ARGUMENT

AGAMEMNON, GENERAL of that noble army of the Greeks which after ten years' siege won Troy, committed the entire government of his country and kingdom during his absence to his wife Clytemnestra, who, forgetting all wifely loyalty and womanly chastity, fell in lawless love and used adulterous company with Aegisthus, son to Thyestes, whom aforetime Atreus (being his own natural brother, and father to this Agamemnon), in revenge of a former adultery, had caused to eat his own two[164] children.

At length, understanding by Eurybates that Troy was won, and that her husband Agamemnon was coming homeward with a young lady named Cassandra, daughter to King Priam, partly enraged with jealousy and disdain thereof, and partly loath to lose the company of Aegisthus her coadulterer, [she] practised with him how to murder her husband, which accordingly they brought to pass; and not resting so contented, they also put Cassandra to death, imprisoned Electra, daughter to Agamemnon, and sought to have slain his son Orestes. Which Orestes, fleeing for safeguard of his life to one Strophius, his dead father's dear friend, was by him secretly kept a long time, till at length coming privily into Mycenae and by his sister's means conducted where his mother Clytemnestra and Aegisthus were, in revenge of his father's death killed them both.

[164] An error, for "three."

The Speakers'[165] Names

Thyestes [brother to Agamemnon's father Atreus, and father (by his own daughter) to Aegisthus; he is dead at the opening of the play, and it is his ghost which appears to spur Aegisthus on to vengeance]

Chorus [of Argive women]

Clytemnestra [wife to Agamemnon and Aegisthus' mistress]

Nutrix[166] [Clytemnestra's nurse]

Aegisthus [first cousin to Agamemnon, and Clytemnestra's lover]

Eurybates [messenger of Agamemnon]

A Company of Greeks

Cassandra [daughter of Priam, King of Troy, and Agamemnon's captive]

Agamemnon [King of Argos]

Electra [daughter of Agamemnon and Clytemnestra]

Strophius [King of Phocis and friend of Agamemnon]

[*Mycenae, before the Palace*]

[165] The "company of Greeks," who have no lines, should not appear on this list, while Studley has omitted from it a Chorus of Trojan Women, who do speak. Besides the speakers there are two nonspeaking roles, those of Orestes, son of Agamemnon, and Pylades, son of Strophius.

[166] "Nutrix" is simply the Latin for "wet-nurse."

The First Act

Thyestes

Thy. Departing from the darkened dens which Ditis low doth keep,
Lo, here I am sent out again from Tartar's dungeon deep,
Thyestes I, that whether coast to shun do stand in doubt:
Th' infernal fiends I fly, the folk of earth I chase about.
My conscience, lo, abhors that I should hither passage make;
Appallèd sore with fear and dread my trembling sinews shake.
My father's house, or rather yet my brother's, I espy;
This is the old and antique porch of Pelops' progeny:
Here first the Greeks on princes' heads do place the royal crown,
And here in throne aloft they lie, they that jet up and down
With stately sceptre in their hand; eke here their courts do lie,
This is their place of banqueting—return therefore will I![167]
Nay, better were it not to haunt the loathsome Limbo lakes?
Whereas the Stygian porter[168] doth advance with lusty crakes,
His triple gorge behung with mane shag-hairy, rusty, black;
Where Ixion's carcase, linkèd fast, the whirling wheel doth rack
And rolleth still upon himself; whereas full oft in vain
Much toil is lost, the tott'ring stone[169] down tumbling back again;
Where growing guts[170] the greedy gripes do gnaw with ravening bites;
Where parchèd up with burning thirst among the waves he[171] sits
And gapes to catch the fleeting flood with hungry chaps beguiled
That pays his painful punishment, whose feast the gods defiled—
Yet that old man so steeped in years at length by tract of time,
How great a part belongs to me, and portion, of his crime!
Account we all the grisly ghosts whom, guilty found of ill,
The Gnosian judge[172] in Pluto's pits doth toss in torments still;

[167] Because this is where he was made to eat his children.
[168] Cerberus, *q.v.* in *Index of Proper Names.*
[169] Of Sisyphus, *q.v.* in *Index of Proper Names.*
[170] Of Tityus, *q.v.* in *Index of Proper Names.*
[171] Tantalus, *q.v.* in *Index of Proper Names.*
[172] Minos, *q.v.* in *Index of Proper Names.*

Thyestes, I, in dreary deeds will far surmount the rest—
Yet to my brother yield I, though I gorged my bloody breast
And stuffèd have my pampered paunch even with my children three
That crammèd lie within my ribs and have their tomb in me.
The bowels of my swallowed babes devourèd up I have,
Nor fickle fortune me alone the father doth deprave,
But enterprising greater guilt than that is put in ure,
To file my daughter's bawdy bed my lust she doth allure.
To speak these words I do not spare: I wrought the heinous deed
That therefore I through all my stock might, parent still, proceed.
My daughter, driven by force of Fates and destinies divine,
Doth breed young bones, and lades her womb with sinful seed of mine.
Lo, nature, changèd upside down and out of order turned,
This mingle-mangle hath she made. O fact to be forlorned!
A father and a grandsire, lo, confusèdly I am,
My daughter's husband both become and father to the same;
Those babes that should my nephews be, when nature rightly runs,
She, being tumbled, doth confound and mingle with my sons:
The crystal clearness of the day, and Phoebus' beams so bright,
Are mixèd with the foggy clouds and darkness dim of night.
When wickedness had wearied us, too late truce taken was,
Even when our detestable deeds were done and brought to pass.[173]
But valiant Agamemnon, he, grand captain of the host
Who bare the sway among the kings, and rulèd all the roost,
Whose flaunting flag and banner brave, displayed in royal sort,
A thousand sail of sousing ships did guard to Phrygian port,
And with their swelling shatling sails the surging sea did hide
That beateth on the banks of Troy, and floweth by her side,
When Phoebus' cart the Zodiac ten times had over run,
And waste the battered walls do lie of Troy destroyed and won,
Returned he is to yield his throat unto his traitress wife,
That shall with force of bloody blade bereave him of his life.
The glittering sword, the hewing axe, and wounding weapons moe,

---

[173] Studley has here misunderstood the Latin, which speaks of the fulfillment
of the oracle that Thyestes' revenge on the house of Atreus would come through
his incestuous union with his own daughter: "When wickedness had wearied
me, though after death and late at length the promise comes to pass of that
uncertain fate: for valiant Agamemnon, ..."

With blood for blood new set abroach shall make the floor to flow.
With sturdy stroke and boist'rous blow of pithy poleaxe given
His beaten brains are pashed abroad, his crackèd skull is riven.
Now mischief marcheth on apace, now falsehood doth appear,
Now butcher's slaughter doth approach, and murder draweth near.
In honor of thy native day, Aegisthus, they prepare
The solemn feast with junketing and dainty toothsome fare.
Fie, what doth shame abash thee so, and cause thy courage quail?
Why doubts thy right hand what to do? To smite why doth it fail?
What he, forecasting, might suspect why shouldst thou take advice?
Why frettest thou, demanding if thou may it enterprise?
Nay; if a mother it beseem thou rather may'st surmise.[174]
What now? How happ'neth it that thus the smiling summer's night,
When Phoebus from th' antipodes should render soon the light,
On sudden, change their turns with nights that last and linger long,
When winter's Boreas bitter blasts doth puff the trees among?
Or what doth cause the gliding stars to stay still in the sky?
We wait for Phoebus.[175] To the world bring day now by and by.

Chorus [of Argive Women]

O Fortune, that dost fail the great estate of kings,
On slippery sliding seat thou placest lofty things
And sett'st on tott'ring sort, where perils do abound.
Yet never kingdom calm nor quiet could be found:
No day to sceptres sure doth shine, that they might say,
"Tomorrow shall we rule as we have done today."
One cloud of crooked care another bringeth in;
One hurly-burly done, another doth begin.
Not so the raging sea doth boil upon the sand
Whereas the southern wind that blows in Afric land
One wave upon another doth heap with sturdy blast;
Not so doth Euxine Sea his swelling waves upcast,
Nor so his belching stream from shallow bottom roll,
That borders hard upon the icy frozen Pole,

[174] *I.e.,* You should rather think if it befit your incestuous birth.
[175] An error for "we hinder Phoebus"; the ghost, seeing that the summer night has grown as long as a winter one, realizes that it is his presence which prevents the coming of the dawn, and so departs.

Whereas Bootes bright doth twine his wain about
And of the marble seas doth nothing stand in doubt.[176]
O how doth Fortune toss and tumble in her wheel
The stagg'ring states of kings that ready be to reel!
Fain would they dreaded be—and yet, not settled so,
Whenas they fearèd are, they fear, and live in woe.
The silent lady, Night, so sweet to man and beast,
Cannot bestow on them her safe and quiet rest:
Sleep, that doth overcome and break the bonds of grief,
It cannot ease their hearts nor minister relief.
What castle strongly built, what bulwark, tower, or town
Is not by mischief's means brought topsy-turvy down?
What rampired walls are not made weak by wicked war?
From stately courts of kings doth Justice fly afar:
In princely palaces of honesty the lore
And wedlock-vow devout is let by little store.
The bloody Bellone those doth haunt with gory hand
Whose light and vain conceit in painted pomp doth stand;
And those Erinys wood turmoils with frenzy's fits,
That evermore in proud and haughty houses sits,
Which fickle Fortune's hand, in twinkling of an eye,
From high and proud degree drives down in dust to lie.
Although that skirmish cease, no banners be displayed,
And though no wiles be wrought, and policy be stayed,
Down, paysèd with their weight, the massy things do sink,
And from her burden doth unstable Fortune shrink.
The swelling sails, puffed up with gale of western wind,
Do yet mistrust thereof a tempest in their mind;
The threat'ning tops, that touch the clouds, of lofty tow'rs
Be soonest paid and beat with south wind's rainy show'rs;
The darksome wood doth see its tough and sturdy oak,
Well woned in years, to be clean overthrown and broke;
The lightning's flashing flame, out-breaking in the sky,
First lighteth on the mounts and hills that are most high;
The bodies corpulent and of the largest size
Are rifest still to catch diseases when they rise;
Whenas the flock to graze in pasture fat is put,

---

[176] *I.e.,* has no fear of; Bootes does not set.

Whose neck is larded best, his throat shall first be cut.
What Fortune doth advance and hoisteth up on high,
She sets it up to fall again more grievously.
The things of middle sort and of a mean degree
Endure above the rest and longest days do see.
The man of mean estate most happy is of all,
Who, pleasèd with the lot that doth to him befall,
Doth sail on silent shore with calm and quiet tide
And dreads with bruisèd barge on swelling seas to ride,
Nor launching to the deep where bottom none is found,
May with his rudder search and reach the shallow ground.

THE SECOND ACT

The First Scene

Clytemnestra, Nutrix

Cly. O drowsy, dreaming, doting soul, what cometh in thy brain
To seek about for thy defense what way thou may'st attain?
What ails thy skittish wayward wits to waver up and down?
The fittest shift prevented is, the best path overgrown:
Thou mightest once maintainèd have thy wedlock-chamber chaste,
And eke have ruled with majesty by faith conjoinèd fast;
Now nurture's lore neglected is, all right doth clean decay,
Religion and dignity with faith are worn away.
And ruddy shame with blushing cheeks, so far, God wot! is past
That when it would it cannot come now home again at last.
O let me now at random run with bridle at my will!
The safest path to mischief is by mischief open still.
Now put in practice, seek about, search out and learn to find
The wily trains and crafty guiles of wicked womankind,
What any devilish traitorous dame durst do in working woe,
Or any wounded in her wits by shot of Cupid's bow,
Whatever rigorous stepdame could commit with desperate hand,
Or as the wench[177] who, flaming fast by Venus' poisoning brand,
Was driven by lewd incestuous love in ship of Thessal land
To flit away from Colchis' isle, where Phasis' channel deep

[177] Medea, *q.v.* in *Index of Proper Names.*

With silver stream down from the hills of Armenie doth sweep.
Get weapons good, get Bilbao blades, or temper poison strong;
Or with some yonker trudge from Greece by theft the seas along—
Why dost thou faint to talk of theft, exile, or privy flight?
These came by hap;[178] thou therefore must on greater mischief light.

   Nut. O worthy Queen, among the Greeks that bear'st the swinging
     sway,
And born of Leda's royal blood, what mutt'ring dost thou say?
What fury fell enforceth thee, bereavèd of thy wits,
To rage and rave with Bedlam brains, to fret with frantic fits?
Though, madame, thou do counsel keep, and not complain thy case,
Thine anguish plain appeareth in thy pale and wanny face;
Reveal therefore what is thy grief. Take leisure good, and stay:
What reason could not remedy, oft curèd hath delay.

   Cly. So grievous is my careful case which plungeth me so sore
That deal I cannot with delay, nor linger any more.
The flashing flames and furious force of fiery fervent heat,
Out-raging in my boiling breast, my burning bones doth beat;
It sucks the sappy marrow out, the juice it doth convey,
It frets, it tears, it rends, it gnaws my guts and gall away.
Now feeble fear still eggs me on, with dolor being pressed;
And cankered hate with thwacking thumps doth bounce upon my
     breast.
The blinded boy[179] that lovers' hearts doth rive with deadly stroke
Entangled hath my linkèd mind with lewd and wanton yoke,
Refusing still to take a foil or clean to be confound.
Among these broils and agonies my mind besieging round,
Lo! feeble, weary, battered-down, and under-trodden shame,
That wrestleth, striveth, struggleth hard, and fighteth with the same.
Thus am I driven to diverse shores and beat from bank to bank
And tossèd in the foamy floods that strive with courage crank.
As when here wind, and there the stream, when both their force will
     try,
From sands a-low do hoist and rear the seas with surges high;
The welt'ring wave doth staggering stand, not witting what to do,

---

[178] The text Studley used reads *sors ista fecit* instead of the correct *soror ista fecit*: "These things thy sister did; thou must on greater mischief light," where the reference is to Helen (*q.v.* in *Index of Proper Names*).

[179] Cupid, *q.v.* in *Index of Proper Names*.

But, hovering, doubts whose furious force he best may yield him to.
My kingdom[180] therefore I cast off, my sceptre I forsake:
As anger, sorrow, hope, me lead, that way I mean to take.
All at a venture to the seas I yield my beaten barge;
At random careless will I run, now will I rove at large.
Whereas my mind to fancy fond doth gad and run astray,
It is the best to choose that chance and follow on that way.

Nut. This desp'rate dotage doth declare and rashness rude and blind,
To choose out chance to be the guide and ruler of thy mind.

Cly. He that is driven to utter pinch and furthest shift of all,
What need he doubt his doubtful lot or how his luck befall?

Nut. In silent shore thou sailest. Yet thy trespass we may hide
If thou thyself detect it not nor cause it be descried.

Cly. Alas, it is more blazed abroad, and further it is blown,
Than any crime that ever in this princely court was sown.

Nut. Thy former fault with pensive heart and sorrow thou dost rue,
And fondly yet thou goest about to set abroach a new?

Cly. It is a very foolishness to keep a mean therein!

Nut. The thing he fears he doth augment who heapeth sin on sin.

Cly. But fire and sword [181] to cure the same the place of salve supply.

Nut. There is no man who, at the first, extremity will try.

Cly. In working mischief men do take the readiest way they find.

Nut. The sacred name of wedlock once revoke and have in mind.

Cly. Ten years have I been desolate, and led a widow's life;
Yet shall I entertain anew my husband as his wife?

Nut. Consider yet thy son and heir whom he of thee begot.

Cly. And eke my daughter's[182] wedding-blaze as yet forget I not;
Achilles eke, my son-in-law, to mind I do not spare,
How well he kept his vow that he to me, his mother, sware.

Nut. Whenas our navy might not pass by wind, nor yet by stream,
Thy daughter's blood in sacrifice their passage did redeem:
She stirred and broke the sluggish seas whose water still did stand,
Whose feeble force might not hoist up the vessels from the land.

Cly. I am ashamèd herewithal, it maketh me repine,

---

[180] Studley loses the figure by this rendering of *regimen*, which can also mean "rudder."

[181] The *ferrum et ignis* of the original could mean "surgery and cautery," which would make more sense in this context.

[182] Iphigenia, *q.v.* in *Index of Proper Names.*

That Tyndaris,[183] who from the gods doth fetch her noble line,
Should give the ghost t'assuage the wrath of gods, and them appease,
Whereby the Greekish navy might have passage free by seas.
My grudging mind still harps upon my daughter's wedding day,
Whom he hath made for Pelops' stock the bloody ransom pay,
Whenas with cruel countenance imbrued with gory blood,[184]
As at a wedding-altar's side, th'unpitiful parent stood.
It irkèd Calchas' woeful heart, who did abhor the same;
His oracle he rued, and eke the back-reflecting flame.
O wicked and ungracious stock, that winnest ill with ill,
Triumphing in thy filthy feats, increasing lewdness still!
By blood we win the wavering winds, by death we purchase war.
    Nut. But by this means a thousand ships at once releasèd are.
    Cly. With lucky fate attempt the seas did not the loosèd rout:[185]
For Aulis' isle th' ungracious fleet from port did tumble out.
As with a lewd unlucky hand the war he did begin,
So fortune favored his success to thrive no more therein:
Her[186] love as captive holdeth him, whom captive he did take;
Not movèd with the earnest suit that could Achilles make,
Of Phoebus' prelate[187] Sminthical he did retain the spoil.
When for the sacred virgin's love his furious breast doth boil,
Achilles' rough and thund'ring threats could not him qualify,
Nor he that doth direct the fates above the starry sky[188]—
To us he is an augur just, and keeps his promise due,
But while he threats his captive trulls of word he is not true.
The savage people fierce in wrath once might not move his sprite,

---

[183] Another name for Clytemnestra, as daughter of Tyndareus.

[184] Studley takes *ore sacrifico* (probably "praying mouth") to mean "bloody face."

[185] *I.e.*, the loosed rout did not attempt the seas with lucky fate; she means that the port itself ejected the fleet because of the sacrilege of the human sacrifice.

[186] Chryseis, *q.v.* in *Index of Proper Names.*

[187] Chryses, father of Chryseis.

[188] This verse and the four following make little, if any, sense, and seem to represent a complete misunderstanding of the text on Studley's part. It is perhaps best merely to provide a paraphrase of the original: "Not he who alone reads the fates of the universe (a prophet trustworthy in the case of me and my family, but untrustworthy in the case of captive women), not the plague-struck people and the blazing funeral pyres." Clytemnestra is complaining that Agamemnon, though willing to obey Calchas' prophecy in sacrificing Iphigenia, ignored him when he ordered the return of Chryseis.

Who did purloin the kindled tents with fire blazing bright:
When slaughter great on Greeks was made in most extremest fight,
Without a foe he, conquerèd, with leanness pines away;
In lewd and wanton chamber tricks he spends the idle day,
And freshly still he feeds his lust. Lest that some other while
His chamber chaste should want a stews that might the same defile,
On Lady Briseis' love again his fancy fond doth stand,
Whom he hath got, that wrested was out of Achilles' hand.
And carnal copulation to have he doth not shame,
Though from her husband's[189] bosom he hath snatched the wicked
    dame—
Tush! he that doth at Paris grudge! With wound but newly struck,
Inflamed with Phrygian prophet's[190] love, his boiling breast doth
    smoke:
Now after Trojan booties brave, and Troy o'erwhelmed, he saw,
Returned he is a prisoner's spouse, and Priam's son-in-law.
Now, heart, be bold! take courage good, of stomach now be stout;
A field that easily is not fought to pitch thou goest about.
In practice mischief thou must put. Why hop'st thou for a day
While Priam's daughter, come from Troy, in Greece do bear the
    sway?
But as for thee, poor silly wretch, ah, waitest at thy place?
Thy widow-virgins and Orest, his father like in face,
Consider their calamities to come, and eke their cares,
Whom all the peril of the broil doth threat in thy affairs.
O cursèd caitiff, woeful wretch, why dost thou loiter so?
Thy little brats a stepdame[191] have whose wrath will work their woe.
With gashing sword, an if thou can none other way provide,
Now thrust it through another's ribs, then lance thy gory side;
So murder twain with bruèd blood, let blood immixèd be,
And by destroying of thyself destroy thy spouse with thee.
Death is not sauced with sups of sorrow, if some man else I have
Whose breathless corpse I wish to pass with me to deadly grave.
    Nut. Queen, bridle thine affections, and wisely rule thy rage,
Thy swelling mood now mitigate, thy choler eke assuage;
Weigh well the weighty enterprise that thou dost take in hand:

---

[189] Achilles, *q.v.* in *Index of Proper Names.*
[190] Cassandra, *q.v.* in *Index of Proper Names.*
[191] Cassandra.

Triumphant victor he returns of mighty Asia land;
Avenging Europe's injury, with him he brings away
The spoils of sackèd Pergama, a huge and mighty prey;
In bondage eke he leads the folk of long-assaulted Troy—
Yet darest thou by policy attempt him to annoy,
Whom with the dint of glitt'ring sword Achilles durst not harm,
Although his rash and desperate dicks the froward knight did arm,
Nor Ajax, yet more hardy man, up yielding vital breath
Whom frantic fury fell enforced to wound himself to death,
Nor Hector, he whose only life procured the Greeks' delay
And long in war for victory enforcèd them to stay,
Nor Paris' shaft, whose cunning hand with shot so sure did aim,
Nor Mighty Memnon, swart and black, had power to hurt the same,
Nor Xanthus' flood, where to and fro dead carcasses did swim,
With armor hewed, and therewithal some maimèd broken limb,
Nor Simois, that purple walms, with slaughter dyed, doth steer,
Nor Cycnus, lily white, the son of fenny god[192] so dear,
Nor yet the mustering Thracian host, nor warlike Rhesus King,
Nor Amazons, who to the wars did painted quivers bring
And bore their hatchets in their hands with target and with shield,
Yet had no power with ghastly wound to foil him in the field?
Since he such scourings hath escaped and plunged, of perils past,
Intendest thou to murder him returning home at last,
And sacred altars to profane with slaughters so impure?
Shall Greece, th' avenger, let this wrong long unrevenged endure?
The grim and fierce courageous horse, the battles, shouts, and cries,
The swelling seas which bruisèd barks do dread when storms arise,
Behold: the fields with streams of blood o'erflowed and deeply
     drowned,
And all the chivalry of Troy in servile bondage bound,
Which Greeks have writ in registers.[193] Thy stubborn stomach bind,
Subdue thy fond affections, and pacify thy mind.

[192] As a translation of *aequorei dei* this seems particularly unfortunate;
Cycnus was the son of Neptune.

[193] Studley has mistaken the sense of the whole preceding passage: the Nurse
is actually asking Clytemnestra to contemplate the possibility of another war
like the Trojan, which may be fought to avenge Agamemnon's death; hence
the emphasis upon the sea rather than the ships, for example, is inappropriate.
He has come to grief in the final clause by rendering *regesta*, "re-enacted,"

The Second Scene

Aegisthus, Clytemnestra

Aeg. The cursèd time that evermore my mind did most detest,
The days that I abhorrèd have, and hated in my breast,
Are come, are come, that mine estate will bring to utter wrack—
Alas, my heart, why dost thou fail, and fainting flyest back?
What dost thou mean, at first assault from armor thus to fly?
Trust this: the cruel gods intend my doleful destiny,
To wrap thee in with perils round and catch thee in a band;
Endeavor, drudge, with all thy power their plagues for to withstand,
With stomach stout, rebellious, to fire and sword appeal.

Cly. It is no plague if such a death thy native dest'nies deal.[194]

Aeg. O partner of my perils all, begot of Leda, thou,
Direct thy doings after mine, and unto thee I vow
This drosel sluggish ringleader, this stout strong-hearted sire,
Shall pay thee so much blood again as shed he hath in fire.
How haps it that thy[195] trembling cheeks to be so pale and white,
Lying aghast as in a trance with fainting face upright?

Cly. His conscience wedlock-vow doth prick and brings him home
    again;
Let us return, the self-same trade anew for to retain
To which at first we should have stuck and ought not to forsake.
To covenant continent anew let us ourselves betake:
To take the trade of honesty at no time is too late.
He purged is from punishment whose heart the crime doth hate.

Aeg. Why, whither wilt thou gad, O rash and unadvisèd dame?
What, dost thou earnestly believe, and firmly trust the same,
That Agamemnon's spousal bed will loyal be to thee,
That nought doth underprop thy mind which might thy terror be?[196]

---

by its medieval meaning of "registered." The sense in the original of this clause
is somewhat as follows: "Imagine the whole fate of the captured House of
Dardanus re-enacted for the Greeks."

[194] This line is now usually considered part of Aegisthus' speech, and in the
original seems to mean, "Death is no punishment for one born thus," the reference being to his birth from an incestuous union.

[195] Studley, apparently by simple error, has "his."

[196] This verse should be in the form of a concessive clause ("Though nought
. . .") and should serve to introduce the next sentence.

His proud success, puffed up too high with lucky blast of wind,
Might make so crank, and set aloft, his haughty swelling mind.
Among his peers he stately was ere Trojan turrets torn;
How think ye then his stomach stout, by nature given to scorn,
In haughtiness augmented is, more in himself to joy,
Through this triumphant victory and conquest got of Troy?
Before his voyage Mycene king most mildly did he reign;
But now a tyrant truculent returned he is again,
Good luck and proud prosperity do make his heart so rise.
With what great preparation, preparèd solemn-wise,
A rabblement of strumpets come that cling about him all!
But yet the prophetess of Phoebe, whom god of truth we call,
Appears above the rest; she keeps the King, she doth him guide.
Wilt thou in wedlock have a mate, and not for it provide?
So would not she! The greatest grief this is unto a wife:
Her husband's minion in her house to lead an open life;
A queen's estate cannot abide her peer with her to reign,
In jealous wedlock will not her companion sustain.

    Cly. Aegist, in desp'rate mood again why set'st thou me afloat?
Why kindlest thou the sparks of ire, in embers covered, hot?
If that the victor's own free will release his captive's care,
Why may not I, his lady spouse, have hope as well to fare?[197]
One law doth rule in royal throne and pompous princely towers;
Among the vulgar sort another, in private simple bowers.
What though my grudging fancy force that, at my husband's hand,
Sharp execution of the law I stubbornly withstand?
Regarding this that heinously offended him I have,
He gently will me pardon grant who needs the same to crave.

    Aeg. Even so on this condition thou may'st with him compound:
To pardon him if he again to pardon thee be bound?
The subtle science of the law, the statutes of our land,
That long ago decreèd were, thou dost not understand.
The judges[198] be malicious men, they spite and envy us;
But he shall have them partial his causes to discuss.

---

[197] The sense of this couplet should be: "A victor, he has indulged himself with a captive girl; it is not right for a wife or a mistress to take any notice of this."

[198] In the original it is kings themselves who are said to be "harsh judges to us, favorable to themselves."

This is the chiefest privilege that doth to kings belong:
What law forbiddeth other men they do, and do no wrong.

Cly. He pardoned Helen. She is wed to Menelas again,
Which Europe all with Asia did plunge alike in pain.

Aeg. No lady's lust hath ravished yet Atrides[199] in his life,
Nor privily purloined his heart, betrothèd to his wife.
To pick a quarrel *he* begins, and matter thee to blame;
Suppose thou nothing hast commit that worthy is of shame:
What booteth him whom princes hate an honest life to frame?
He never doth complain[200] his wrong, but ever bears the blame.
Wilt thou repair to Sparte, and to thy country trudge aright?
Wilt thou become a renegade from such a worthy wight?
Divorcement made from kings will not so let the matter scape;
Thou easest fear by fickle hope that falsely thou dost shape.

Cly. My trespass is disclosed to none but to a trusty wight.

Aeg. At princes' gates fidelity yet never enter might.

Cly. I will corrupt and feed him so with silver and with gold
That I, by bribing, bind him shall, no secrets to unfold.

Aeg. The trust that hirèd is, and bought by bribes and money's fee,
Thy counsel to betray again by bribes enticed will be.

Cly. The remnant left of shamefacedness, of those ungracious tricks
Wherein of late I did delight, my conscience freshly pricks.
Why keep'st thou such a busy stir, and, with thy flatt'ring speech
Instructing me with lewd advice, dost wicked counsel preach?
Shall I forsooth, of royal blood, with all the speed I can,
Refuse the king of kings and wed an outcast banished man?

Aeg. Why should you think, in that Thyest was father unto me,
And Agamemnon Atreus' son, he should my better be?

Cly. If that be but a trifle small, and nephew[201] to the same.

Aeg. I am of Phoebus' lineage[202] born, whereof I do not shame.

---

[199] It is clear from the context that "Atrides" here refers to Menelaus, not Agamemnon.

[200] Studley translates *quaeritur* ("investigation is made") as if it were *queritur* ("he complains"). The sense of the line should be: "Where there is the hatred of a master, a man is condemned, the case is not looked into."

[201] *I.e.,* "grandson" (see *Glossary*); Clytemnestra taunts Aegisthus with his incestuous birth.

[202] A mistranslation; *auctore Phoebo* refers rather to the fact that Thyestes committed incest by the advice of Apollo's oracle.

Cly. Why mak'st thou Phoebus author of thy wicked pied-de-grue
Whom out of heaven ye[203] forced to fly, when bridle back he drew,
When Lady Night with mantle black did spread her sudden shade?
Why makest thou the gods in such reproachfulness to wade,
Whose father hath thee cunning made, by slight and subtle guile
To make thy kinsman cuckold while his wife thou do defile?
What man is he whom we do know to be thy father's mate
Abusing lust of lechery in such unlawful rate?
Avaunt! Go pack thee hence in haste, dispatch out of my sight
This infamy, whose blemish stains this blood of worthy wight.[204]

Aeg. This is no new exile to me, that wickedness doth haunt;
But if that thou, O worthy Queen, command me to avaunt,
I will not only straight avoid the house, the town, and field;
My life on sword at thy request I ready am to yield.

Cly. This heinous deed permit shall I, most churlish cruel drab?
Against my will[205] though I offend, the fault I should not blab.
Nay, rather come apart with me, and let us join our wits
To rapt ourselves out of this woe and per'lous threat'ning fits.

Chorus

Now chant it, lusty lads, Apollo's praise suborn!
To thee the frolic flock their crownèd heads adorn,
To thee King Inach's stock, of wedlock chamber void,
Braid out their virgins' locks, and thereon have employed
Their savory garlands green, ytwist of laurel bough.
Draw near with us, O Thebes, our dancing follow thou;
Come also, ye that drink of Ismen's bubbling flood
Whereas the laurel tree full thick on banks doth bud;
Eke ye whom Manto mild, the prophetess divine
Foreseeing fate, and born of high Tiresias' line,

---

[203] *I.e.,* your family, referring to the fact that the sun had fled from the sight of Thyestes' banquet.

[204] Studley omits Clytemnestra's final sentence: "This house awaits its king, my husband."

[205] Studley's text wrongly reads *invita* (unwilling) for *iuncta* (joined); the sense of the line should be: "She who sins jointly owes loyalty to the crime."

Hath stirred to celebrate with sacred use and rite
Apollo and Dian, born of Latona bright.
O victor Phoebe, unbend thy notchèd bow again,
Since quietness and peace anew we do retain;
And let thy twanging harp make melody so shrill,
While that thy nimble hand strike quavers with thy quill.
No curious descant I, nor lusty music, crave,
No jolly rumbling note, nor trolling tune, to have;
But on thy treble lute, according to thy use,
Strike up a plainsong note, as when thy learned Muse
Thy lessons doth record, though yet on baser string
It liketh thee to play the song that thou did sing
As when from fiery heaven the dint of lightning flew,
Sent down by wrath of gods, the Titans overthrew,
Or else when mountains were on mountains heapèd high
That raise for Giants fell their steps into the sky:
The mountain Ossa stood on top of Pelion laid;[206]
Olympe (whereon the pines their budding branches braid)
Down paysèd both. Draw near, O Juno, noble dame,
Both spouse of mighty Jove and sister to the same.
Thou that dost rule with him, made jointer of his mace,
Thy people we of Greece give honor to thy grace;
Thou only dost protect from perils Argos land,
That ever careful was to have thine honor stand,
Most suppliant thereunto. Thou also with thy might
Dost order joyful peace and battles fierce of fight;
Accept, O conquering Queen, these branches of the bays
That Agamemnon here doth yield unto thy praise.
The hollow boxen pipe that doth with holes abound
In singing unto thee doth give a solemn sound;
To thee the damsels eke that play upon the strings
With cunning harmony melodious music sings;
The matrons eke of Greece, by riper years more grave,
To thee the taper pay that vowèd oft they have.
The heifer young and white, companion of the bull,
Unskillful yet by proof the painful plow to pull,
Whose neck was never worn nor galled with print of yoke,

[206] Studley here reverses the text, which follows the usual tradition that Pelion
was piled upon Ossa.

Is in thy temple slain, receiving deadly stroke.
O lady Pallas, thou of most renownèd hap,
Bred of the brain of Jove that smites with thunderclap,
Thou lofty Trojan tow'rs of craggy knotty flint
Hast beat with batt'ring blade and struck with javelin-dint;
The elder matrons, with the dames that younger be,
Together in mingled heaps do honor due to thee;
When, thou approaching nigh, thy coming is espied
The priest unbars the gate and opes the temple wide;
By clust'ring throngs the flocks thine altars haunt apace
Bedecked with twisted crowns so trim with comely grace;
The old and ancient men well steeped and grown in years,
Whose feeble trembling age procureth hoary hairs,
Obtaining their request craved of thy grace divine,
Do offer up to thee their sacrificèd wine.
O bright Dian, whose blaze sheds light three sundry ways,
We mindful are of thee, and render thankful praise.
Delos, thy native soil, thou diddest firmly bind
That to and fro was wont to wander with the wind
Which, with foundation sure, main ground forbids to pass;
For navies, after which to swim it wonted was,
It is become a road defying force of wind.
The mother's funerals of Tantalus's kind,
The daughters seven, by death thou, victress, dost account,
Whose mother, Niobe, abides on Sipyl's mount,
A lamentable rock, and yet unto this hour
Her tears new gushing out the marble old doth pour.
The godhead of the twins[207] in sumptuous solemn wise
Both man and wife adore with savory sacrifice.
But thee above the rest, O father great, and guide,
Whose mighty force is by the burning lightning tried,
Who when thou gavest a beck, and didst thy head but shake,
At once th'extremest poles of heaven and earth did quake,
O Jupiter, the root that of our lineage art,
Accept these offered gifts and take them in good part,
And thou, O grandsire[208] great, to thy posterity
Have some remorse, that do not swerve in chivalry.

[207] Apollo and Diana.
[208] Jupiter, as ancestor of the Argive nation.

But yonder, lo! with stiving steps the soldier comes amain
In all post-haste, with token that good news declareth plain:
A laurel branch that hangeth on his spear-head he doth bring—
Eurybates is come, who hath been trusty to the King.

The Third Act

Eurybates, Clytemnestra

Eur. Sore tirèd after many years with travail and with toil,
Scant crediting myself, the gods of this my native soil,
The temple, and the altars of the saints that rule the sky,
In humble sort with reverence devoutly worship I.
Now pay your vows unto the gods. Returnèd is again
Unto his country's court, where wont he was to rule and reign,
Prince Agamemnon, victor, he of Greece the great renown!
  Cly. The tidings of a message good unto mine ears is blown.
Where stays my spouse, whom longing for ten years I have out
     scanned?
What, doth he yet sail on the seas, or is he come on land?
Yet hath he fixed and set his foot back-stepping home again
Upon the sandy shore that long he wishèd to attain?
And doth he still enjoy his health, enhanced in glory great
And painted out in pomp of praise whose fame the sky doth beat?
  Eur. Bless we with burning sacrifice at length this lucky day!
  Cly. And eke the gods, though gracious, yet dealing long delay.
Declare if that my brother's wife[209] enjoy the vital air,
And tell me to what kind of coast my sister[210] doth repair.
  Eur. God grant and give us better news than this that thou dost
     crave:
The heavy hap of fighting floods forbids the truth to have.
Our scattered fleet the swelling seas attempts in such a plight
That ship from ship was taken clean out of each others' sight.
Atrides, in the waters wide turmoiled and straying far,
More violence by sea sustained than by the bloody war,
And, as it were a conquered man, escaping home all wet
Now bringeth in his company, of such a mighty fleet,

---

[209] An error for "my husband's brother," *i.e.,* Menelaus.
[210] Helen.

A sort of bruisèd broken barks, beshaken, torn, and rent.

Cly. Show what unlucky chance it is that hath our navy spent,
What storm of seas dispersèd hath our captains here and there.

Eur. Thou willest me to make report of heavy woeful gear;
Thou biddest me most grievous news with tidings good to part.
For utt'ring of this woeful hap my feeble mind doth start
And horribly appallèd is with this so monstrous ill.

Cly. Speak out and utter it. Himself with terror he doth fill
Whose heart his own calamity and cark doth loath to know;
The heart whom doubted damage dulls with greater grief doth glow.

Eur. When Trojan buildings blazing bright did burn away and broil
Enkindled first by Greekish brand, they fall to part the spoil;
Repairing fast unto the seas again, we come aboard,
And now the soldier's weary loins were easèd of his sword;
Their bucklers, cast aside, upon the hatches lie above.
Their warlike hands in practice put, and oars learn to move;
Each little hindrance seems too much to them, in hasty plight.
When of recourse the Admiral gave watchword, by his light,
And trumpet blast began to call our army from delay,
The painted poop[211] with gilded snout did first guide on the way
And cut the course, which following on a thousand ships did rive.
Then first a wind with pipeling puffs our launching ships did drive,
Which glided down upon our sails, the water being calm,
With breath of western wind so mild scant movèd any walm.
The shining sea, bespread about with ships, doth glister bright,
And also, covered with the same, lay hid from Phoebus' light.[212]
It doth us good to gaze upon the naked shore of Troy;
The desert Phrygian plots, so bare, to view we hop for joy.
The youth, each one, bestir themselves and, striking all together,
They tug their oars, and with their toil they help the wind and
     weather;
They tug and cheer'ly row by course. The spurting seas up dash;
Against the rattling ribs of ships the flapping floods do flash;
The hoary froth of wrestling waves, which oars aloft do raise,
Do draw and trace a furrow through the marble-facèd seas.
When stronger blast with belly swoll'n our hoisted sails did fill,
They row no more, but let the poop to go with wind at will,

[211] Like the equivalent Latin, *puppis,* by synecdoche for the ship.
[212] *I.e.,* the sea reflects the ships, which are so many as to hide it.

Their shearing oars laid aside. Our pilot doth espy
How far from any land aloof our sails recoiling fly,
Or bloody battles doth display, the threats of Hector stout
Or of his rattling wagons tells, wherein he rode about,
Or how his gashèd carcass, slain and trained about the field,
To funeral flames and obit rites for coin again was yield,
How Jupiter embathèd was in all his[213] royal blood.
The frolic fish disposèd was to mirth in Tyrrhene[214] flood
And, fetching frisks both in and out, plays on the water's brim,
And on his broad and finny back about the seas doth swim
With gambols quick, in rings around and side to side inclined,
Erewhile he sports afront the poop, and whips again behind;
Now sidling on the snout before, the dallying wanton rout
With jocundary jolly tricks doth skip the fleet about;
Sometime he standeth gazing on, and eyes the vessels bright.[215]
Now every shore is covered clean, and land is out of sight,
The per'lous point of Ida's rock in sight doth open lie;
And, that alone espy we could with firmly fixèd eye,
A dusky cloud of stifling smoke from Troy did smolder black.
When Titan from the weary necks the heavy yoke did slack,
The fading light did groveling bend, and down the day did shroud;
Against the stars a-mounting up, a little misty cloud
Came belching out in irksome lump, and Phoebus' gallant beams
He spewed upon, bestaining them ducked down in western streams.
The sunset, swerving in such sort with diverse change of face,
Did give us cause to have mistrust of Neptune's doubted grace.[216]
The evening first did burnish bright, and paint with stars, the sky;
The winds were laid, and clean forsook our sails that quiet lie—
When cracking, rattling, rumbling noise rushed down with
     thund'ring sway
From top of hills, which greater stir doth threaten and betray.
With bellowings and yellings loud the shores do grunt and groan,

[213] This should read "all the royal blood"; the reference is to the death, not of Hector, but of Priam, who was slain at the altar of Jupiter in the courtyard of his palace.

[214] The epithet has been transposed by Studley: it should be "Tyrrhene fish," *i.e.*, the dolphin.

[215] This verse has been added by Studley.

[216] A many-colored sunset was thought to be a sign of a coming storm.

The craggy cliffs and roaring rocks do howl in hollow stone,
The bubbling waters swell, up-reared before the wrestling wind,
When suddenly the lowering light of moon is hid and blind,
The glimpsing stars do go to glade, the surging seas are tossed
Even to the skies, among the clouds the light of heaven is lost,
More nights in one compacted are with shadow dim and black,
One shadow upon another doth more darkness heap and pack,
And, every spark of light consumed, the waves and sky do meet.[217]
The ruffling winds range on the seas, through every coast they flit,
They heave it up with violence, o'erturned from bottom low;
The western wind flat in the face of eastern wind doth blow,
With hurly-burly Boreas set ope his blasting mouth,
And girdeth out his boisterous breath against the stormy south.
Each wind with all his might doth blow, and worketh dangers deep:
They shake the floods, a sturdy blast along the seas do sweep
That rolls and tumbles wave on wave. A northern tempest strong
Abundance great of flaky snow doth hurl our ships among;
The south wind, out of Libya, doth rage upon a shoal,
And with the puissant force thereof the quicksands up do roll,
Nor bideth in the south, which doth with tempest lump and lower
And force the flowing floods to rise by pouring out a shower;
The stubborn Eurus earthquakes made, and shook the countries east
And Eos' coast, where Phoebus first ariseth from his rest;
How violent Corus stretched and tore his yawning breast full wide!
A man would sure have thought the world did from his center slide
And that, the frames of heaven brok'n up, the gods adown would fall,
And Chaos' dark confusèd heap would shade and cover all.
The stream strove with the wind; the wind did bear it down again.
The springing sea within his banks cannot itself contain;
The raging shower his trilling drops doth mingle with the seas.
And yet, in all this misery, they find not so much ease
To see and know what ill it is that worketh their decay.
The darkness dim oppresseth still and keeps the light away;
The black-faced night with hellish hue was clad, of Stygian lake.
And yet full oft with glimpsing beams the sparkling fire outbrake,

[217] The sense of the original is that, in the dark, sea and sky are indis-
tinguishable.

The cloud doth crack and, being rent, the lightning leapeth out;
The wretches like the same so well, it shining them about,
That still they wish such light to have, although, God wot! but ill.
The navy, swaying, down itself doth cast away and spill;
One side with other side is cracked, and helm is rent with helm,
The ship itself the gulping seas do headlong overwhelm.
Erewhile a greedy gaping gulf doth sup it up amain,
Then by and by, tossed up aloft, it spews it out again;
She, with her swaying full of sea, to bottom low doth sink
And drencheth deep aside in floods her tott'ring broken brink
That underneath a dozen waves lay drownèd out of sight.
Her broken planks swim up and down; spoiled is her tackle quite:
Both sail and oars clean are lost, the mainmast eke is gone
That wonted was to bear upright the sailyard thereupon,
The timber and the broken boards lie on the water's brim—
When cold and shivering fear in us doth strike through every limb;
The wisest wits, intoxicate, dare nothing enterprise
And cunning practice naught avails, when fearful storms arise.
The mariners, letting duty slip, stand staring all aghast;
Their scooping oars suddenly out of their hands are wrast.
To prayer then apace we fall, when other hope is none;
The Greeks and Trojans to the gods alike do make their moan.
Alack, what succor of the fates may we poor wretches find?
Against his father Pyrrhus bears a spiteful cankered mind;
At Ajax doth Ulysses grudge; King Menelaus doth hate
Great Hector; Agamemnon is with Priam at debate.[218]
"Oh, happy man is he that doth lie slain in Trojan ground
And hath deserved by handy stroke to take his fatal wound,
Whom fame preserveth, taking up his tomb in conquered land!
Those momes whose melting cowards' heart durst never take in hand
Or enterprise no noble act, those force of floods shall drown;
But Fate, forebearing long, will take stout brutes of high renown.[219]

[218] In the original the point is that the Greeks, about to drown, envy those, both Greek and Trojan, who have died at Troy; Studley has obscured this by replacing envy with hatred.

[219] Studley has almost reversed the sense of the original, which is: "The sea and its floods bear those who have enterprised no noble act, while a coward's fate will destroy brave men."

Full well we may ashamèd be in such a sort to die!
If any man[220] his spiteful mind yet cannot satisfy
With these outrageous plunging plagues that down from gods are
    sent,
Appease at length thy wrathful god again, and eke relent—
Even Troy for pity would have wept to see our woeful case!—
But if that in thy boiling breast black rancor still have place,
And that the Greeks to ruin run it be thy purpose bent,
Why do these Trojans go to wrack, for whom thus are we spent?[221]
Assuage the rigor of the sea that threat'ning hills uprears:
This drenchèd fleet the Trojan folk and Greeks together bears."
Then from their prayers are they put, their falt'ring tongues do stay;
The roaring sea doth drown their voice and carries their cries away.
Then mighty Pallas, armèd with the leaping lightning-fire
(That testy Jove doth use to hurl, provoked to swelling ire),
With threat'ning javelin in her hand her prowess means to try,
And eke her force, whose boiling breast with Gorgon's fits doth fry,
Or what with target[222] she can do, and with her father's fire.
Then from the skies another storm begins abroad to spire;
But Ajax, nothing yet dismayed, all force withstandeth stout,
Whom, when he spread his swelling sails with cable stretchèd out,
The lightning down did wring him hard and wrapped him in her
    flame
And flung another flashing dint of lightning on the same.
With all her force and violence, her hand brought back again,
She tossed him out, as late that feat her father taught her plain;
Both over Ajax and his poop she flyeth overthwart,
And, rending man and ship, of both she bears away a part.
His courage naught abated, yet he all to-singed doth seem;
Even like a stubborn rugged rock amid the striving stream,
He trains along the roaring seas, and eke the welt'ring wave
By shoving on his burly breast in sunder quite he drave;
The bark with hand he caught, and on itself did rip it over;[223]
Yet Ajax shineth in the flood which darkness blind doth cover.

[220] This should read, "If any god . . ."; and the rest of the speech is meant
to be a prayer addressed to the unknown god who is causing the disaster.
[221] The Greeks assume that the storm has been sent to avenge the Trojans.
[222] *I.e.,* her Aegis, *q.v.* in *Index of Proper Names.*
[223] This rather obscure clause represents no statement in the original.

At length attaining to a rock his thund'ring cracks were these:
"I conquered have the force of fire and rage of fighting seas;
It doth me good to master thus the anger of the sky,
With Pallas' wrath, the lightning-flames, and floods tumulting high.
The terror of the warlike god once could not make me fly:
The force of Mars and Hector both at once sustained have I,
Nor Phoebus' darts could me constrain from him one foot to shun;[224]
All these beside, the Phrygians subdued we have, and won.
When other meacock flings his[225] darts, shall I not them withstand?
Yea, what if Phoebus[226] came himself to pitch them with his hand?"
When in his melancholy mood he boasted without mean,
Then Father Neptune lift his head above the waters clean;
The beaten rock with forkèd mace he undermining plucked
From bottom loose, and sunk it down when down himself he ducked.
There Ajax lay, by land, by fire, and storm of seas, destroyed;
But we by suffering shipwreck are with greater plagues annoyed:
A subtle shallow flood there is, flowed on a stony shoal
Where crafty Caphar out of sight the lurking rocks doth hold
Upon whose sharp and ragged tops the swelling tide doth flow.
The boiling waves do beat thereon, still swaying to and fro.
A turret nodding over it doth hang with falling sway,
From whence on either side, from high prospect, espy we may
Two seas, and on this hand the coast where Pelops once did reign,
And Isthmus' flood,[227] in narrow creek recoiling back again,
Doth stop Ionian Sea, lest into Hellespont it run.
On th' other part is Lemnos' flood,[228] that fame by bloodshed won;
On th' other side Chalcedon[229] town doth stand against this fort,

[224] This incident does not occur in the *Iliad* or any other extant account of the war. In *Iliad* VII, the other Ajax fights a duel with Hector, but there is no mention of the intervention of Mars or Apollo.

[225] Jupiter's.

[226] An error for "Jupiter."

[227] There is nothing in the original ("Isthmus, curved back with its narrow soil") to have given Studley the impression that it is a river or inlet.

[228] Studley may have taken Lemnos to be a river; or perhaps he means to refer to the sea near Lemnos.

[229] So also in the original; but since the only known city of that name is too far to be seen from Caphareus by any stretch of rhetorical exaggeration, we should perhaps assume the existence of another city by that name or that Seneca has used it by mistake for Chalcis.

And Aulis' isle,[230] that stayed our ships that thither did resort.
This castle here inhabit doth our Palamedes' sire,
Whose cursèd hand held in the top a brand of flaming fire
That did allure our fleet to turn on lurking rocks aright,
Enticing them with wily blaze to come unto the light.
All into fitters shaken are the vessels on the shoal,
But other some do swim, and some upon the rocks are rolled,
And other, slipping back again so to eschew the rocks,
His bruisèd ribs and rattling sides against each other knocks,
Whereby the other he doth break, and broken is himself;
Then would they launch into the deep, for now they dread the shelf.
This peck of troubles chanced to hap in dawning of the day;
But when the gods, besought of us, began the rage to stay,
And Phoebus' golden beams began afresh to render light,
The doleful day descrièd all the damage done by night.
     Cly. Oh, whether may I now lament and weep with wailing sad,
Or shall I else, in that my spouse returnèd is, be glad?
I do rejoice, and yet I am compellèd to bewail
My country's great calamity that doth the same assail.
O Father great, whose majesty doth thund'ring sceptres shake,
The lowering gods unto the Greeks now favorable make!
With garlands green let every head rejoicing now be crowned;
To thee the pipe in sacrifice melodiously doth sound,
And on thine altar lieth slain an heifer lily-white.
Before the same do present stand, with hanging locks undight,
A care-full Trojan company in heavy woeful plight,
On whom from high the laurel tree with spreading branch doth shine,
Whose virtue hath inspirèd them with Phoebus' grace divine.[231]

Chorus,[232] *Cassandra*

Alas, the cruel sting of love![233] how sweetly doth it taste,
A misery to mortal man annexed while life doth last!

[230] There is nothing in the original to justify Studley's calling Aulis an isle.
[231] Studley has considerably confused the meaning here; it should be: "But see, a sad throng, the daughters of Ilium with unkempt hair, are here, over whom the proudly stepping daughter [*i.e.,* priestess] of Phoebus wildly shakes the inspiring laurels."
[232] This is the Chorus of Trojan women not included on Studley's list of speakers.
[233] *I.e.,* love of life; Studley has not translated *vitae.*

The path of mischief for to fly now since[234] there is a gap,
And wretched souls be frankly called from every woeful hap
By death, a pleasant port, for aye in rest themselves to shroud
Where dreadful tumults never dwell, nor storms of Fortune proud;
Nor yet the burning fiery flakes of Jove the same doth doubt
When wrongfully with thwacking thumps he raps his thunder out.
Here Lady Peace th' inhabitors do never put in flight,
Nor yet the victor's threat'ning wrath approaching nigh to sight;
No whirling western wind doth urge the ramping seas to prance,
No dusty cloud that raisèd is by savage demilance
On horseback riding rank by rank, no fierce and cruel host,
No people slaughtered, with their towns clean topsy-turvy tossed—
While that the foe with flaming fire doth spoil and waste the wall,
Untamèd and unbridled Mars destroys and batters all.[235]
That man alone who forceth not the fickle Fates a straw,
The visage grim of Acheron whose eyes yet never saw,
Who never viewed with heavy cheer the ugsome Limbo lake,
And, putting life in hazard, dare to death himself betake,
That person is a prince's peer, and like the gods in might.
Who knoweth not what death doth mean is in a piteous plight!
The ruthful ruin of our native country we beheld,
That woeful night in which the roofs of houses overquelled
In Dardan's city blazing bright with flashing fiery flames,
Whenas the Greeks with burning brands enkindle did the frames.
That Troy, whom war and deeds of arms might not subdue and take
(As once did mighty Hercules, whose quiver caused it quake),
Which neither he that Peleus' son and son to Thetis was,
Nor whom Achilles loved so well[236] could ever bring to pass
When, glittering bright, in field he wore false armor on his back
And, counterfeiting fierce Achill, the Trojans drove to wrack.
Nor when Achilles, he himself, his mind from sorrow wrast,

[234] An error for "although." The *cum* of the original may introduce either a causal or a concessive clause, but the sense clearly demands the latter: "How love of life holds us, although death offers such an easy release!"

[235] In this and the next six verses Studley muddles the meaning. The sense is: ". . . nor untamed Mars. The scorner of the fickle gods will break out of any servitude, he who looks on the face of dark Acheron and, unfearful himself, upon fearful Styx, and who dares to put an end to his life. He will be equal to a king, equal to the gods. Oh, how wretched it is not to know how to die!"

[236] Patroclus, *q.v.* in *Index of Proper Names.*

And Trojan women to the walls did scudding leap in haste,[237]
In misery she lost her proud estate, and last renown
By being stoutly overcome, and hardly pullèd down.
Years five and five did Troy resist, that yet hereafter must
In one night's space by destiny be layèd in the dust.
Their feignèd gifts well have we tried, that huge and fatal gin;
We, light of credit, with our own right hand have haulèd in
That fatal gift of Greeks, what time at entry of the gap
The huge horse did shivering stand, wherein themselves did wrap
The captains close, in hollow vaults with bloody war yfreight,
When lawfully we might have tried and searchèd their deceit:
So by their own contrived snares the Greeks had been confound.
The brazen bucklers being shook did give a clatt'ring sound,
A privy whispering oftentimes came tickling in our ear,
And Pyrrhus, in a murrain's name! so ready for to hear
The crafty counsel pickèd out of false Ulysses' brain,
Did jangle in the hollow vaults that rang thereof again.
But, fearing and suspecting naught, the heady youth of Troy
Laid hands upon the sacred ropes, to haul and pull with joy:
On this side young Astyanax came guarded with his train,
On th' other part Polyxena (desponsèd to be slain
Upon Achilles' tomb); she comes with maids and he with men,
A jolly flock with equal years as young as they were then.
Their vowed oblations to the gods in holiday attire
The matrons bring; and so to church[238] repaireth every sire.
And all the city did alike. Yea, Hecuba, our Queen,
That since the woeful Hector's death ere now was never seen,
She merry is. O grief accursed, of all thy sorrows deep,
For which, that first or last befell, intendest thou to weep?
Our battered walls, which heavenly hands erected have and framed?
Or else the burning temples which upon their idols flamed?
Lamenting these calamities we have not time and space—
O mighty parent, Priam, we poor Trojans wail thy case:
The old man's throttling throat I saw, alas! I saw ybored
With cruel Pyrrhus' blade, that scant with any blood was gored.

---

[237] Studley has muddled this hopelessly; the meaning should be: "and the Trojan women even from the top of the walls feared him, swift in leaping."
[238] An anachronistic rendering of *aras*, "altars."

Cas. Refrain your tears that down your cheeks should trickle
   evermore;
With woeful wailings piteously your private friends deplore.
My miseries refuse a mate (so much accursed am I)
To rue my care-full case. Refrain your lamentable cry;
As for mine own distress to mourn I shall suffice alone.

Cho. To mingle tears with other tears it doth us good, to moan;
In those the burning teary streams more ardently do boil
Whom secret thoughts of lurking cares in privy breast turmoil.
Though that thou were a gossip stout, that brook much sorrow may,
I warrant thee, thou mightest[239] well lament this sore decay.
Not sad and solemn Aedon[240] that in the woods doth sing
Her sugared ditties finely tuned on sweet and pleasant string,[241]
Recording Itys' woeful hap in divers kind of note,
Whom Procne, though he were her child and of her womb begot,[242]
For to revenge his father's fault she did not spare to kill,
And gave his flesh and blood for food the father's maw to fill,
Nor Procne who, in swallow's shape, upon the ridges high
Of houses sits, in Bistones' town, bewailing piteously,
With chattering throat, of Tereus, her spouse, the cruel act,
Who did by strength and force of arms—a shameful, brutish fact![243]—
Defile the sister of his wife, fair Philomel by name,
And eke cut out her tongue, lest she should blab it, to his shame,
Though Procne, this her husband's rape lamenting very sore,
Do wail and weep with piteous plaint, yet can she not deplore
Sufficiently, though that she would, our country's piteous plight;
Though he himself, among the swans, Sir Cycnus, lily-white,
Who dwells in streams of Ister's flood and Tanais' channel cold,
His weeping voice most earnestly though utter out he would,
Although the mourning halcyons with doleful sighs do wail
At such time as the fighting floods their Ceyx did assail,
Or, rashly waxing bold, attempt the seas now laid at rest,

[239] Studley omits a negative here; the sense should be that Cassandra, however strong, will not be able sufficiently to lament such great disasters.

[240] The nightingale. Studley proceeds to relate the story, not of Aedon, but of Philomel, *q.v.* in *Index of Proper Names.*

[241] The sweet and pleasant string is Studley's own addition, and an inappropriate one.

[242] This and the next two verses are added by Studley.

[243] This and the following two verses have been added by Studley.

Or, being very fearful, feed their brood in tott'ring nest,
Although, as squeamish-hearted men,[244] those priests in bedlam rage
Whom mother Cyb'le, being borne on high in lofty stage,[245]
Doth move to play on shawms Attis the Phrygian to lament,
Yet cannot they this lot bewail, though brawn from arms they rent.
Cassandra, in our tears there is no measure to refrain;
Those miseries all measure pass that plungèd us in pain.
The sacred fillets from thy head why dost thou haul and pull?
They chiefly ought to worship God whose hearts with grief be dull.
   Cas. My fear by this affliction is clean abated all
Nor, praying to the heavenly ghosts, for mercy will I call:
Although they were disposed to chase and fret with fustian fumes,
They nothing have me to displease. Fortune her force consumes,
Her spite is worn unto the stumps. What country have I left?
Where is my sire? Am I of all my sisters quite bereft.
The sacred tombs[246] and altar-stones[247] our blood have drunk and
   swilled.
Where are my brethren, blessed knot? Destroyèd in the field.
All widowed wives of Priam's sons may eas'ly now behold
The palace void, and cast of court of silly Priam old;[248]
And by so many marriages so many widows are,
But only Helen, coming from the coast of Lacone far.
That Hecuba, the mother of so many a princely wight,
Whose fruitful womb did breed the brand of fire blazing bright,
Who also bore the swing in Troy, by practice now doth learn
New laws and guise of destiny in bondage to discern.
On her she taketh heart of grace with looks so stern and wild,[249]

---

[244] "Squeamish-hearted" is not a bad translation for *molles*; but here the adjective (a standard epithet for Cybele's priests) probably refers to their emasculate state.

[245] The picture of Cybele on a high building is probably derived from her epithet *turrita* ("turreted" or "towered") which actually refers, however, to her crown, which was in the shape of a fortification tower or a city wall.

[246] Referring to the death of Polyxena.

[247] Referring to the deaths of Priam and Polites.

[248] This erroneous translation is due to a textual corruption. Reading *senes* for *senis* we would have: "Only pitiable old men are left in the empty palace."

[249] This interpretation cannot be justified by the original, which means simply: "She has put on the appearance of an animal" (a reference to Hecuba's metamorphosis into a bitch).

And barketh as a bedlam bitch about her strangled child,[250]
Dear Polydorus, remnant left and only hope of Troy
Hector and Priam to revenge and to restore her joy.

   Cho. The sacred Phoebus' prophet is with sudden silence hushed;
A quaking, trembling, shivering fear throughout her limbs hath
   rushed;
Her face as pale as ashes is, her fillets stand upright;
The soft and gentle goldy locks start up of her affright;
Her panting breathing breast, stuffed up within, doth grunt and groan;
Her glaring, bright, and steaming eyes are hither and thither thrown,
Now glancing up and down they roll, now standing stiff they stare.
She stretcheth up her head more straight than commonly she bare;
Bolt up she goes. Her wrestling jaws that fast together cling
She doth attempt by divers means asunder how to wring;
Her mumbling words in gabbling mouth shut up she doth assuage,
As Maenad mad that Bacchus' ares doth serve in furious rage.

   Cas. How doth it hap, O sacred tops of high Parnassus' hill,
That me, bereft of sense, with pricks of fury fresh ye fill?
Why do you me with ghost inspire that am beside my wits?
O Phoebus, none of thine I am; release me from the fits!
Infixèd in my burning breasts, the flames extinguish out!
Who forceth me with fury fell to gad and trot about?
Or for whose sake, inspired with sprite, mad mumbling make must I?
Why play I now the prophet cold, since Troy in dust doth lie?
The day doth shrink for dread of war, the night doth dim mine eyes,
With mantle black of darkness deep clean covered are the skies,
But lo! two shining suns at once in heaven appeareth bright;
Two Grecian houses muster do their armies twain to fight.[251]
Among the mighty goddesses in Ida's woods I see
The fatal shepherd,[252] on his throne as umpire placed to be—

---

[250] There is no reference, implied or explicit, to Polydorus in the original.
This and the next two verses should have this sense: "Mad, she barked around
her ruins, the survivor of Troy, Hector, Priam, even of herself," *i.e.,* by chang-
ing her form she has outlived even herself.

[251] The original does not justify this interpretation, but rather seems merely
to continue the description of double vision of the preceding verse: ". . . and
a twin Argos lifts up double palaces." Seeing double was considered a symptom
of madness.

[252] Paris.

I do advise you to beware, beware I say! of kings,[253]
A kindred in whose cankered hearts old privy grudges springs—
That country clown, Aegisthus, he this stock shall overthrow . . .
What doth this foolish desp'rate dame her naked weapons show?
Whose crown intendeth she to crack, in weed of Lacone land[254]
With hatchet (by the Amazons invented first) in hand?
What face of mighty majesty bewitchèd hath mine eyes?
The conqueror of savage beasts, Marmaric lion, lies,
Whose noble neck is worrièd with currish fang and tooth;
The churlish snaps of eager lioness abide he doth—
Alack, ye ghosts of all my friends, why should ye say that I
Among the rest am only safe, from perils far to lie?
Fain, father,[255] follow thee I would, Troy being laid in dust!
O brother,[256] terror of the Greeks, O Trojans' aid and trust,
Your ancient pomp I do not see, nor yet thy warmèd hands
That fierce on Greekish flaming fleet did fling the fiery brands,
But mangled members, scorchèd corpse, and eke thy valiant arms
Hard-pinioned and bound in bands, sustaining grievous harms!
O Troilus, a match unfit encountering with Achill,
That mighty man of arms, too soon come unto thee I will![257]
I do delight to sail with them on stinking Stygian flood;
To view the churlish mastiff cur[258] of Hell, it doth me good,
And gaping-mouthèd kingdom dark of greedy Ditis' reign.
The barge of filthy Phlegethon this day shall entertain

---

[253] This verse and the following are probably a mistranslation; the original seems to mean: "I warn you, kings, beware the thievish race" (*genus furtivum*, a reference to the Trojans, but since the phrase could also mean "the illicit birth," it provides a kind of transition to the mention of Aegisthus, the child of incest). In the original, the ambiguity is continued in the next verse, "The man brought up in the country will overturn the house," which could refer to either Paris or Aegisthus. Studley loses the ambiguity by introducing Aegisthus' name.

[254] In Cassandra's prophetic vision, Clytemnestra, though dressed as a Spartan, is armed as an Amazon.

[255] Priam.

[256] Hector.

[257] Here Studley omits a verse and a half of the original: "Deiphobus, you wear an unrecognizable face, the gift of your new wife."

[258] Cerberus.

Me conquering and conquerèd, and princes' souls withal.[259]
You flittering shades, I you beseech; and eke on thee I call,
O Stygian pool, whereon the gods their solemn oaths do take:
Unbolt a while the brazen bars of darksome Limbo lake,
Whereby the Phrygian folk in Hell may Mycene state behold.
Look up, ye silly wretched souls, the Fates are backward rolled![260]
The squalid sisters[261] do approach, and deal their bloody stroke,
Their smold'ring faggots in their hands, half burnt to ashes, smoke,
Their visages so pale do burn, with fiery flaming eyes,
A garment black their gnawèd guts doth gird, in mourning guise!
Dire dread of night begins to howl! The bones of body vast
With lying long do rot, corrupt, in miry puddle cast . . .[262]
Behold, the weary aged man,[263] his burning thirst forgot,
The waters dallying at his lips to catch endeavors not,
But mourneth for the funeral that shall ensue anon;
The Trojan prince[264] his royal robes triumphant putteth on.
  Cho. The furious rage, clean overpassed, begins itself to slake
And slips away, even as a bull that deadly wound doth take
On gashèd neck afront the ares. Come let us ease at last
Her limbs that of the sprite of God have felt the mighty blast.
Returning home again at length, and crowned with laurel bough,
A sign of worthy victory, is Agamemnon now;
The wife to meet her husband doth her speedy passage ply,
Returning hand in hand, and foot by foot, most lovingly.

THE FOURTH ACT

Agamemnon, Cassandra

  Aga. At length I do arrive again upon my native soil;
God save thee, O dear lovèd land! to thee so huge a spoil
So many barbarous peoples yield! The flower of Asia, Troy,

[259] Wrongly rendered; it should mean. ". . . shall entertain royal souls, one conquering [Agamemnon's] and one conquered [her own]."
[260] *I.e.,* Agamemnon, who destroyed Troy, is soon to be destroyed himself.
[261] The Furies.
[262] It is not known to what myth Seneca alludes here.
[263] Tantalus.
[264] Dardanus, according to the original.

To bear thy yoke submits herself, that long did live in joy.
Why doth this prophet, on the ground her sprawling body laid,
Thus reel and stagger on her neck, all trembling and dismayed?
Sirs, take her up, with liquor warm let her be cherishèd.
Now peeps she up again, with drooping eyes sunk in her head—
Pluck up thy sprite! here is the port wished for in misery;
This day is festival.

    Cas. At Troy so was it wont to be[265]

    Aga. Let us to th' altars worship give.

    Cas. At th' altars died my sire.

    Aga. Pray we to Jove.

    Cas. To Jove whose grace divine doth me inspire?[266]

    Aga. Dost thou suppose that Troy thou seest?

    Cas. And Priam eke I see.[267]

    Aga. Troy is not here.

    Cas. Where Helen[268] is, there I take Troy to be.

    Aga. Fear not as maid to serve thy dame.

    Cas. Nay, freedom draweth nigh.

    Aga. Take thou no thought how thou shalt live.

    Cas. All cares for to defy,
Death gives a courage unto me.

    Aga. Yet say I once again,
There is no danger left whereby thou mightest hurt sustain.

    Cas. But yet much troublous danger doth hang over thy head, I wot.

    Aga. What mischief may a victor dread?

    Cas. Even that he dreadeth not.

    Aga. Ye trusty many of my men, come, carry her away
Till of the sprite she rid herself, lest fury force her say
That may be prejudicial; her tongue she cannot frame.
To thee, O Father, flinging forth the lightning's flashing flame,
That dost disperse the clouds and rule the course of every star
And guide the globe of earth, to whom the booties won by war

[265] Probably referring to the rejoicing that followed the feigned departure of the Greeks, when the horse was brought within the walls.

[266] Cassandra should say, "To Hercean Jove?" (at whose altar Priam died).

[267] *I.e.,* another doomed king, Agamemnon.

[268] *I.e.,* a wicked woman, perhaps with reference to the fact that Clytemnestra is Helen's sister.

With triumph victors dedicate; to thee, O Juno, hight
The sister dear of doughty Jove, thy husband full of might;
Both I and Greece, with flesh and blood, and eke our vowèd beast,
And gorgeous gifts of Araby,[269] give worship to thy hest.

Chorus

O Greece,[270] by noble gentlemen in honor shining clear,
O Greece, to wrathful Juno[271] thou that art the darling dear,
Some jolly worthy lusty blood thou foster'st evermore;
Thou hast made even the gods, that were a number odd before:
That puissant mighty Hercules, a noble imp of thine,
Deservèd, by his travails twelve, rapt up in heaven to shine,
For whom the heavens did alter course, and Jupiter withal
Did iterate the hours of night, when dampish dew doth fall,
And charged Phoebus' chariot swift to trot with slower pace,
And leisurely, bright lady Moon, thy homeward wain to trace.
Bright Lucifer, that year by year[272] his name anew doth change,
Came back again, to whom the name of Hesperus seemed strange.[273]
Aurora to her common course her rearèd head addressed,
And, couching backward down again, the same she did arrest
Upon the shoulder of her spouse,[274] whose years with age are worn.
The East did feel, so felt the West, that Hercules was born.
Dame Nature could not clean dispatch to utter in one night
That boist'rous lad; the whirling world did wait for such a wight.
O babe, whose shoulders underprop the ample spacious sky,[275]
In claspèd arms thy prowess did the crushèd lion[276] try,

[269] *Arabum donis, i.e.,* incense.
[270] In the original the chorus apostrophizes not Greece, but Argos, the scene of the play and (according to some accounts) Hercules' birthplace.
[271] The original says "dear to the angered stepmother"; Juno hated Hercules as the product of one of Jupiter's infidelities, but was eventually reconciled to him.
[272] An error; the point of the original is that Hesperus, the evening star, and Lucifer, the morning star, are one and the same.
[273] *I.e.,* he is still called Hesperus, since the morning has not come. For the story of the lengthening of the night of Hercules' begetting, *v. Index of Proper Names, s.v.* Hercules.
[274] Tithonus, *q.v.* in *Index of Proper Names.*
[275] A mistranslation. The original says, "O boy destined to rise to heaven."
[276] The Nemean lion, *s.v.* Nemea in *Index of Proper Names.*

Whom from his fiery yawning throat spews out his broiling brand;
The nimble hind on Maenal Mount hath known thy heavy hand;
The boar hath felt thy fist, which did Arcadia destroy;
The monstrous conquered bull hath roared, that Creta did annoy;
The dragon dire, that breeding beast,[277] in Lerna's pool he slew
And, chopping off one head, forbade thereof to rise anew;
With clubbèd, bruising, batt'ring bat he crankly did subdue
The brethren twins that tugged on teat whereof three monsters
    grew,[278]
Of triple-formèd Geryon the spoil, into the East,
A drove of cattle, Hercules did fetch out of the West;
Away from tyrant Diomed the Thracian horse he led,
Which neither with the grass that grew by Strymon's flood he fed
Nor yet on Hebrus' banks, but them the villain did refresh,
His greedy, munching, cramming jades, with aliens' blood and flesh—
Their raw-fed jaws imbrued were with the car-man's blood at last;
The spoils and shafts Hippolyte saw from her bosom wrast;
As soon as he with clatt'ring shaft the dusky cloud did smite,
The Stymphal bird, that shadowèd the sun, did take her flight;
The fertile tree that apples bears of gold did fear him sore,
Which never yet acquaintance had with taster's tooth before,
But, whipping up with lively twigs, into the air she flies,
And while the chinking plate doth sound, then Argus, full of eyes,[279]
The watchman shrinking close for cold, that sleep yet never knew,
Doth hear the noise while Hercules, with metal of yellow hue
Well laden, packs away, and left the grove befilchèd clean;
The hound of Hell[280] did hold his tongue, drawn up in triple chain,
Nor bark with any boughing throat, nor could abide the hue
Or color of the heavenly light, whose beams he never knew—
When thou[281] wert captain-general, and didst conduct our host,

[277] The Hydra, *q.v.* in *Index of Proper Names*; she is called "breeding" from
her ability to grow new heads.

[278] It is hard to see what meaning Studley intended to convey by this verse.
The original describes Geryon, "triplet brothers, three monsters springing from
one breast."

[279] Seneca's "cold watchman" refers to the serpent of the Garden of the
Hesperides, not Argus.

[280] Cerberus, *q.v.* in *Index of Proper Names*.

[281] Hercules.

They that of Dardan's line to come their stock do falsely boast[282]
Were vanquishèd by force of arms; and since they felt again
Thy grey goose wing,[283] whose bitterness to fear might them constrain.

The Fifth Act

The First Scene

Cassandra

Cas. Within a revel rex is kept, as sore as ever was
Even at the ten years' siege of Troy! What thing is this? Alas,
Get up, my soul, and of thy rage avengement worthy crave;
Though Phrygians we be vanquishèd, the victory we have.
The matter is well brought about. Up, Troy, thou risest now;
Thou flat on floor hast pulled down Greece, to lie as low as thou.
Thy conqueror doth turn his face.[284] My prophesying sprite
Did never yet disclose to me so notable a sight.
I see the same, and am thereat, and busied in the broil;
No vision fond, fantastical, my senses doth beguile.
Such fare as Phrygians feasted with on last unhappy night
At Agamemnon's royal court full daintily they dight.
With purple hangings all adorned the broidered beds[285] do shine;
In old Assarac's goblets gilt they swink and swill the wine.
The King, in gorgeous royal robes, on chair of state doth sit,
And pranked with pride of Priam's pomp, of whom he conquered it.
"Put off this hostile weed," to him the Queen his wife gan say,
"And, of thy loving lady wrought, wear rather this array,
This garment knit." It makes me loath, that shivering here I stand—
Oh, shall a king be murdered by a banish'd wretch's hand?
Out! shall th' adulterer[286] destroy the husband of the wife?

---

[282] This is Studley's rendering of "the lying house of the descendant of Dardanus," the reference being to Laomedon (*q.v.* in *Index of Proper Names*) and his deceitfulness.

[283] Presumably a reference to the feathered shafts of Hercules' arrows; the Trojans are said to have felt them again since then because Hercules' arrows were brought to Troy by Philoctetes (*q.v.* in *Index of Proper Names*) in the Trojan War.

[284] *I.e.,* turn away in flight or fear.

[285] *I.e.,* dining couches.

[286] Aegisthus.

The dreadful destinies approached! The food that last in life
He tasted of before his death the master's blood shall see;
The gobs of blood down dropping on the wine shall pourèd be.
By trait'rous trick of trapping weed his death is brought about,
Which being put upon his head, his hands could not get out;
The stoppèd poke with mouth set ope[287] his muffled head doth hide.
The man-kind dame[288] with trembling hand the sword drew from her
    side;
Nor to the utmost of her might it in his flesh she thrust,
But in the giving of the stroke she stayèd all aghast.
He, as it were a bristled boar, entangled in the net
Among the briers in bushy woods, yet tryeth out to get,
With struggling much the shrinking bands more straitly he doth bind;
He strives in vain, and would slip off the snare that doth him blind,
Which catcheth hold on every side. But yet th' entangled wretch
Doth grope about, his subtle foes with gripping hand to catch.
But furious Tyndaris prepared the poleaxe in her hand;
And, as the priest to sacrifice at th' altar-side doth stand
And views with eye the bullock's neck, ere that with axe he smite,
So to and fro she heaves her hand to strike and level right.
He hath the stroke! Dispatched it is. Not quite chopped off, the head
It hangeth by a little crop. Here from the carcass dead
The spouting blood came gushing out; and there the head doth lie
With wallowing, babbling, mumbling tongue. Nor they do by and by
Forsake him so; the breathless corpse Aegist doth all to-coil,
And mangled hath the gashèd corpse. While thus he doth him spoil,
She putteth to her helping hand. By detestable deed
They both accord unto the kind whereof they do proceed:
Dame Helen's sister right she is, and he Thyestes' son.
Lo, doubtful, Titan standeth still, the day now being done,
Not knowing whether best to keep still on his wonted way
Or turn his wheels unto the path of dire Thyestes' day.[289]

---

[287] Seneca describes the folds, not as open, but as loose, hence voluminous
and enveloping.

[288] Seneca's *semivir,* "half-man," refers to Aegisthus; Studley takes it to mean
Clytemnestra.

[289] The Sun is undecided whether to set or to turn back, as he did when
Thyestes ate his own sons.

The Second Scene

Electra, Orestes

Ele. O thou, whom of our father's death the only help we have,
Fly, fly from force of furious foes! make haste thyself to save.
Our house is topsy-turvy tossed, our stock is cast away,
Our ruthful realms to ruin run, our kingdoms do decay . . .
Who cometh here, in chariot swift thus galloping amain?
Brother, disguisèd in thy weed let me thy person feign—
O buzzard blind, what dost thou mean from foreign folk to fly?
Whom dost thou shun? it doth behove to fear *this* family.
Orestes, now be bold and set all shivering fear aside;
The certain succor of a trusty friend I have espied.

The Third Scene

Strophius, Electra

Str. With solemn pomp, I, Strophius, forsaking Phocis' land,
Bearing a branch of palm that grows at Elis in my hand,[290]
Returnèd back I am. The cause that willed me hither wend
Is with these gifts to gratify and welcome home my friend,
Whose valiant army scaled and shook the tattered Trojan walls
(Who,[291] wearied with the ten years' war, now flat on floor she falls).
What woeful wight is this that stains her mourning face with tears,
And, drownèd deep in drowsy dumps, oppressèd is with fears?
I know full well this damsel is of prince's lineage born—
What cause Electra hath this joyful family to mourn?

Ele. By treason that my mother wrought my father lieth slain,
And, drinking of their father's cup, the children do complain.[292]
Aegist engrosseth castles got by fornication.

Str. Alack! that of so long a time felicity is none!

Ele. I thee request, even for the love my father thou dost owe,

---

[290] Strophius is returning from the Olympic games, where he has won the palm of victory.

[291] Troy.

[292] This verse should convey that "the son is being sought to share his father's death."

And for the honor of the crown, whose bruit abroad doth grow
In every coast, and by the gods that diversely do deal:
Take into thy tuition, convey away, and steal
This poor Orest. Such kind of theft is piety indeed.

   Str. Although that Agamemnon's death doth teach me to take heed,
Yet will I undertake the same; and with all diligence,
Orestes, shall I go about with strength to have thee hence.
Prosperity requireth faith, but trouble *exacts* the same.
Have here a prize[293] for those that do contend and wage in game,
An ornament with comely grace ordained to deck the brow,
And let thy head be covered with this green and pleasant bough;
And carry this victorious triumphant branch[294] in hand—
God grant this palm, that planted was in fertile Pisa's land,
Where solemn games were celebrate, Jove's honor to express,
May both a safeguard be to thee, and bring thee good success![295]
Thou that bestrid'st thy father's steeds, as he before hath done,[296]
Go, strike a league of amity with Pylades, my son.
Now, nimble nags (let Greece, hereof recording, testify),[297]
With headlong scouring course amain this trait'rous country fly!

   Ele. He is escaped and gone, and with unmeasurable might
The chariot-horse, with rein at will, do scud out of my sight.
Now, free from peril, on my foes attendance will I make,
And offer willingly my head the deadly wound to take.
The cruel conqueress of her spouse is come, whose spotted weed
With sprinkles, sign of slaughter, do bear record of her deed.
Her gory hands, new-bathed in blood (as yet they be not dry),
Her rough and churlish rigorous looks the fact do notify.
Unto the temple[298] will I trudge. Cassandra, suffer me,
Oppressed with equal grief, take part of sacrifice with thee.

   [293] The olive crown, a prize from the Olympic games, to be worn by Orestes as a disguise.

   [294] The palm of Olympic victory.

   [295] *I.e.,* be an omen of victory.

   [296] This verse and the following are wrong. The Latin means: "And you, Pylades, your father's charioteer, learn loyalty from your father's example."

   [297] *I.e.,* all Greece, having seen the prowess of these horses at the Olympic games, can testify to their swiftness.

   [298] "To the altars," to take sanctuary as Cassandra has done.

The Fourth Scene

Clytemnestra, Electra, Aegisthus, Cassandra

Cly. O thou, thy mother's enemy, ungracious, saucy face,
After what sort dost thou, a maid, appear in public place?

Ele. I have, with my virginity, the bow'rs of bawds forsook.

Cly. What man is he that ever thee to be a virgin took?

Ele. What, your own daughter?[299]

Cly. With thy mother more modest shouldst thou be.

Ele. Do you at length begin to preach such godliness[300] to me?

Cly. A manly stomach stout thou hast, with swelling haughty heart;
Subdued with sorrow, learn thou shalt to play a woman's part.

Ele. A sword and buckler very well a woman do beseem,
Except I dote.[301]

Cly. Thyself dost thou hail-fellow with us esteem?

Ele. What Agamemnon new is this whom thou hast got of late?[302]

Cly. Hereafter shall I tame and teach thy girlish tongue to prate,
And make thee know how to a queen thy taunting to forebear.

Ele. The whilst, thou widow, answer me directly to this gear:
Thy husband is bereavèd quite of breath; his life is done.

Cly. Inquire where thy brother is; so seek about my son.

Ele. He is departed out of Greece.

Cly. Go fetch him out of hand!

Ele. Fetch thou my father unto me.

Cly. Give me to understand
Where doth he lurking hide his head; where is he shrunk away?

Ele. All plunge of perils past he is, and at a quiet stay,

---

[299] Electra would imply that no daughter of Clytemnestra's could be thought chaste.

[300] *Pietas*, a word which includes the concepts of fidelity to a husband and of duty to a parent.

[301] This is a threat: Electra is willing to play a woman's part if this includes, as in her mother's case, the right to kill.

[302] This verse and the next four are the result of a corruption in the text Studley used. The order should be: "*Ele.* Who is that other Agamemnon of yours? Speak as a widow; your husband is dead. Cly.: Afterwards, as Queen, I shall break the untamed words of an unfilial girl; meanwhile quickly tell me where is my son, where your brother."

And in another kingdom, where no harm he doth mistrust.
This answer were sufficient to please a parent just;
But one whose breast doth boil in wrath it cannot satisfy.

Cly. Today by death thou shalt receive thy fatal destiny.

Ele. On this condition am I pleased the altar to forsake:
If that this hand shall do the deed, my death when I shall take.
Or else, if in my throat to bathe thy blade thou dost delight,
Most willingly I yield my throat, and give thee leave to smite.
Or if thou wilt chop off my head in brutish beastly guise,
My neck, a-waiting for the wound, outstretchèd ready lies.
Thou hast committed sinfully a great and grievous guilt;
Go purge thy hardened hands, the which thy husband's blood have
     spilt.[303]

Cly. O thou, that of my perils all doth suffer part with me
And in my realm dost also rule with equal dignity,
Aegisthus, art thou glad at this? As doth her not behoove,
With checks and taunts the daughter doth her mother's malice move:
She keeps her brother's counsel close, conveyed out of the way.

Aeg. Thou malapert and witless wench, thine elvish prating stay;
Refrain those words unfit thy mother's glowing ears to vex!

Ele. What? shall the breeder of this broil control me with his checks,
Whose father's guilt hath causèd him to have a doubtful name,
Who both is to his sister son, and nephew to the same?

Cly. To snap her head off with thy sword, Aegist, dost thou refrain?
Let her give up the ghost, or bring her brother straight again.
Let her be locked in dungeon dark, and let her spend her days[304]
In caves and rocks. With painful pangs torment her every ways.
I hope him whom she hidden hath she will again descry,
Through being clapped in prison strong, and suff'ring poverty,
With irksome and unsavory smells on every side annoyed,
Enforced to wear a widow's weed ere wedding-day enjoyed,
Put in exile and banishment, when each man doth her hate.
So shall she be by misery compelled to yield, too late,
Prohibited of wholesome air fruition to have.

Ele. Grant me my doom, by means of death to pass unto my grave!

[303] The Latin for this verse means: "Purge the hand, sprinkled and defiled with a husband's murder, in this blood."

[304] Modern editors assign this verse and the rest of this speech to Aegisthus.

Cly. I would have granted it to thee, if thou shouldst it deny;
Unskillful is the tyrant who, by suff'ring wretches die,
Doth end their pains.

Ele. What, after death doth anything remain?[305]

Cly. An if thou do desire to die, the same see you refrain.
Lay hands, sirs,[306] on this wondrous wretch, whom, being carried on
Even to the furthest corner of my jurisdiction,
Far out beyond Mycenae's land in bonds let her be bound;
With darkness dim, in hideous hold, let her be closèd round.
This captive spouse[307] and wicked quean, the trull of prince's bed,
Shall pay her pains, and suffer death by losing of her head.
Come, hale her on, that she may follow that way my spouse is gone,
Whose love from me enticèd was.

Cas. Do not thus hale me on;
I will before you take the way, these tidings first to tell
Unto my countrymen of Troy, beneath in lowest Hell:
How overwhelmèd ships eachwhere are spread the seas upon,
And Mycene country, conquered, is brought in subjection.
He that of thousand captains was grand captain-general,
Come to as great calamity as Troy itself did fall,
Entrappèd was by trait'rous train, and whoredom of his wife,
And by a gift received of her deprivèd of his life.
Let us not linger. On with me, and thanks I do you give:
I joy that it might be my hap *thus* after Troy to live.

Cly. Go to, prepare thyself to die, thou frantic raging wight!

Cas. The frenzy fits of Fury fell on you shall also light.[308]

Eurybates

(added to the tragedy by the translator)

Eur. Alas, ye hateful hellish hags, ye Furies foul and fell,
Why cause ye rusty rancor's rage in noble hearts to dwell,
And cankered hate in boiling breasts to grow from age to age?

---

[305] *I.e.,* what can be worse than death?

[306] The palace servants.

[307] Cassandra.

[308] Cassandra refers prophetically to the murder of Clytemnestra and Aegisthus by the maddened Orestes.

Could not the grandsire's[309] painful pangs the children's wrath
   assuage,
Nor famine faint of pining paunch, with burning thirst of Hell,
Amid the blackest stream of Styx, where pois'ning breaths do dwell,
Where vapors vile parbraking out from dampish miry mud
Increase the pains of Tantalus, deserved by guiltless blood?[310]
Could not thine own offense suffice, Thyestes, in thy life,
To file thy brother's spousal bed, and to abuse his wife?
But after breath from body fled, and life thy limbs hath left,
Cannot remembrance of revenge out of thy breast be reft?
What? yet hast thou not laid thy lips to taste of Lethe's flood?
Now after death why dost thou come to move thy son to blood?
Could cruel Ditis grant to thee thy passport back again
To work this woe upon the world, and make such rigor reign
That Clytemnestra is become the fifty'th sister dire
Of Danaus' daughters, that did once their husbands' death conspire?
Lo here, how fickle Fortune gives but brittle, fading joy:
Lo, he who late a conqueror triumphèd over Troy,
Enduring many sturdy storms with mighty toil and pain
To sow the seeds of fame, hath reaped small fruit thereof again!
Whenas his honor, budding forth with flow'r, began to bloom,
Alas! the stock was hewèd down and sent to deadly doom.
And they that of his victory and coming home were glad
To sudden mourning change their mirth, with heaviness bestead.
The lusty pomp of royal court is dead—O doleful day!—
The people moan their prince's death with woe and wellaway,
With howling, crying, wringing hands, with sobs, with sighs and
   tears;
And with their fists they beat their breasts, they pull and haul their
   hairs.
And, as the sheep amazèd run and ramp about the field
Whenas their shepherd to the wolf his gory throat doth yield,
Even so, as mad, they rage and rave throughout Mycenae's land;
Deprivèd of their prince, they fear the bloody tyrant's hand.
While thus were woeful wailings heard in every place about,
The good Cassandra, come from Troy, to death is halèd out.
Like as the swan, who, when the time of death approacheth nigh,

[309] Tantalus'.
[310] *I.e.,* the blood of his son Pelops.

By nature warnèd is thereof, and, pleasèd well to die,
Doth celebrate her funeral with dirge and solemn song,
Even so the noble virgin, who in woe hath livèd long,
Most joyful goes she to her death with mild and pleasant face,
Stout bolst'ring out her burly breast with princely port and grace.
Nothing dismayed, with courage bold and cheerful countenance,
On stage ordainèd for her death she gan herself advance,
As though she had not thither come to leave her loathsome life,
As though she had not come to taste the stroke of fatal knife,
But even as if in bridal bed her journey were to meet
Coroebus dear, not having mind of death or winding-sheet.
When, looking round on every side, she took her leave of all,
From vapor'd eyes of young and old the trickling tears do fall.
The Greeks themselves to grief are moved, to see this heavy sight.
So pity pierced the headman's heart that thrice, about to smite,
He stayed the smite. With shivering hand yet once again he tried,
And from her shoulders struck her head; and thus the virgin died.
But now the Greeks another cause of mourning have in hand:
Orestes, Agamemnon's son, is forced to fly the land.
Among old rotten, ragged rocks there lies an ugly place,
A dungeon deep, as dark as Hell, unknown to Phoebus' face,
A hollow, huge, wide-gaping hole, with way still bending down,
Whose mouth with venomous withered weeds is hid and overgrown,
Where stinking smells come belching out from filthy, dirty dike,
Where vermin vile do creep and crawl—in Hell is not the like!
Ill-favored, foul, misshapen bugs do lurk about this cave;
With dreadful sounds and roaring noise within the pit they rave.
Even hither is Electra sent, in darkness deep to lie
In poverty, and comfortless without the light of sky,
Fast clogged with iron bolts and chains, thus by her mother laid
In torments, till by her to death Orestes be betrayed,
Who, as Cassandra telleth, shall revenge his father's death,
Deprive, with sword, th' adulterer and mother both of breath.
So, after all these bloody broils Greece never shall be free;
But blood for blood, and death by turns, the after-age shall see.

FINIS

GLOSSARY

This Glossary contains (1) words now obsolete or archaic, (2) latinisms, coinages, and nonce-words which never became part of the language, and (3) words still in common use whose meanings have shifted since Tudor times. *N.B.* Most words of this third type have their modern meanings as well as the old ones given here.

Abbreviations

a. adjective	n. noun	vb. n. verbal noun
adv. adverb	p. participle	v.i. intransitive verb
conj. conjunction	p.a. participial adjective	v.t. transitive verb
interj. interjection	prep. preposition	

abject, n. A castaway; a derelict.
accord to, v.t. Accord with.
account, v.t. Count.
adown, adv. Downward.
advice, n. Consideration. *Take advice,* take into consideration.
afeared, a. Afraid.
affraid, n. Affray, fright.
affront, prep. In front of.
agrise, v.t. Terrify (*cf. grisly*).
a-low, adv. Below.
amaze, v.t. Stupefy.
amid, prep. Midway in, having half completed.
an, conj. If. *An if,* provided that; *an whether,* whether.
annoy, v.t. Impede.
apparent, a. Conspicuous.
are, n. Altar.
aright, adv. Straight; straightway.
as, conj. As if.
assoil, v.t. Solve; absolve.
attempt, v.t. Attack.
avoid, v.t. Withdraw from.
aye, adv. Always, ever.

band, n. Bond, fetter.
bank, n. Bench; platform.
bedlam, n. Madness.
befilched, p. Robbed of all possessions.
beset, p. Surrounded.
beshaken, p. Thoroughly shaken.
betrap, v.t. Entrap.
bewray, v.t. Betray.
bide, v.t. Await; encounter; withstand; suffer.
blain, n. A sore, a pustule.
blaze, n. A torch.
blaze, v.t. Make public.
blear, v.i. Be dim-sighted or watery-eyed.
blood, n. Offspring.
boisterous, a. Strong.
bolt, v.t. Utter unthinkingly. *Bolt out,* blurt out.
boot, v.t. Benefit.
bough, v.i. Make the sound *bough* (an imitation of the bark of a dog, the
  gh representing a guttural aspirate).
boxen, a. Of boxwood.
brake, v.t. past tense. Broke
brand, n. A burning ray; a flame.
breast, n. Courage.
broil, v.t. Burn.
brue, v.t. Imbrue.
bruit, n. Fame.
bug, n. A hobgoblin; a spectre.
burly, a. Noble; excellent.
bustle, v.i. Struggle.
buzzard, n. A worthless, stupid, or ignorant person (often with *blind*).
by and by, adv. phrase. Immediately, straightway.

car, n. Chariot.
care, v.t. Care for, take care of.
careful, a. Full of care, anxious.
cark, n. Care; pains; heed.
car-man, n. Charioteer.
case, n. Fate; accident.
cast, v.t. Ponder, consider; forecast.
cast, p. Rid.

casualty, n. Chance, precariousness, uncertainty.
cease of, v.t. Cease.
celebrate, p. Celebrated.
chance, v.i. Happen.
charge, n. A burden.
chase, v.t. Harass, annoy.
check, n. Taunt, insult.
cheer, n. Countenance; expression.
chill, v.i. Grow cold.
church, n. Temple.
clean, adv. Entirely.
clerk, n. Scholar, man of letters.
close, a. Secret.
coast, n. Side.
commonalty, n. The common people, the commons.
complain, v.t. Lament, bewail.
conceive, v.t. Perceive.
confound, p. Confounded.
convey, v.t. Steal.
corn, n. Grain (especially wheat).
course, n. A turn. *By course*, in order, in turn.
crack, n. A boast.
crake, n. A croaking; a barking.
crank, a. Vigorous.
crankly, adv. Lustily, vigorously.
crave, v.t. Demand, ask as a right.
crime, n. An accusation.
crop, n. Neck.
cue, n. Temperament; character. *Out of one's cue*, out of character, abnormal.
cunning, a. Learned; skillful.

dally at, v.t. Make sport of.
danky, a. Moist.
debate, n. Fight; strife.
decree, v.i. Decide, determine.
default, n. Fault.
demilance, n. A cavalryman armed with a light lance.
deny, v.i. Refuse, decline.
deprave, v.t. Speak ill of, depreciate.
descry, v.t. Disclose, reveal.
desponsed, p. Betrothed.

detect, v.t. Reveal, expose.
dick, n. Lad.
dight, v.t. Arrange, set out.
discuss, v.t. Scatter, dispel.
disdain, n. The feeling of injured pride.
dispatch, v.i. Make haste.
dispoint, v.t. Dismiss; disappoint.
dor, n. Mockery. *To give one the dor,* to make a fool of; *to take a dor,* to be made a fool of.
dotage, n. Folly.
doubt, v.i. Hesitate.
doubt, v.t. Fear.
dreary, a. Cruel; dire.
drench, v.i. and t. Submerge, sink, drown.
drift, n. Scheme, plot.
drosel, a. Slovenly.
dug, n. Teat; breast.

eager, a. Savage, fierce.
eftsoons, adv. Again; soon after.
eke, adv. Also.
elvish, a. Irritating; perverse.
enclose, v.t. Protect.
ensample, n. Example, instance.
enterprise, v.t. Undertake.
erst, adv. First, formerly.
estate, n. State.
everduring, p.a. Everlasting.
except, except that, conj. If . . . not, unless.
expound, p. Expounded.

fact, n. Deed.
fain, a. Eager.
fall, v.t. Befall.
falsehood, n. Treachery.
fame, n. Rumor, report.
fear, v.t. Terrify, frighten.
fetch, n. Trick, stratagem.
fetch, v.t. Make; take; achieve.
fierce, a. Proud, haughty.
file, v.t. Defile.
fit, n. Crisis; outburst.

fitter, n. A fragment.

flite, v.i. Contend.

flood, n. A stream, a torrent.

foil, v.t. Stain.

fond, a. Foolish.

fondly, adv. Foolishly.

fool, n. A wretch, an innocent (a term of endearment).

fordo, v.t. Abolish; undo.

forlorn, v.t. Lament.

for why, conj. Because.

frame, v.i. Progress.

frame, v.t. Produce; direct, control.

frankly, adv. Freely.

fray, v.t. Frighten.

frequent, v.t. Crowd, fill.

frisk, n. A caper.

fry, v.i. Seethe.

fume, n. A rage.

fustian, a. Bombastic; worthless.

gan, v.i. past tense. Began; did. *Gan say*, did say.

gape, v.i. Pant.

gear, n. Affair, doings.

get, v.t. Beget.

ghost, n. Soul; divine spirit.

gin, n. A device; a trick.

gin, v.i. Begin.

gird, v.t. Pull; thrust, drive.

glade, n. The sinking below the horizon of a heavenly body. *To go to glade*, to set.

gob, n. A gobbet, a lump; a clot.

gone, v.i. Go.

good, n. Goods.

gore, v.t. Cover with blood.

gossip, n. A godparent; a close friend. The word is inexplicably used by Studley to translate the Latin *virago*, heroic woman, applied in the text to Cassandra.

go to, interj. denoting impatience or scorn.

gratify, v.t. Welcome, greet with pleasure.

grudge, n. Misgiving; reluctance.

guard, v.t. Escort.

guise, n. Wise, way; method, custom.

hale, v.t. Pull, tug.

hand, with turn of, prep. phrase. At the turning of a hand, in a moment, instantly.

handy, a. Performed by the hand.

hap, n. Fortune.

hap, v.i. Happen.

happy, v.t. Make happy.

heap, n. Band, crowd.

hest, n. Command.

hight, v.i. Be called or named.

hight, v.t. Call or name.

hinder, a. Rearward.

holden, p. Held.

hugy, a. Huge.

ill, a. Evil, iniquitous; vicious.

imp, n. Offspring.

invent, v.t. Find.

irk, v.t. Disgust.

irksome, a. Disgusting.

jet, v.i. Strut, swagger.

jocundary, a. Jocund.

jointer, n. Sharer.

jolly, a. Gallant; bold.

kind, n. Nature.

knit, v.t. Weave.

lake, n. A pit; a river.

latest, a. Last.

leam, v.i. Gleam.

leave, v.i. and t. Cease.

let, v.t. Lose; impede.

lewd, a. Stupid; lawless, wicked.

lift, p. Lifted.

lights, n. Lungs (the tautological *lungs and lights* is common in the sixteenth and seventeenth centuries).

liking, a. Preferred.

limit, p.a. Limited.

list, v.i. and t. Please; choose; like; wish; incline to.

lively, a. Living, alive.

loath, a. Disgusted; indignant, angry.
loose, v.t. Solve.
lump, n. A bump, the sound *lump;* a mass.
lump, v.i. Mass, bulk, grow.
lust, n. Pleasure. *In liking lust,* at one's pleasure, according to one's taste.
lust, v.i. and t., a variant of *list, q.v.*

main, a. Solid.
man-kind, a. Like a man.
marble, a., used by Studley to translate *caeruleus,* deep blue.
marble-faced, a. see *marble.*
maze, v.t. Stupefy; amaze.
meacock, n. Coward.
mean, n. Moderation.
meat, n. Food.
mends, n. Amends.
mingle-mangle, n. A confused mixture, a hodgepodge.
minion, n. Mistress; paramour.
minister, v.t. Furnish.
mischief, n. An evil; wickedness; a mishap.
miser, n. An unhappy or wretched person.
mishap, n. Misfortune.
moe, n., a., adv. More.
moil, v.i. Be muddied; muddy oneself.
moil, v.t. Muddy.
mome, n. Blockhead.
monster, n. Prodigy; omen.

nephew, n. Grandchild.
nobility, n. Fame.
nonce, for the, prep. phrase. All at once.
nurture, n. Moral training.

obit, n. Funeral.
ope, a. Open.
oppress, v.t. Extinguish, suppress.
ordain, v.t. Put in order; prepare.
out, interj. denoting grief, horror, or indignation.
outlive, v.t. Live out, live through.
overhill, v.t. Cover over.
overquell, v.i. Be overcome; perish.

overshed, v.t. Shed over. *E.g.*, *overshed my thoughts with woes*, shed woes over my thoughts.
overstride, v.t. Walk beyond.

pack away, v.i. Depart in haste.
pain, n. Penalty.
parbrake, v.i. Vomit.
part, n. Side; direction.
part, v.t. Mix.
pash, v.t. Throw violently.
patter, v.i. Talk rapidly, chatter gibberish.
payse, n. Weight.
payse, v.t. Weigh upon, burden.
peevish, a. Silly, senseless.
pestered, p. Thronged, crowded.
piecemeal, n. Fragment, fragments.
pied-de-grue, n. Pedigree.
pipeling, p.a. Whistling.
pitch, v.t. Set in order for battle, as *to pitch a field*.
pithy, a. Strong.
playfere, n. Playmate; companion.
plight, n. Condition; health; mood.
plump, n. Clump; flock, group.
plunge, n. A submergence in danger or difficulty; straits.
plunge, v.t. Overwhelm, overcome.
ply, v.i. Travel, direct one's course.
poke, n. A fold of cloth; a pocket; a sleeve; a bag.
pole, n. Sky, heavens.
policy, n. Craft, strategy, trick.
pomp, n. Show.
portly, a. Dignified, majestic, stately.
post, v.i. Hasten.
preposterous, a. Hindside foremost, inverted in order; contrary to nature.
presently, adv. In person.
press, v.t. Oppress.
pretend, v.t. Present, offer.
prevail, v.i. Avail.
prevent, v.t. Anticipate; precede.
prey, n. Spoil, booty, plunder.
prick, v.t. Spur.
proof, n. Trial; experience.
protest, v.i. Promise solemnly.

protest, v.t. Call to witness.
prove, v.t. Try.
purple, n. Cloth dyed with an expensive crimson dye.
purple, a. Crimson; colored with an expensive crimson dye.
push, n. Assault, attack.

qualify, v.t. Pacify.
quaver, n. An eighth-note.
quean, n. Slut; harlot.
quick, a. Living, alive.
quite, v.t. Requite.

rage, n. Madness.
rampire, n. A rampart.
rampired, a. Having ramparts.
rapt, v.t. Carry away.
rate, n. Manner.
ray, v.t. Soil.
reave, v.t. Rob.
rebel, v.i. Fight back, make war in return.
record, v.t. Recall, remember.
recourse, n. Return; flow, movement.
reflect, v.i. Bend back, be bent back.
refrain, v.t. Check, rein.
remediless, a. Without hope of relief, beyond help.
remorse, n. Pity, compassion.
rent, v.t. Rend, tear.
represent, v.t. Cause to be present; exhibit, display.
reprove, v.t. Reject; refute; correct.
require, v.t. Seek; ask; summon.
resort, n. A throng; a retinue.
respect, n. Relationship. *In respect of,* in comparison with.
respect, v.t. Look upon.
revel, a. Riotous.
rex, n. Prank, pranks.
rife, a. Ready.
rig, v.t. Ransack, rifle.
ripe, v.t. Ripen.
rive, v.t. Pierce.
road, n. Harbor.
rock, n. A distaff with wool or flax on it.
roge, n. A funeral pyre.

room, n. Stead. *Supply the room to,* take the place of.
rout, n. Troop, throng.
rue, v.i. Feel pity.
rusty, a. Foul, vile; stained.

safeguard, n. Safety.
scant, adv. Scarcely.
scape, v.i. and t. Escape.
sceptres, n. plural with singular meaning. Sceptre.
score, v.t. Punish.
season, n. Time. *In the mean season,* meanwhile.
seem, v.t. Beseem.
shatling, p.a. Rattling; shaking; fluttering.
shawm, n. A wind instrument with reeds (the Roman *tibia*).
shear, v.t. Pierce; cleave.
shet, p. Shut.
shright, n. A shriek.
shun, v.i. Shrink back.
sign, v.t. Assign.
silly, a. Innocent, harmless; pitiful.
since that, conj. Since.
slack, v.t. Slow.
slander, n. Scandal, disgrace.
snout, n. Prow.
sometime, adv. Once, formerly.
sore, adv. Sorely; very, much.
sort, n. Lot; way, manner; group, flock. *On such a sort,* in such a way.
spare, n. Restraint; parsimony, economy.
spire, v.i. Blow.
spite, n. Injury; disgrace.
splay, v.t. Display; adorn.
spoil, n. Earth thrown up in excavating.
sprite, n. Ghost, spirit.
squat, v.i. Squeeze.
squat, v.t. Squeeze, crush.
stately, a. Noble, high-born.
stay, v.i. Stop, cease; stand; wait.
stay, v.t. Await.
steam, v.t. Emit.
stews, n. A prostitute.
stick, v.i. Hesitate.
still, v.i. Drip.

stiving, p.a. Hasty.
stomach, n. Pride, arrogance.
stound, n. Moment, instant.
straight, adv. Straightway.
strain, v.t. Distrain, restrain.
strake, v.t. past tense. Struck.
strake, p. Stricken.
stripe, n. Blow, stroke.
suborn, v.t. Provide, furnish.
subtle, a. Elusive; sly.
swing, n. Control.
swing, v.i. Exercise control.
swing, v.t. Control.
swink, v.t. Drink heavily.

targe, n. A shield, especially a small round one; a protection.
target, n. A shield, especially a small round one.
temper, v.t. Compound, blend.
thoroughout, prep. Throughout.
though, conj. If.
threat, v.i. and t. Threaten, menace.
throughly, adv. Thoroughly.
thrust, v.t. Force.
to-, prefix. Asunder, apart; completely.
to-broke, see *to-.*
to-coil, v.t. Beat thoroughly.
to-rent, see *to-.*
to-singed, see *to-.*
to-spattered, see *to-.*
tract, n. Lapse of time, period of time.
trade, n. Course of action; way of life.
train, n. Treachery; stratagem; trap.
train, v.t. Drag, draw along.
treat, v.t. Pull, draw.
trill, v.i. Trickle; stream.
trow, v.i. Trust, suppose.
turmoil, v.t. Harass, disquiet.
turn of hand, with, prep. phrase, see *hand, with turn of.*

ugsome, a. Frightful, abhorrent.
ungracious, a. Graceless; wicked.
unknowen, a. Unknown.

unware, a. Unaware, unwary; unforeseen.
updo, v.t. Put away; bury, plunge.
ure, n. Use; operation.
use, v.i. Be accustomed.
utter, v.t. Put forth.

vail, n. Advantage; advance; success.
vail, v.t. Avail.
vantage, n. Advantage.
venom, v.t. Poison.

wage, v.i. Engage; take risks.
wagon, n. A chariot.
wallow, v.i. To flounder in speech.
walm, n. A boiling, a bubbling; a whirlpool; a wave.
wanny, a. Wan.
want, v.i. Be lacking.
want, v.t. Lack.
waste, v.t. Consume.
wealth, n. Welfare.
wedding-blaze, n. Nuptial torch; a marriage.
weed, n. A garment. *Wailing weed,* mourning clothes.
ween, v.i. Suppose; expect; hope.
wellaway, n. Lamentation.
whereas, conj. Where.
whether, pronoun and a. Which (of two).
whilst, n. While. *The whilst,* meanwhile.
whisht, v.t. Be silent concerning.
who that, pronoun. Whoever.
widow, a. Unmarried.
wight, n. Human being.
will, v.t. Wish, desire, want.
wist, v.i. and t. past tense. Knew; learned.
wit, v.i. and t. Know; learn.
wite, v.i. and t. present plural. Know; learn.
witen, see *wite.*
witting, p. Knowing; learning.
woned, p.a. Plentifully or generously supplied, well endowed.
wood, a. Mad.
worried, p. Wasted; mangled, torn.
wost, v.i. and t. Wottest (see *wot*).
wot, v.i. and t. Know; learn.

wrack, n. Ruin, calamity.
wrast, p. Wrested.
wreak, v.t. Avenge (a person).
wreck, n. Vengeance.
wreckful, a. Vengeful.
wrest, v.t. Twist; wield.
writ, n. Writing; a written document.
writhen, p. Twisted.

y-, prefix, vaguely intensive, attached to past participles and occasionally
    to other verb forms.
ybored, see *y-.*
ycarved, see *y-.*
ycharm, see *y-.*
yclad, see *y-.*
yfreight, p. Laden, fraught.
younker, n. A young gallant.
yscorched, see *y-.*
ytossed, see *y-.*
ytwist, see *y-.*

INDEX OF PROPER NAMES*

Acheron. "River of Woe," one of the rivers of the Lower World, the realm of Dis (*q.v.*).

Achill. Achilles (*q.v.*).

Achilles. The son of Peleus, King of the Myrmidons in Phthia in Thessaly (*v.* Table D, p. 197) and of the sea-nymph Thetis. By birth he was thus connected with all three worlds, through his mother with the sea, through his grandfather Aeacus (*q.v.*) with the Lower World, and with the Upper World through Jupiter, his great-grandfather. His mother, realizing by her prophetic powers that his life would be long if obscure but short if glorious, attempted to save him from taking part in the Trojan War by hiding him, disguised as a girl, among the daughters of Lycomedes, King of Scyros, by one of whom, Deidamia, he became the father of Pyrrhus. Calchas betrayed his hiding-place to Ulysses who, together with Diomedes, unmasked him by displaying (while disguised as a merchant) female ornaments and a shield and spear or sword to Lycomedes' daughters. At a sudden trumpet-call the girls fled, but Achilles seized the arms. At the delaying of the Greek fleet at Aulis, it was by a pretended betrothal to Achilles that Iphigenia (*q.v.*) was lured to the sacrifice. When the Greek forces landed in Mysia and Telephus (*q.v.*), its king, opposed them, Achilles wounded him and took his land. In raids around Troy he took the islands of Tenedos, Scyros, and Lesbos, the city of Thebes or Thebe in Cilicia, and the cities of Cilla, Lyrnesos,

* The large number, and the obscurity, of Seneca's mythological references, as well as the fact that the translators have in some cases misunderstood the reference, have made it necessary to give rather full versions of many of the myths involved in this index; but the index should nevertheless not be taken to be a dictionary of mythology, since only such parts of the various stories are given as serve to clarify references in the text. Interpretations are not provided, and variants are given only when it is uncertain to which version Seneca refers, or when the translator has had in mind another version than that intended by Seneca. A system of cross-references is used so that stories need not be repeated: it is in many cases necessary to read more than one entry in order to have the whole story. The somewhat inconsistent use of forms and spellings (sometimes Greek, sometimes Latin) of the proper names follows that of the translators, who themselves usually follow Seneca.

and Chryse in the Troad. In the last two he took captive Briseis and
Chryseis respectively. The former girl he kept for himself; the latter
fell to the lot of Agamemnon, who brought the wrath of Apollo on the
Greek army by refusing to allow her father Chryses, a priest of Apollo,
to ransom her. Forced eventually to return her, Agamemnon demanded
Achilles' captive, Briseis, as compensation. Achilles in his anger withdrew
himself and his forces from the war. The affairs of the Greeks de-
clined in consequence, and Agamemnon was forced to capitulate, sending an embassy of Ulysses, Ajax the Greater, and Achilles' paedagogue
Phoenix to Achilles, who, although he refused to fight himself, allowed
his dearest friend Patroclus, disguised in his armor, to lead the Myrmidons to battle. When Patroclus was killed by Hector, Achilles was
roused to anger, slew Hector, and mutilated his body by dragging it
around Patroclus' tomb (or around the city) tied to his chariot. When
Priam attempted to buy back Hector's body for burial, Achilles was
moved to pity and gave it up without ransom. Besides Hector he also
slew before Troy Penthesilea the Amazon, Memnon, and Troilus. He
was betrothed to Priam's daughter Polyxena and, lured unarmed to the
temple of Thymbraean Apollo to wed her, was treacherously slain by
Paris. On the eve of the Greeks' departure from Troy after their victory
his ghost appeared and demanded the sacrifice of Polyxena on his tomb.

Aeacus. Son of Jupiter and Aegina, a daughter of Asopus, a river god, was
King of the Myrmidons. His son was Peleus, the father of Achilles
(*q.v.*). Because of his just mind, Aeacus after his death became, along
with Minos and Rhadamanthus, one of the three judges of the Lower
World.

Aedon. The wife of Zethus, King of Thebes, and mother of Itys. She
became jealous of Niobe (*q.v.*), wife of Zethus' brother Amphion (*q.v.*),
because she had six sons and six daughters, and attempted to kill
Niobe's eldest son. When by mistake she killed her own son Itys,
Jupiter changed her to a nightingale, in which form she still mourns
her loss.

Aegean Sea. A part of the Mediterranean, lying to the south of Thrace
and Macedonia and between Greece on the west and Asia Minor to
the east. It was said to have received its name from Aegeus (*q.v.*)
because he committed suicide by throwing himself into it.

Aegeus. King of Athens, and father of Theseus. When Theseus went to
Crete to free Athens from the tribute it had to pay to Minos (*q.v.*; *v.*
also *Minotaur*), he promised to change the black sails of his vessel for
white ones on his return, if he should survive. He forgot his promise,
and Aegeus, seeing the black sails and assuming that his son was dead,
threw himself into the sea called thereafter the Aegean from his name
(*v.* also *Medea*).

Aegis. A shield or breastplate covered with goatskin and bearing the head of Medusa, carried or worn by Jupiter and Athena. It caused panic or destruction to fall on those to whom it was displayed.

Aegist. Aegisthus (*q.v.*).

Aegisthus. Son of Thyestes (*q.v.*) by his own daughter Pelopia (*v.* Table C, p. 194). With his father he slew Atreus (*q.v.*), and his father reigned in Mycenae until expelled by the return of Agamemnon (*q.v.*) from exile. During Agamemnon's absence at the Trojan War Aegisthus seduced Clytemnestra, Agamemnon's wife, and helped her to murder him on his return. He then reigned at Mycenae for seven years, but was slain by Orestes in the eighth.

Aeneas. Son of Anchises (*v.* Table A, p. 190) and the goddess Venus, Troy's greatest hero after Hector. Priam is said to have distrusted him, thinking that he desired the kingship; this and the fact that he, with Antenor (*q.v.*), had always counseled against the war and advocated the return of Helen, led to a late legend that he had betrayed Troy to her enemies. After the fall of Troy he migrated with his followers to Latium in Italy; the Romans were thought to be descended from him.

Aethiopia. The ancients applied this name to two regions, the first south of Egypt and the second north of the Persian Gulf, extended from the mouth of the Tigris up the valley of the Choaspes and including the ancient city of Susa. Both areas were thought to be inhabited by dark-skinned people. At the time of the Trojan War the eastern Aethiopia was ruled by Memnon (*q.v.*).

Afric. African. By *Africa* the Romans meant, not the whole continent (*v. Libya*), but the province which they had made of the former territory of Carthage.

Agamemnon. Son of Atreus (*q.v.*; *v.* also Table C, p. 194). On the death of Atreus he and his brother Menelaus left Mycenae for Sparta, where Tyndareus gave them his daughters in marriage, Clytemnestra to Agamemnon and Helen to Menelaus. Agamemnon drove Thyestes (*q.v.*) from Mycenae and became its king, extending his power over all Argos as well. When his brother's wife was abducted by the Trojan Paris, Agamemnon led the Greek forces in the war fought to recover her. He allowed his daughter Iphigenia to be sacrificed at Aulis to obtain favorable winds for the Greek fleet. At Troy he brought a pestilence on the Greek forces by refusing to allow the priest Chryses, father of his captive Chryseis, to ransom her. Forced to return her, he incurred the wrath of Achilles (*q.v.*) by taking his captive, Briseis, in compensation. At the capture of Troy he received Cassandra (*q.v.*) as his prize. On his return from Troy he was murdered, along with Cassandra, by his wife and her lover, his cousin Aegisthus (*q.v.*).

Agave. Daughter of Cadmus (*q.v.*), wife of Echion, and mother of Pentheus (*q.v.*).

Ajax. (*1*) Son of Telamon and King of Salamis. At Troy he was considered second only to Achilles in strength and bravery. After the fall of Troy Thetis offered the arms of Achilles as a prize to whichever hero, after Achilles, had done most to win the war. Ajax and Ulysses (*q.v.*) competed, and the arms were awarded to the latter when Trojan prisoners testified that their city had suffered more from his cunning than from Ajax's bravery. The decision drove Ajax mad, and he slaughtered the sheep of the Greek forces under the delusion that they were his enemies. When he came to himself he committed suicide in mortification. (*2*) Ajax "the Lesser," son of the King of Locris, also took part in the Trojan War. Because he violated the temple of Athena (*v. Cassandra*) the goddess in her wrath wrecked the Greek fleet off Caphareus in Euboea. Neptune rescued Ajax, but when he boasted that he had escaped against the will of the gods, Neptune split the rock on which he stood, and he drowned.

Alcides. "Descendant of Alcaeus," *i.e.,* Hercules (*q.v.*).

Amazons. A race of female warriors, dwelling in the Caucasus or on the shores of the Black Sea. They allowed no men in their kingdom and perpetuated their race by mating with neighboring tribes. They fought armed with crescent-shaped shields, two-bladed battle-axes, spears, and bows and arrows.

Amphion. Son of Antiope (*v.* Table B, p. 192) and Jupiter. Nycteus, Antiope's father, was regent at Thebes during the minority of Labdacus. Enraged by his discovery of her pregnancy by Jupiter, he threatened to punish her. She fled to Sicyon, whose King, Epopeus, married her, begetting Zethus by superfetation. When Nycteus tried to recover her he was killed by Epopeus, who was then himself killed by Lycus, Nycteus' brother. Lycus, regent at Thebes for the boy Laius, imprisoned Antiope there, where she was cruelly treated by Dirce, Lycus' wife. Antiope finally escaped to Mt. Cithaeron, where she found her twin sons Amphion and Zethus, whom Lycus had exposed on the mountain as soon as they were born. Now grown, they took Thebes, killed Dirce by tying her to a wild bull, and assumed the regency of the city, which they fortified with walls and towers, Amphion causing the stones to fit themselves together by the magical music of his lyre. Zethus married Aedon (*q.v.*); Amphion, Niobe (*q.v.*).

Amyclae. A town of Laconia on the Eurotas River, southeast of Sparta; it was the landing-place of Paris when he came to abduct Helen.

Andromacha. Andromache (*q.v.*).

Andromache. Daughter of Eetion (*q.v.*), King of Thebes or Thebe in Cilicia, married to Hector (*q.v.*) of Troy, by whom she had a son,

Astyanax (*q.v.*). After the Trojan War she was awarded as a prize to Pyrrhus (*q.v.*), the son of the man who had killed her father, her seven brothers, and her husband. Pyrrhus took her to Epirus where, after begetting a son on her, he gave her to another Trojan captive, Helenus (*q.v.*), a brother of Hector. On Pyrrhus' death she and Helenus reigned in Epirus.

Antenor. A wise elder at Troy and a kinsman of Queen Hecuba (*q.v.*), he was an advocate of peace and the surrender of Helen, in recognition of which he was spared by the Greeks. A late legend has him betray Troy to the Greeks.

Apollo. A god, the son of Jupiter (*q.v.*) and Latona (*q.v.*); his twin sister was Diana. As god of light, both in the physical and the spiritual sense, he was the divinity of the sun and also the chief god of prophecy. His principal oracle, at Delphi, he won by killing the huge serpent, Python, which guarded it. His oracles, usually ambiguous, were delivered there by a prophetess called the Pythia. With Neptune he built the walls of Troy for Laomedon (*q.v.*) and was a supporter of the city in the Trojan War. One of his many loves was Priam's daughter Cassandra (*q.v.*). He was armed with the bow and played the lyre, his attributes as god of disease and health and of song and music. In this latter aspect he was often accompanied by the Muses.

Araby. Arabia, thought by the ancients to be a fertile peninsula, the source of precious incense and spices.

Arcadia. A country in the middle of the Peloponnesus, the scene of two of Hercules' (*q.v.*) labors, that of the Erymanthian Boar and that of the Cerynian or Maenalian Hind.

Argos. A geographical term which the ancients applied in various ways, occasionally confusing them. It referred (*1*) to the whole Peloponnesus (hence *Argives* as a term for Greeks in general), (*2*) to Agamemnon's kingdom, the eastern peninsula of the Peloponnesus, whose capital was Mycenae, or (*3*) to the town of Argos, which lay to the south of Mycenae in the kingdom of Argos.

Argus. A monster of human form but having a hundred eyes. Juno (*q.v.*) set him to guard Io, Jupiter's (*q.v.*) love whom he had changed into a heifer in the hope of protecting her from Juno's wrath. When Mercury, at Jupiter's command, killed him, Juno placed his eyes in the tail of her bird, the peacock.

Armenia. A high table-land between Asia Minor and the Caspian Sea, containing the sources of five major rivers, the Tigris, Euphrates, Cyrus, Araxis, and Phasis.

Armenie. Armenia (*q.v.*).

Asia. A geographical term used by the Romans with various meanings, to refer to (*1*) the continent, pictured as occupying either the eastern half or the southeastern quarter of the land surface known to the ancients (in either case it was separated from Europe by the Bosporus and Hellespont and from Libya by the Red Sea), *(2)* Asia Minor, or *(3)* Pergamum.

Assarac. Assaracus (*q.v.*).

Assaracus. Son of Tros (*v.* Table A, p. 190) and the second King of Troy.

Astyanax. Son of Hector (*q.v.*) and Andromache (*q.v.*). After the fall of Troy he was killed by being thrown from a tower, having been pointed out by Calchas as destined to restore the kingdom of Troy.

Athena, Pallas Athena. The goddess of wisdom, and hence patroness of all arts, crafts, and sciences, both of war and of peace. Born full-grown from the head of her father Jupiter (who had swallowed her mother Metis) she was his favorite of his children, and was allowed to bear his Aegis (*q.v.*) and to wield his thunderbolts. Although a chief goddess of Troy, she supported the Greeks in the Trojan War.

Atreus. The son of Pelops (*v.* Table C, p. 194), King of Pisa; he and his brother Thyestes murdered their stepbrother and fled, to escape Pelops' wrath, to Mycenae. On the death of its king, Atreus assumed the throne, which he kept by virtue of a magical golden lamb which Mercury had given him in order to cause discord in Pelops' family and thus avenge the death of Myrtilus (*v. Pelops*). Thyestes, coveting the royal power, obtained the golden lamb by seducing Aerope, Atreus' wife, a deed which caused Jupiter in horror to turn the sun and the moon back in their courses. Atreus succeeded in recovering the kingship, and banished Thyestes. Thyestes sent Atreus' son Plisthenes, whom he had raised as his own son, to murder his true father Atreus; Atreus, not knowing that Plisthenes was his own son, killed him. To avenge Plisthenes' death, Atreus recalled Thyestes, pretending to offer him a share in the kingship, but slew his sons, cooked their flesh, and served it to their father at a banquet of pretended reconciliation, a deed which made the sun recoil and turn backward in his course. Thyestes fled, and, told by an oracle that in this way he could have revenge on Atreus, lay with his own daughter Pelopia. As a result, Mycenae was afflicted with a famine and Atreus, on consulting an oracle for the cause, was told to seek his brother. He did not find him, but did find Pelopia, whom he married, believing her to be a daughter of King Thesprotus. When she gave birth to Aegisthus (*q.v.*), her son by her own father, Atreus adopted him and raised him as his own son, later sending him to kill Thyestes, who had been found and imprisoned by Atreus' sons, Agamemnon and Menelaus. But Thyestes recognized Aegisthus as his own son, and Pelopia, who had witnessed their meeting and was overcome with horror, killed herself with a sword. By displaying the bloody sword

Aegisthus convinced Agamemnon that Thyestes was dead, then, with Thyestes, murdered him as he was sacrificing to the gods in thanksgiving. Thyestes and Aegisthus then banished Agamemnon and Menelaus, and Thyestes was left to be King of Mycenae.

Atrid. Atrides (*q.v.*).

Atrides. "Son of Atreus," *i.e.,* Agamemnon (*q.v.*) or Menelaus (*q.v.*).

Attis. A beautiful Phrygian youth beloved by the goddess Cybele (*q.v.*) who, to prevent him from marrying the daughter of the King of Pessinus, drove him mad and caused him to castrate himself. He died as a result and was metamorphosed into a fir or pine tree.

Aulis. A port town of Boeotia, the mustering-place of the Greek ships at their departure for the Trojan War. It was here that Iphigenia (*q.v.*) was sacrificed.

Aurora. Goddess of the dawn, the mother by Tithonus (*q.v.*) of Memnon (*q.v.*).

Avern. Avernus (*q.v.*).

Avernus. A lake near Cumae and Puteoli in Italy, though because of its gloomy appearance and its mephitic vapors (which were believed to kill any bird which flew over it) to be an entrance to the Lower World; hence the word is sometimes applied to the Lower World in general.

Bacchus. God of wine, the son of Jupiter (*q.v.*), by Semele, daughter of Cadmus (*q.v.*). After his invention of wine he traveled over the world, accompanied by a rout of Maenads (*q.v.*), Satyrs, Sileni, Hermaphrodites, and others, teaching the cultivation of the vine and instituting his cult and rites. Where his worship was opposed he could take a fearful vengeance (*v. Pentheus*). When, on one occasion, he had been captured by Tyrrhene or Phoenician pirates, he caused the rigging of the ship to be overgrown with vines and changed the pirates themselves into dolphins. The chief centers of his worship were Boeotia (the country of his birth), Phocis, Argos, Laconia, and Naxos (where he found his bride Ariadne).

Bedlam (Bethlehem). The Hospital of St. Mary of Bethlehem in London, hence *(1)* a madhouse, *(2)* a madman, or *(3)* (as adjective) mad.

Bellona. Goddess of war, the sister or wife of Mars (*q.v.*).

Bellone. Bellona (*q.v.*).

Bilbao. A Spanish port, famous in the sixteenth and seventeenth centuries for the quality of the swords manufactured there.

Bistones. A people of Thrace (*q.v.*).

Bootes. "The Herdsman," a constellation of the Northern Hemisphere which does not set below the horizon.

Boreas. The North Wind.

Briseis. Daughter of Briseus of Lyrnesos; taken prisoner by Achilles (*q.v.*), she was the cause of the quarrel between him and Agamemnon (*q.v.*).

Busiris. A King of Egypt; when Egypt was afflicted with a nine-year famine, he was advised by Phrasius, a prophet, to sacrifice a stranger to Jupiter each year. Busiris followed the advice, beginning by sacrificing Phrasius himself. He was eventually killed by one of his intended victims, Hercules (*q.v., the Eleventh Labor*).

Cadmus. A prince of Phoenicia, the brother of Europa. When she was carried off by Jupiter in the form of a bull, Cadmus was sent to find her. He was unsuccessful, and upon applying to the Delphic oracle for advice, was told to abandon the search and instead to follow a cow which would meet him and to found a city on the spot where she would lie down. This was Cadmea, later to become the citadel of Thebes. Near the city Cadmus slew a dragon which had killed his men, and on Athena's advice planted its teeth. A race of warriors sprang up from them, and fell to killing each other until only five, the ancestors of the future aristocracy of Thebes, were left; one of them, Echion (*v.* Table B, p. 192), married Cadmus' daughter Agave. Cadmus was through her and his son Polydorus the ancestor of the Kings of Thebes. He was credited with having brought the alphabet to the Greeks from Phoenicia.

Caicus. A river of Mysia (*q.v.*).

Calchas. A Mycenean soothsayer who accompanied the rest of the Greeks to the Trojan War. It was he who revealed the hiding place of Achilles (*q.v.*), who at Aulis demanded the sacrifice of Iphigenia (*q.v.*), who insisted on the return of Chryseis (*q.v.*) to her father, and who called for the deaths of Polyxena (*q.v.*) and Astyanax (*q.v.*) after the fall of Troy.

Caphar. Caphareus (*q.v.*).

Caphareus. A promontory on the southeast coast of Euboea, where the Greek fleet was wrecked on its return from Troy (*v. Ajax, 2*), by the trickery of Nauplius (v. *Palamedes*).

Cassandra. A daughter of Priam (*q.v.*) and Hecuba (*q.v.*). Because of her beauty Apollo (*q.v.*) fell in love with her and bestowed upon her the gift of prophecy in exchange for a promise of her love. She broke her promise, and Apollo decreed that no one would ever believe her prophecies. She prophesied the doom of Troy both at Paris' birth and at the arrival of Helen. When Troy fell she was dragged from the temple of Athena, where she had taken sanctuary, by the lesser Ajax. Her betrothed, Coroebus (*q.v.*), died trying to rescue her. She fell as a prize to Agamemnon (*q.v.*) and was murdered with him by Clytemnestra (*q.v.*).

Castalia. A spring on Mt. Parnassus, north of Delphi. It was sacred to Apollo and the Muses.

Cephallenia. An island near Ithaca, part of the realm of Ulysses (*q.v.*).

Cephally. Cephallenia (*q.v.*).

Cerberus. The dog which guarded the entrance to the Lower World; he had three heads and a mane and tail of serpents. The Twelfth Labor of Hercules (*q.v.*) was to drag him to the Upper World. The appearance of Cerberus was so dreadful that the Sun hid his face from the sight.

Ceyx. Son of Lucifer, the Morning Star, and King of Trachis. When he was drowned at sea his wife Alcyone threw herself into the sea. The gods in pity changed the pair into birds, halcyones; and when the halcyones are hatching their eggs there is always calm at sea, effected by Alcyone's father, Aeolus, the wind-god. Hence the expression "halcyon days."

Chalcedon. A city in Asia Minor on the coast of the Propontis (the Sea of Marmora), opposite Byzantium.

Chalcis. The chief town of Euboea.

Chaos. A personification of the primeval mixture of all matter out of which the universe was created, he was the father of Night and Erebus (*q.v.*).

Chryse. A city of the Troad, with a temple of Apollo Smintheus. It was taken by Achilles, who took prisoner Chryseis (*q.v.*), daughter of Chryses, the priest of Apollo.

Chryseis. Daughter of Chryses, priest of Apollo at Chryse; she was taken prisoner by Achilles (*q.v.*).

Cilla. A town in the Troad, famous for the temple of Apollo Cillaeus; it was taken in a raid by Achilles (*q.v.*).

Cithaeron. A mountain between Boeotia and Attica, sacred to Bacchus (*q.v.*) and the Muses. Oedipus (*q.v.*), Amphion (*q.v.*), and Zethus were exposed here in infancy. For the Lion of Cithaeron, *v. Hercules*.

Clotho. One of the Fates (*q.v.*).

Clytemnestra. Daughter of Tyndareus of Sparta and wife to Agamemnon (*q.v.*), King of Mycenae and Argos. After her murder of Agamemnon she ruled at Mycenae for seven years with her lover Aegisthus (*q.v.*) but was then slain by her son Orestes (*q.v.*).

Colchis. A country of Asia east of the Black Sea and south of the Caucasus. Its people were considered savage and cruel. It was the land from which Jason (*q.v.*) brought the Golden Fleece (*v. Medea*).

Colchus. An inhabitant of Colchis (*q.v.*).

Corinth. A city on the isthmus between the Peloponnesus and Attica (*v. Oedipus*).

Coroebus. Son of Mygdon, King of the Phrygians. Mygdon was an ally of Priam, who had helped him in a war with the Amazons, and sent his son to the Trojan War. Coroebus was betrothed to Priam's daughter Cassandra (*q.v.*).

Corus. The Northwest Wind.

Creon. "Ruler," a name given to several kings in ancient myth, two especially: *(1)* The son of Menoecus (*v.* Table B, p. 192) and brother of Jocasta (*v. Oedipus*). Oedipus, on his departure for exile, left the government of Thebes in the hands of his two sons Eteocles and Poly-nices. Eteocles drove out Polynices, who fled to Adrastus, King of Sicyon. Adrastus organized an expedition to take Thebes for Polynices (the *Seven Against Thebes*). Eteocles and Polynices perished in single combat in this war. Creon then seized the throne and refused burial to Polynices, even sentencing Antigone to death for attempting to bury her brother's body. His own son, Haemon, killed himself in grief at Antigone's death. *(2)* King of Corinth, father of Glauce, the bride of Jason (*v. Medea*).

Creta. Crete (*q.v.*).

Crete. A large island in the eastern Mediterranean. It was ruled before the Trojan War by Minos (*q.v.*; *v.* also *Theseus*), and was the scene of the Seventh Labor of Hercules (*q.v.*), the capture of the Cretan or Marathonian Bull.

Cupid. The god of love, son of Venus and Mars, Mercury, or Jupiter. He was a capricious boy, feared by all gods and men, armed with a bow and arrows and carrying a burning torch, his instruments for inspiring love. Later legend ascribed his capriciousness to blindness.

Cybel. Cybele (*q.v.*).

Cybele. A Phrygian nature-goddess, the Great Mother of the gods. She roamed the woodlands of Mt. Ida in Crete or Mt. Ida in the Troad, wearing a turreted crown, in a chariot drawn by lions, accompanied by the Galli, male devotees who had castrated themselves in her honor and that of her beloved, Attis (*q.v.*). The priests of her cult bore the same name, Galli, and practised the same self-mutilation.

Cycnus. A son of Neptune and Calyce. He was invulnerable and his body was as white as snow. King of Colonae in the Troad, he came to the aid of Troy in the Trojan War, where he was killed by Achilles who, unable to wound him, strangled him with his own helmet-strap, where-upon Neptune changed him into a swan.

Danaus. Son of Belus, King of Egypt. He was himself King of Libya, but, fearing his brother Aegyptus and his fifty sons, fled with his fifty daughters to Argos, where he was elected King. The fifty sons of Aegyptus followed him and demanded his daughters in marriage. He agreed, but gave each of his daughters a dagger, and on their bridal night they slew their husbands, all but one, Hypermnestra, who spared her husband Lynceus. Lynceus later killed Danaus. The Danaids (daughters of Danaus), in punishment for their crime, were condemned in the Lower World to the hopeless task of fetching water in bottomless vessels.

Dardan. Dardanus (*q.v.*).

Dardanus. Son of Jupiter and Electra, one of the Pleiades (*v.* Table A, p. 190). Bringing the Palladium (*q.v.*), he came from Samothrace to the Troad, where he founded Dardania on Mt. Ida. Through his great-grandsons Ilus and Assaracus he was the ancestor of both royal lines at Troy.

Dares the Phrygian. A priest of Vulcan at the Trojan War, thought to be the author of an eye-witness account of the war. A spurious Latin version of this supposed work was a popular source for the history of the Trojan War in the Middle Ages.

Death. Son of Night and brother of Sleep. He was a youth with black wings, and carried a knife and an extinguished torch.

Deianira. Daughter of Oeneus, King of Calydon, and Althaea. The river-god Achelous and Hercules fought for the possession of her. She was won by Hercules and became his wife, but later caused his death by giving him the Shirt of Nessus (*v. Hercules*).

Deiphobus. Son of Priam and Hecuba (*q.v.*), he led the Trojan army after Hector's death. After the death of Paris he married Helen (*q.v.*), who at the fall of Troy betrayed him as he slept to Menelaus (*q.v.*), who killed and mutilated him.

Delos. An island, one of the Cyclades, in the Aegean Sea. It had been a floating island, but was chained to the bottom of the sea by Jupiter, so that Latona (*q.v.*) might there give birth to Apollo and Diana. It was thereafter sacred to these two gods.

Delphi. A city of Phocis, where there was an oracular shrine of Apollo (*q.v.*), who won the oracle by killing the serpent Python. The oracles were given by the Pythia (*q.v.*), who sat upon a sacred tripod to receive the inspiration of the god, and were of tremendous importance in classical myth and history.

Deucalion. Son of Prometheus, husband of Pyrrha, the daughter of Prometheus' brother Epimetheus. When Jupiter (*q.v.*) proposed to punish the wickedness of mankind by sending a universal flood, Deucalion, on the advice of his father, shut himself and Pyrrha in a chest, which floated on the flood and was eventually deposited on Mt. Parnassus. Consulting the oracle at Delphi, Deucalion and Pyrrha were told to repopulate the earth by throwing the bones of their mother behind them. They obeyed by throwing stones (the bones of Earth); those thrown by Deucalion became men; by Pyrrha, women.

Dian. Diana (*q.v.*).

Diana. Daughter of Latona (*q.v.*) and twin sister of Apollo (*q.v.*). Like him she was a divinity of both health and disease, armed, as he was, with bow and arrows. She is sometimes called the Triple Goddess from her three aspects: *(1)* as goddess of light she was the deity of the moon and of the night sky; *(2)* as a nature goddess she was the huntress and protectress of wild beasts; and *(3)* as a chthonic deity she reigned in the Lower World as goddess of darkness and witchcraft. It was she who demanded, as recompense for Agamemnon's killing of a hind sacred to her, the sacrifice of Iphigenia (*q.v.*).

Dictys of Crete. A companion of Idomeneus, leader of the Cretan forces at the Trojan War. It was said that his diary of the war was discovered in the reign of Nero and translated into Greek. The extant version (in Latin), however, dates from no earlier than the fourth century A.D. It was much used as a source for the history of the Trojan War in the Middle Ages.

Diomed. Diomedes (*q.v.*).

Diomedes. There were two heroes with this name: *(1)* A son of Mars, King of the Bistones in Thrace. He owned some man-eating mares, to which he used to feed the bodies of strangers who came to his land. The capturing of these mares and the killing of Diomedes were the Eighth Labor of Hercules (*q.v.*). *(2)* King of the city of Argos, he took part in the Trojan War. He helped Ulysses to discover the disguised Achilles (*q.v.*). At Troy he was one of the bravest heroes; with the aid of Athena he defeated Aeneas (*q.v.*) and even wounded Mars and Venus when they mingled in the mortal battle. With Ulysses he made his way into Troy by night and stole the Palladium (*q.v.*). As punishment for this impiety and for his wounding of Venus, his wife was tempted to unfaithfulness, and Diomedes was forced to go into exile to escape the fate of Agamemnon (*q.v.*). He eventually reached Italy, where he reigned in Apulia.

Dis. *(1)* The god of the Lower World, brother of Jupiter and Neptune. His consort was Proserpina, the daughter of Ceres, with whom he ruled over the shades of the dead. He was cruel and inexorable. *(2)* Hence the name *Dis* was also applied to his realm. This was entered at several places in the upper world, such as Taenarus (*q.v.*) and Avernus (*q.v.*). It was bounded and intersected by six great rivers (*v. Acheron, Lethe, Phlegethon, Styx*), across which the shades, guided by Mercury, were ferried by Charon. They then passed Cerberus (*q.v.*) and were brought to their judges, Minos (*q.v.*), Rhadamanthus, and Aeacus (*q.v.*), and were by them assigned to Elysium (*q.v.*) or Tartarus (*q.v.*).

Ditis. Dis (*q.v.*).

Eetion. King of Thebes or Thebe in Cilicia, and father of Andromache (*q.v.*). Achilles (*q.v.*) killed him and his seven sons.

Elean. Of Elis (*q.v.*).

Electra. Daughter of Agamemnon (*q.v.*) and Clytemnestra (*q.v.*). After her father's murder she helped her brother Orestes (*q.v.*) to escape from Mycenae, and afterwards helped him to avenge the death of Agamemnon. She married Orestes' friend Pylades (*q.v.*).

Elis. Country on the west coast of the Peloponnesus, just west of Arcadia; Olympia, the site of the Olympic Games (*q.v.*) was here.

Elysium. The abode of the blessed in the Lower World (*v. Dis*). Here the shades of the guiltless lived in tranquillity in meadows of asphodel.

Eos. Greek name for Aurora (*q.v.*).

Erebus. (*1*) The god of darkness, the son of Chaos. He begot Day and Aether on his sister Night. (*2*) Because the Lower World was perpetually dark, the name *Erebus,* like *Dis* or *Orcus,* was also applied to it.

Erinys. Fury (*q.v.*).

Europe. A name applied to the northern half or northeastern quarter of the land mass known in antiquity. Its boundary with Asia was at the Hellespont and Bosporus.

Eurus. The Southeast Wind.

Eurybates. The herald of Ulysses (*q.v.*); he took part in the Trojan War.

Euxine. The Black Sea.

Fates. Three goddesses who determined the length of human life. They were Clotho ("Spinner") who spun the thread of life, Lachesis ("Assigner of Lots") who measured the thread, and Atropos ("Inevitable") who cut it off. They were euphemistically called Parcae ("Sparers") by the Romans.

Fortune. The goddess of chance or luck. She had many attributes: the cornucopia, as the giver of blessings; a steering-oar, as the pilot of the world's affairs; wings, and a wheel (or ball), as being variable and fickle.

Fury. A goddess of vengeance. The Furies, who dwelt in Tartarus (*q.v.*), had snakes for hair and twined around their waists and arms, and blood dripping from their eyes. They carried torches and scourges, with which they punished the damned in Tartarus or emerged into the upper world to strike the guilty with madness. The crimes which they punished include those which the Romans called *impia, i.e.,* any failure of respect toward relatives, old people, guests, suppliants, or anyone to whom a special loyalty was owed, as well as perjury.

Geryon. A giant with three bodies, who lived on the western island of Erythia. There he kept a herd of cattle. guarded by a giant cow-herd and a two-headed dog. The capture of his cattle and the slaying of Geryon were the Tenth Labor of Hercules (*q.v.*).

Giants. A race of monsters sprung from Earth when she was fertilized by the blood of the castrated Uranus. Some of them had human shapes, monstrous only in their size; others were monsters of various kinds, with wings, with serpents for legs, with multiple heads, hands, or bodies. They revolted against the gods, piling Mt. Pelion upon Mt. Ossa in their attempt to reach Olympus; but the gods defeated them with the aid of Hercules (*q.v.*). Some were killed and condemned to Tartarus (*v. Tityus*), some were buried alive, and some were set to perform various tasks for the gods (*v. Geryon*).

Gnosian. Of Gnossus, or Cnossus, the chief city of Crete (*q.v.*; *v.* also *Minos*).

Gorgons. Three sisters, two of whom were immortal, having golden wings, bronze claws, huge teeth, and hair composed of serpents. The third, Medusa, was a mortal maiden who enraged Athena by lying with Neptune in one of her temples. Athena turned her hair to snakes and cursed her so that anyone who looked upon her face was turned to stone. She was beheaded by Perseus with the aid of Athena, whereupon her children by Neptune, Chrysaor (the father of Geryon, *q.v.*) and Pegasus (*q.v.*) sprang from her neck. Perseus presented her head to Athena, who placed it on the Aegis (*q.v.*).

Grecia. Greece (*q.v.*).

Grecian. Greek (*q.v.*).

Greece. A name not restricted in antiquity to the Balkan Peninsula, but applied to all that part of the world where Greeks lived.

Greek. A term having no political significance in antiquity, but applied to certain peoples who had common descent, language, and set of religious beliefs.

Harpies. Monsters, half bird, half woman, with pale faces and long claws, who carried off human beings or befouled or snatched from them their food. They were sent to torment King Phineus of Thrace; driven off by the Argonauts (*v. Jason*), they settled in the Strophades. They also appeared in Tartarus (*q.v.*) as tormentors of the damned.

Hecate. One of the Titans (*q.v.*), a goddess of ghosts and witchcraft. She is often identified with the triple Diana (*q.v.*), and so was goddess of the moon, as well as a ruler of the Lower World. She was thought to roam the earth by night, accompanied by demons and ghosts.

Hector. Eldest son of Priam and Hecuba (*v.* Table A, p. 190), husband of Andromache (*q.v.*) and father of Astyanax (*q.v.*); he was Troy's greatest hero. After slaying Patroclus he ventured out against Achilles (*q.v.*) himself, in spite of the pleas of his wife and parents. Overcome by panic at Achilles' terrible approach, he was pursued by him thrice around the walls of Troy and finally killed. Achilles dragged his body behind his chariot around Patroclus' tomb (or around the city), but later gave it up for burial to Priam.

Hecuba. Wife of Priam (*q.v.*) and mother of nineteen of his fifty sons. At the birth of Paris (*q.v.*) she dreamt that she had given birth to a firebrand. After the fall of Troy she fell to the lot of Ulysses. On the way to Ithaca, Ulysses put in at Thrace, where she avenged the death of her son Polydorus (*q.v.*) by putting out King Polymestor's eyes. She was then metamorphosed into a bitch and threw herself into the sea.

Helen. Daughter of Jupiter and Leda (*v.* Table C, p. 194); she was the most beautiful woman of classical myth. In girlhood she was carried off to Attica by Theseus and Pirithous, whence she was rescued by her brothers Castor and Pollux. All the nobles of Greece sued for her hand; she was married to Menelaus (*q.v.*), who thus became King of Sparta at the death of her mother's husband Tyndareus, and to whom she bore a daughter, Hermione. When she was seduced and carried off to Troy by Paris (*q.v.*) her former suitors vowed to avenge her abduction; their war of vengeance was the Trojan War. After the death of Paris she married his brother Deiphobus (*q.v.*); at the fall of Troy she was handed over to Menelaus and returned to Sparta with him.

Helena. Helen (*q.v.*).

Helenus. A son of Priam and Hecuba; a prophet. Upon the death of Paris (*q.v.*) he contended with Deiphobus (*q.v.*) for the hand of Helen (*q.v.*). Defeated, he fled to Mt. Ida, where he was captured by Ulysses, who wished to obtain his prophecy concerning the fall of Troy. He revealed that Troy could not be conquered without the aid of Pyrrhus (*q.v.*) and the cooperation of Philoctetes (*q.v.*). He became the slave of Pyrrhus, to whom he prophesied the disaster of the Greek fleet (*v. Caphareus*), persuading him to go to Epirus by land. Upon Pyrrhus' death he married Andromache (*q.v.*) and reigned with her in Epirus.

Hell. The place of torment for sinners in Christian theology, hence used by the translators as a synonym for Tartarus (*q.v.*) or Dis (*q.v.*) in general.

Helle. Daughter of Athamas and Nephele and sister of Phrixus (*q.v.*).

Hellespont. The strait connecting the Propontis (Sea of Marmara) with the Aegean; it was the boundary between Europe and Asia (for its name, *v. Phrixus*).

Hercean. "Of the Courtyard," an epithet of Jupiter as protector of the house. An altar to Hercean Jupiter stood in the central courtyard of Priam's palace.

Hercules. The most famous of the heroes of classical mythology. Originally an Argive hero, Hercules was also claimed by the Boeotians; therefore his birthplace is variously given as Tiryns, Argos, and Thebes. According to the most common version of his story, he was born at Thebes, the son of Jupiter (*q.v.*) and Alcmene (*v.* Table B, p. 192), the wife of Amphitryon, whose form Jupiter had counterfeited. Jupiter also miraculously lengthened the night of Hercules' conception. When he was about to be born, Jupiter swore an oath that the descendant of Perseus to be born that day would rule over all the others. Juno, in jealousy of Alcmene, kept Alcmene in labor for seven days, delaying the birth of Hercules, and caused the premature birth of Eurystheus, a grandson of Perseus, thus giving him power over Hercules. The angry goddess also sent two serpents to kill the new-born Hercules and his twin brother Iphicles (the son of Amphitryon by superfetation); they were strangled by the infant Hercules. In adolescence he was tutored in the arts of war, athletics, and music by the best-known heroes of the day. When in a fit of anger he killed Linus, his music-teacher, with a lyre, his father sent him to Mt. Cithaeron to tend his flocks; when these were harassed by a monstrous lion he killed it, taking its skin for his garment. Thus he earned the gratitude of Thespius, King of Thespiae, who allowed him to enjoy his fifty daughters. At eighteen Hercules returned to Thebes, whence he went against Orchomenos, to which Thebes paid tribute, and killed Erginus, its king. For this Creon (*q.v.*), King of Thebes, gave him his daughter Megara in marriage. Juno, resenting his prosperity, sent a fit of madness, in which he killed his three children by Megara and two children of Iphicles. Recovering, he went into exile from Thebes, was purified by Thespius, and went to consult the Delphic oracle as to where he should settle. The oracle commanded him to serve for twelve years Eurystheus, now King of Tiryns. In his service he performed the famous Twelve Labors of Hercules: *(1)* Eurystheus first ordered him to bring him the skin of the Nemean Lion, a monstrous beast which haunted the valley of Nemea. Hercules strangled it when his club and arrows had no effect. *(2)* He was next ordered to kill the Hydra, a monstrous nine-headed serpent which dwelt in the marsh of Lerna, near Argos. He struck off its heads with his club, but for each head lost two new ones grew in its place. To prevent this he had his companion Iolaus burn the necks of the monster with a torch as each head was struck off. The ninth head, which was immortal, he buried beneath a rock. He then dipped his arrows in the gall of the Hydra, so that wounds inflicted by them were incurable. *(3)* Eurystheus now ordered him to capture the Cerynian Hind (called also Arcadian or Maenalian), which lived in Arcadia, had golden horns and bronze hoofs, and was sacred to Diana. Hercules pursued it for a whole year to the source of the Danube River, finally disabled it with an arrow, and so caught it. *(4)* He was next sent to capture the Erymanthian Boar, which had come from Mt. Erymanthus and was devastating Arcadia. On his way he was the guest of the Centaur Pholus, to whom had been entrusted a jar of wine belonging to all the Centaurs, the gift of Bacchus. Hercules broached the jar, whereupon all the other Centaurs, drawn by the smell of the wine, attacked him. He killed them, even his old friend Chiron, with his poisoned arrows. Pholus also fell, accidentally poisoned by an arrow he had drawn from the body of a friend. Hercules, having found the boar, drove it into the snow, where he captured it with a noose. Eurystheus was so terrified when he dragged it back that he hid in an underground refuge. *(5)* Augeas, King of Elis, had a herd of three thousand oxen, whose stalls had not been cleaned for thirty years. Hercules was now commanded by Eurystheus to cleanse the Augean Stables in one day. First he bargained with Augeas for one tenth of the herd for his pay, then cleaned the stalls by diverting the rivers Alpheus and Peneus through them. Augeans, who had discovered that the labor was being performed at Eurystheus' command, refused to pay, and Hercules left vowing vengeance. *(6)* He was now ordered to kill the man-eating Stymphalian Birds, who had claws, wings, and beaks of bronze and could shoot their feathers like arrows. They inhabited the lake of Stymphalis, in Arcadia. With a rattle given him by Athena he scared them into flight, killed some with his arrows, and drove the rest to an island in the Black Sea. *(7)* The Cretan (or Marathonian) Bull was the white bull which Neptune had sent to Minos *(q.v.)*. To punish Minos for his disobedience Neptune drove the bull mad so that it ravaged the island of Crete. Hercules was told to bring the bull back alive; he caught it, crossed the sea on its back, and carried it to Eurystheus. He then released it; it wandered to Marathon where it was eventually killed by Theseus. *(8)* Eurytheus now ordered Hercules to bring him the man-eating Horses of Diomedes *(q.v.)*. He captured them, was pursued by Diomedes, defeated him and fed him to his own mares, which he then brought back and released in the Peloponnesus (they had become tame upon eating their master's body). *(9)* Hercules then had to bring back the Girdle of Hippolyte, Queen of the Amazons *(q.v.)*, who, on his arrival, received him kindly and offered him the belt of her own free will. Juno, enraged, spread a rumor amongst the Amazons that their queen was in danger, and a battle followed in which Hercules slew Hippolyte and many other Amazons. Returning with the girdle, he arrived at Troy as Laomedon *(q.v.)* was offering his daughter Hesione to the sea monster. Hercules killed the monster, and was to receive as a reward the horses which Jupiter had given Laomedon. When Laomedon refused them Hercules swore to make war on Troy. *(10)* Hercules now had to bring back the Oxen of Geryon *(q.v.)*. On his

way to Erythia he passed through Europe and Libya, setting up the
Pillars of Hercules (Gibraltar and Jebel Musa) at the boundary between the continents. Oppressed by the heat of the sun he shot an
arrow at it, whereupon the Sun, in admiration, presented him with a
golden bowl, in which he sailed to Erythia, where he killed the giant
cowherd Eurytion and his two-headed dog, and drove off the herd. He
killed the pursuing Geryon with his arrows. Landing at Tartessos he
returned the golden bowl to the Sun, and started back with the cattle
by way of the Iberian peninsula and Gaul into Italy. On the future
site of Rome the Giant Cacus stole some of the cattle while Hercules
slept, dragging them backwards into his lair so that their footmarks
would not lead Hercules there. Led by the lowing of the imprisoned
cattle, Hercules found, fought, and killed Cacus; in gratitude the in-
habitants of the area instituted a cult in his honor. He then proceeded
to Sicily, where one of the bulls wandered off and was appropriated
by King Eryx, a son of Venus; Hercules killed him in a boxing-match.
At the mouth of the Rhone he was forced to fight the Ligyes, who also
wanted the herd; having exhausted his arrows, he was on the verge of
defeat when Jupiter sent a rain of stones, with which he vanquished
them. As he was finally nearing the Balkan peninsula, Juno sent a
gadfly which scattered the herd through Thrace as far as the Hellespont.
Hercules painfully got together a part of the herd, only to have it
stolen by the Giant Alcyoneus. In the fight which followed Alcyoneus
hurled a huge crag at Hercules, who batted it back with his club,
killing the Giant. He then drove the cattle to Eurystheus, who sacrificed
them to Juno. (11) On her marriage to Jupiter, Juno had received from
Earth as a gift a number of golden apples. These she had entrusted
to the Hesperides (q.v.), who hung them on a tree in their garden,
setting a large serpent, Ladon, to guard them. Hercules, instructed to
bring to Eurystheus the Apples of the Hesperides, did not know where
to find their garden. He finally captured Nereus, the Old Man of the
Sea, and clinging to him in spite of his metamorphoses into many
shapes, compelled him to reveal the location of the Garden of the
Hesperides on Mt. Atlas in the country of the Hyperboreans. Passing
through Libya on his way, he was challenged to a wrestling match by
Antaeus, a Giant who renewed his strength every time he touched
Earth, his mother. Hercules killed him by holding him off the ground
until he became weak enough to be strangled. Arriving in Egypt he
was captured by Busiris (q.v.); he allowed himself to be led to the
altar, where he burst his bonds and killed his captors, including Busiris
and his sons. In Aethiopia (the eastern one) he killed Emathion and
restored the government to Memnon (q.v.). Passing next through the

Caucasus, he freed Prometheus from his crag, and finally reached the garden, where he killed Ladon and plucked the apples. Eurystheus allowed him to keep the apples; he gave them to Athena, who restored them to the Hesperides. *(12)* The last of the Labors was the most difficult, to bring the dog Cerberus *(q.v.)* from the Lower World. Hercules descended to the Realm of Dis *(q.v.)* at Taenarus *(q.v.)*. There he freed Theseus from his imprisonment, and persuaded Dis to let him take Cerberus, provided that he used no weapons. By his own strength he dragged the dog to Eurystheus, and then brought him back to Dis. The Labors over, Hercules returned to Thebes, where he gave his wife Megara to Iolaus, and set out for Oechalia to woo Iole, the daughter of King Eurytus, who had been promised to any suitor who could defeat her father and brothers in contests with the bow. He won, but was refused (because he had killed his children) by Eurytus, although his suit was supported by Iphitus, Iole's brother. Hercules then went as a guest to King Admetus; hearing that Admetus' wife Alcestis was dead, having volunteered to die in her husband's place, he went once more to the Lower World and brought her back. Iphitus then asked Hercules' help in recovering Eurytus' cattle, which had been stolen by Autolycus. Hercules, in a fit of madness sent by Juno, murdered Iphitus. As a punishment, a sickness fell upon him, and he went to Delphi to ask the oracle how he might be cured. Apollo refused to respond, whereupon Hercules in a rage stole the oracular tripod of the Pythia and fought Apollo when he attempted to recover it. Jupiter stopped the fight, and Apollo revealed that Hercules could be cured if he would serve Omphale, Queen of Lydia, for three years, turning his wages over to Eurytus. At Omphale's court he was forced to wear female dress and sit amongst the women spinning, while the Queen took his club and lion's skin. He next took part in the expedition of the Argonauts and in the Calydonian Boar hunt. With other heroes of these exploits, including Telamon and Peleus (the fathers respectively of the greater Ajax and of Achilles), he led an expedition against Troy to punish Laomedon for his false dealing; the city was taken and Laomedon was slain along with all his sons except Priam *(q.v.)*. Returning, Hercules was shipwrecked by a storm sent by Juno on the island of Cos, where he was nearly defeated by Neptune's son Eurytion and his sons. He was then called by Athena to help the gods in their fight against the Giants *(q.v.)*. He next invaded Elis and killed Augeas and his sons in revenge for Augeas' broken promise; he then instituted there the Olympic Games *(q.v.)*. Next he invaded Pylus, whose king, Neleus, had refused to purify him after the murder of Iphitus, and killed Neleus and all his sons but Nestor, who was away at the time.

He avenged the murder of his cousin Oeonus by King Hippocoon of Sparta by killing him and his sons and restoring Tyndareus (*q.v.*) to the throne. He was assisted in this war by King Cepheus of Tegea, by whose sister Auge he became the father of Telephus (*q.v.*). Hercules now wooed and won Deianira (*q.v.*), but while residing at her father's court accidentally killed a boy and was exiled with Deianira and their son Hyllus. On his way to his friend Ceyx (*q.v.*), King of Trachis, he met at the River Evenus the Centaur Nessus who carried travelers across on his back; Deianira was to cross with Nessus while Hercules went ahead with Hyllus. Nessus attempted to violate Deianira and was shot in the heart with a poisoned arrow by Hercules; dying, Nessus persuaded Deianira to take some of his blood (now poisoned by the arrow), telling her that it would be a powerful potion to retain Hercules' love. Once settled at Trachis, Hercules set out against Eurytus of Oechalia, killed him and his sons, and captured Iole, whom they had previously refused him. Returning home he prepared to sacrifice to Jupiter in Euboea and sent to Trachis for a fresh robe for the ceremony. Deianira, jealous of Iole, sent him a robe (the so-called "Shirt of Nessus") dipped in the blood of Nessus. When he donned the robe the poison penetrated his skin, and when he attempted to tear it off it took with it great pieces of his flesh. Dying, he was brought to Trachis, where Deianira hanged herself in horror. At Apollo's bidding a funeral pyre was built on Mt. Oeta, and he was laid on it. He gave Iole to Hyllus as his bride and presented his bow and arrows to his attendant Poeas, the father of Philoctetes (*q.v.*), bidding him light the pyre. As the flames rose a cloud descended and carried Hercules to heaven, where, reconciled with Juno, he married her cupbearer Hebe and was received as a god.

Hermiona. Hermione (*q.v.*).

Hermione. Daughter of Menelaus (*q.v.*) and Helen (*q.v.*). She was betrothed to Orestes (*q.v.*), but on his return from the war Menelaus married her to Pyrrhus (*q.v.*). Orestes murdered Pyrrhus and carried her off to be his wife.

Hesperides. The daughters of Atlas and Hesperis, they guarded the golden apples which Earth had given Juno as a wedding present (*v. Hercules, Eleventh Labor*).

Hesperus. Son of Atlas and Hesperis, brother of the Hesperides. The name was given to the planet Venus as Evening Star; as Morning Star it was called Lucifer.

Hippolyte. Queen of the Amazons (*q.v.*). She invaded Attica with her army in an attempt to recover her sister Antiope, who had been carried off by Theseus, but was defeated. She was later slain by Hercules (*q.v., the Ninth Labor*).

Hydra. A nine-headed serpent which dwelt in the marsh of Lerna. It was slain by Hercules (*q.v.*, the Second Labor).

Ida. The name of two mountains, both sacred to Cybele (*q.v.*), one in Crete and one in the Troad. The latter was the scene of the rape of Ganymede (*v. Laomedon*) and the Judgment of Paris (*q.v.*).

Inach. Inachus (*q.v.*).

Inachus. The son of Oceanus and Tethys and the father of Io (*v. Argus*); he was the first King of Argos (*q.v.*).

Ionian Sea. The sea between Italy and the Balkan peninsula, south of the Adriatic.

Iphigenia. Daughter of Agamemnon (*q.v.*) and Clytemnestra. When the Greek fleet on its way to Troy was assembled at Aulis, Diana, to avenge the killing by Agamemnon of a hind sacred to her, caused a calm which kept the fleet in port. The seer Calchas (*q.v.*) announced that Iphigenia must be sacrificed; Agamemnon sent Ulysses, who persuaded her that she was to be married to Achilles. After her death the longed-for winds began to blow; but her death was later to be one of Clytemnestra's motives for the murder of Agamemnon.

Ismen. Ismenus (*q.v.*).

Ismenus. A river of Boeotia, near Thebes.

Ister. The Danube River, or that part of it nearest its mouth in the Black Sea.

Isthmus. The Isthmus of Corinth, the neck of land connecting the Peloponnesus with the rest of the Balkan Peninsula.

Ithaca. (*1*) An island in the Ionian Sea, the home of Ulysses; (*2*) The chief city of this island, Ulysses' capital.

Itys. (*1*) Son of Aedon (*q.v.*); (*2*) Son of Procne (*q.v.*).

Ixion. King of the Lapiths who, in order to avoid paying the bride-price, invited his father-in-law to his house and threw him into a pit of fire. Jupiter himself offered to purify him from this dreadful breach of the laws of hospitality, and invited him to the table of the gods. Ixion thereupon attempted to seduce Juno; but Jupiter created Nephele, a creature made of clouds to resemble Juno, by whom Ixion became the father of the Centaurs. He was punished by being fastened to a wheel on which he revolves eternally. Later ages pictured him rather as having his flesh torn by a turning toothed or spiked wheel.

Jason. Son of Aeson, King of Iolcus in Thessaly. Aeson was expelled by his half-brother Pelias. Jason, when he came of age, demanded the kingdom from Pelias, who promised to surrender it if Jason would bring him the Golden Fleece (*v. Phrixus*). This fleece was the property of King Aeetes of Colchis and was guarded by a never-sleeping dragon. For his expedition, in which he was helped by Juno and Athena, Jason enlisted the aid of all the best-known heroes of the time, among whom were Hercules, Castor and Pollux, Peleus, Laertes, and Orpheus. The Argonauts, after many adventures (*v. Lemnos*), arrived in Colchis, where Jason was assigned several seemingly impossible tasks by Aeetes; but with the help of the enchantress Medea, Aeetes' daughter, who had fallen in love with him, he performed them, put the dragon to sleep, and escaped with Medea and the fleece. In Iolcus Jason found that Pelias had murdered Aeson, and determined to have his revenge through Medea's magic art. She cut up an old he-goat and boiled its limbs in a cauldron, from which it emerged as a young kid; Pelias' daughters, seeing this, begged her to rejuvenate their father, but when they had cut him into pieces Medea left them. As a result she and Jason were banished and took refuge in Corinth, where, after ten years had passed, Jason determined to marry Glauce, daughter of King Creon of Corinth. In jealously Medea sent Glauce a poisoned robe and crown which burnt her up (her father was also consumed in the flames), murdered her own sons by Jason in his sight, and escaped to Athens in a serpent-drawn chariot sent by her grandfather the Sun. Jason was later accidentally crushed by his old ship, the Argo.

Jocasta. Wife of Laius and mother of Oedipus (*q.v.*).

Jove. Jupiter (*q.v.*).

Juno. Daughter of Saturn, sister and wife of Jupiter. She was the Queen of Heaven and protectress of all women, especially in her capacities as goddess of the sanctity of marriage and of childbirth. Her jealousy of Jupiter's frequent love affairs often caused her to persecute his paramours and their offspring. In the Trojan War she sided with the Greeks.

Jupiter. Son of Saturn (*q.v.*) and Ops, he shared the rule of the universe with his brothers Neptune and Dis, but had precedence even over them. He was known as King and Father of Gods and Men. As god of the sky he had the thunderbolt as his weapon. Suppliants and guests were especially under his protection. His amorous propensities frequently led him into love affairs both with goddesses and with mortal women, and many gods and heroes were his children.

Justice. A goddess, sister of Jupiter and mother of the Fates. She was represented as carrying a pair of scales and a cornucopia.

Lacone. Laconia (*q.v.*).

Laconia. A country in the southeast Peloponnesus, consisting of a long valley running south to the sea and surrounded on the other three sides by mountains. Its capital was Sparta (*q.v.*).

Laertes. King of Ithaca and father of Ulysses (*q.v.*).

Laius. Son of Labdacus (*v.* Table B, p. 192). When his guardian Lycus was banished by Amphion (*q.v.*) and Zethus, he fled to the protection of Pelops, returning after their deaths. He married Jocasta and was the father of Oedipus (*q.v.*), by whom he was afterwards killed.

Laomedon. Son of Ilus and Eurydice (*v.* Table A, p. 190) King of Troy. His son Ganymede was carried off by Jupiter, who was enamored of him, and who gave Laomedon some marvelous horses (*v. Hercules,* the Ninth Labor) in compensation. Apollo and Neptune agreed, for pay, to fortify his city for him; when he refused to pay, Neptune sent a sea monster, to which Laomedon was forced to offer his daughter Hesione. She was rescued by Hercules; but when Laomedon refused him the promised reward, Hercules made war on Troy and killed him and all his sons but Priam (*q.v.*). Because of his false dealing both with Apollo and Neptune and with Hercules, his name came to stand for untrustworthiness.

Latona. One of the Titans (*q.v.*). By Jupiter she was the mother of Apollo and Diana. Driven from land to land by the jealous persecutions of Juno, she eventually came to Delos (*q.v.*), where she gave birth to the twin deities.

Leda. Wife of King Tyndareus of Sparta. Jupiter fell in love with her and visited her in the form of a swan. She gave birth at one time to Clytemnestra (*q.v.*) and Castor, the children of Tyndareus, and to an egg containing the children of Jupiter, Helen (*q.v.*) and Pollux.

Lemnos. An island in the Aegean. The Lemnian women killed all the men on the island out of jealousy, except for King Thoas, who was saved by his daughter Hypsipyle. Jason (*q.v.*) visited Lemnos on his way to Colchis and became by Hypsipyle the father of twin sons.

Lerna. A district near Argos where there was a marsh inhabited by the Hydra (*v. Hercules,* the Second Labor).

Lesbos. An island of the Aegean Sea off the coast of Mysia. It was taken by Achilles (*q.v.*) in a raid during the Trojan War.

Lethe. "Forgetfulness," one of the rivers of the Realm of Dis (*q.v.*). The shades of the dead drank from it and so forgot their past existences.

Libya. The ancient name for the continent of Africa, which occupied the southwest quarter of the known land mass. Egypt is sometimes not included in the term.

Limbo. In Christian terminology, the edge of Hell. The term is used by the translators to refer to the realm of Dis (*q.v.*) or to the outer borders thereof.

Lucifer. The name given to the planet Venus as Morning Star; as Evening Star it was called Hesperus.

Lycomedes. King of Scyros. The young Achilles (*q.v.*) was hidden at his court to prevent his taking part in the Trojan War.

Lyrnesos. A town in the Troad taken by Achilles (*q.v.*); it was here that he captured Briseis.

Maenad. The term for a woman in Bacchic ecstasy, applied either to *(1)* the frenzied women who, clad in animal skins, with vine leaves in their hair, and brandishing the thyrsus, accompanied Bacchus in his wanderings, tearing to pieces such small animals as came in their way, or *(2)* the priestesses of Bacchus' cult.

Maenal. Maenalian, of Maenalus, a mountain in Arcadia.

Manto. A Theban prophetess, the daughter of Tiresias.

Marmaric. Of Marmarica, a north African land lying between Egypt and Cyrenaica.

Maro. Vergil (*q.v.*).

Mars. The quarrelsome, hot-tempered god of war, son of Jupiter and Juno or of Juno alone. He was hated by Jupiter and Athena, and was the friend and lover of Venus. In the Trojan War he sided with the Trojans and on one occasion actually took the field on their behalf, when he was wounded by Diomedes.

Medea. Daughter of King Aeetes of Colchis, and wife of Jason (*q.v.*). When she escaped to Athens she became the mistress of King Aegeus, but was forced to flee when discovered in a plot against his son Theseus.

Memnon. The son of Tithonus (*q.v.*) and Aurora, and King of the eastern Aethiopia. His brother Emathion seized the kingship; but when Hercules (*q.v.*, the Eleventh Labor) killed the usurper he regained his throne. On the death of Hector he went to Troy to help his uncle Priam (*v.* Table A, p. 190). Achilles, enraged by his killing of his friend Antilochus, slew him, but at Aurora's request Jupiter made him immortal.

Menelas. Menelaus (*q.v.*).

Menelaus. King of Sparta by his marriage to Helen (*q.v.*), a son of Atreus (*q.v.*; *v.* also Table C, p. 194) and younger brother of Agamemnon (*q.v.*). At the fall of Troy he was one of the heroes of the Trojan Horse, and was thereafter reconciled to his wife by her betrayal of Deiphobus (*q.v.*). He wandered the seas for eight years on his way home, but dwelt in peace with Helen in Sparta thereafter.

Merope. Wife of King Polybus of Corinth, and foster-mother of Oedipus (*q.v.*).

Minos. The son of Jupiter and Europa (*v. Cadmus*), whose husband Asterion was King of Crete. On Asterion's death, Minos, with Neptune's support, seized the kingship from his half-brothers, Asterion's sons Sarpedon and Rhadamanthus. In response to his prayer for an animal to sacrifice in thanksgiving, Neptune sent from the sea a magnificent white bull. Minos kept the bull and sacrificed another, and Neptune punished him by causing his wife Pasiphae to fall in love with the bull. By it she became the mother of a man-eating monster, the Minotaur, which was half bull and half man. Neptune also drove the bull mad so that it ravaged Crete; it was captured and brought to the Peloponnesus by Hercules (*q.v.,* the Seventh Labor).

Minotaur. The monstrous son of Pasiphae, wife of Minos (*q.v.*) and the Cretan Bull. He was eventually slain by Theseus of Athens because he had yearly devoured seven Athenian youths and seven maidens, Athens' tribute to Crete.

Mycenae. A town of the Peloponnesus, the capital of Argos (*q.v.*), the kingdom of Agamemnon (*q.v.; v.* also *Atreus, Pelops,* and *Tantalus*).

Mycene. Of Mycenae (*q.v.*).

Mysia. A country in the northwest corner of Asia Minor, the kingdom of Telephus (*q.v.*).

Nemea. A valley in Argos (*q.v.,* 2) where Hercules (*q.v.,* the First Labor) slew the Nemean Lion.

Neptune. Brother of Jupiter and Dis, he received all the seas, lakes, and rivers as his share in their division of the universe. He was also god of earthquakes and, as creator of the horse, patron of equestrian accomplishments. As the builder of Troy (*v. Laomedon*) he supported the Trojans in the war.

Neptunus. Neptune (*q.v.*).

Nereus. A sea god, dwelling especially in the Aegean, he was the father of two hundred beautiful sea nymphs, the Nereids, one of whom was Thetis (*q.v.*); he was therefore the grandfather of Achilles (*q.v.*).

Night. A goddess, the daughter of Chaos. By her brother Erebus (*q.v.*) she became the mother of Day and Aether.

Niobe. Daughter of Tantalus (*q.v.*) and wife of Amphion (*q.v.*). She had seven sons and seven daughters, and boasted that she was superior to Latona (*q.v.*), who had only two children. To punish her Apollo slew her sons and Diana her daughters. She herself was changed into a rock on Mt. Sipylus, a rock which continued to shed tears.

Oedipus. Son of Laius, King of Thebes, and of his wife Jocasta (*v.* Table B, p. 192). Laius, warned by an oracle of Apollo that his son was destined to kill him, had a thong run through the infant's feet and gave him to his shepherd Phorbas to expose on Mt. Cithaeron. Phorbas, moved by pity, gave the baby to a shepherd of King Polybus of Corinth, who took it to his master. Polybus and his wife Merope, being childless, raised the child, whom they called Oedipus ("Swollen-foot"), as their own. Taunted by other young men who called him a foundling, Oedipus went without his supposed parents' knowledge to Delphi to enquire about his parentage, and was given the terrifying response that he would kill his father and marry his mother. Supposing his parents to be Polybus and Merope, he did not dare return to Corinth, but went from Delphi toward Daulis. Meanwhile a dreadful monster with the body of a winged lion and the head and breast of a maiden, the Sphinx, had appeared near Thebes. To every passer-by she proposed a riddle, "What animal goes on four legs in the morning, two at noon, and three in the evening?" casting him to his death from her rock when he could not answer. Laius, on his way to Delphi to ask the meaning of this portent, met Oedipus at a forking of the road; when Oedipus would not move aside for him a quarrel arose and Oedipus killed Laius and his attendant. The Thebans, left without a king, offered the kingship and Jocasta's hand in marriage to anyone who could rid them of the Sphinx. This Oedipus did by correctly answering her riddle, whereupon she cast herself from her rock and perished. Oedipus ruled Thebes well for some years, and Jocasta bore him four children, Eteocles, Polynices, Antigone, and Ismene; but in time Thebes began to be wasted by a plague. Oedipus, investigating the cause of the pestilence, learned his true parentage. Jocasta killed herself; he put out his own eyes and went into voluntary exile. He wandered over the earth in his blindness until he came to Attica, where the Furies removed him from the world.

Olenia. The territory of the city of Olenus in Aetolia, west of Delphi.

Olympe. Olympus (*q.v.*).

Olympic Games. A Panhellenic festival in honor of Jupiter, held at Olympia, near Pisa in Elis. They were supposed to have originated as the funeral games of Pelops (*q.v.*) and to have been established as regularly held competitions by Hercules (*q.v.*). They were held every four years and consisted at first of various athletic events, especially foot and chariot races.

Olympus. The abode of the gods, either *(1)* the range of mountains between Macedonia and Thessaly, on the summits of which the gods had their palaces, or *(2)* the vault of the sky, "Heaven."

Orcus. Dis (*q.v.*).

Orest. Orestes (*q.v.*).

Orestes. Son of Agamemnon (*q.v.*; *v.* also Table C, p. 194) and Clytemnestra (*q.v.*). After the murder of the father he was saved from the murderers by his sister Electra (*q.v.*) and conveyed to his uncle King Strophius of Phocis, where he became a close friend of Pylades, Strophius' son. Eight years later he returned with Pylades and avenged his father's murder by slaying Aegisthus (*q.v.*) and Clytemnestra. For killing his mother he was maddened and pursued by the Furies. In his madness he slew Pyrrhus (*q.v.*), who had married his betrothed, Hermione (*q.v.*). He was eventually rescued and cured by the intervention of Apollo and Athena, married Hermione, and recovered his father's kingdom by killing Aletes, the son of Aegisthus.

Orpheus. A legendary Thracian poet, whose singing was so enchanting that it not only charmed birds and beasts but moved trees, rocks, and rivers to follow him. On his return from the expedition of the Argonauts (*v. Jason*) he married Eurydice. When she died he followed her to the Lower World, charmed Dis with his music, and won her back, on condition that he not look upon her until she had reached the upper world. At the last moment he looked back, and so lost her again. His grief made him scorn the women of Thrace, who in their fury tore him to pieces in a Bacchic frenzy. His head was thrown into the Hebrus River and was borne eventually to the island of Lesbos.

Ossa. A mountain in the north of Thessaly, near Mt. Olympus (*v. Pelion*).

Palamedes. Son of Nauplius; the craftiest of the Greeks next to Ulysses (*q.v.*). When Ulysses, to avoid joining the Greek expedition to Troy, feigned madness by ploughing his fields with salt, Palamedes exposed him by placing the infant Telemachus (*q.v.*) before the plough, which Ulysses turned aside, thus showing that he was not mad. In revenge Ulysses bribed a slave of Palamedes to hide a letter, supposedly from Priam (*q.v.*), under his bed. When Ulysses accused him of treachery and produced the letter the Greeks stoned Palamedes to death. Palamedes' brother, afraid to send the facts of his brother's death home by a messenger, wrote the story on an oar and cast it into the sea. The oar fell into the hands of Nauplius, who wrecked the Greek fleet in revenge by displaying false beacons on Cape Caphareus. In this he was inspired by Athena (*v. Ajax* 2). Palamedes was the inventor of lighthouses, weights and measures, dice, draughts, and the discus; he also added four letters to Cadmus' alphabet.

Palladium. An ancient image of Pallas Athena sent down from heaven by Jupiter to Ilus (*q.v.*). Troy could not fall so long as it possessed the Palladium. Accordingly Ulysses and Diomedes stole it, but in handling it with bloody hands polluted it and so brought the displeasure of Athena upon the Greeks.

Pallas. Athena (*q.v.*).

Parcae. The Fates (*q.v.*).

Paris. Son of Priam and Hecuba (*v.* Table A, p. 190). Before his birth Hecuba dreamed that she had given birth to a firebrand which set the whole city of Troy on fire. The newborn child was therefore exposed on Mt. Ida; but he was found and raised by a shepherd. It was to him as judge that Mercury brought Juno, Athena, and Venus when they had quarreled as to which was the most beautiful (the "Judgment of Paris"; *v. Peleus*). The goddesses offered bribes: Juno, wealth and power; Athena, wisdom and fame; and Venus, the love of the most beautiful woman in the world. He chose Venus, and so brought upon Troy the hatred of the other two goddesses. When Priam was holding games in memory of Paris, whom he supposed dead, Paris, who was a herdsman himself, was chosen to bring to Troy a bull for the sacrifice. He joined the games and defeated his brothers, being especially accomplished in archery, at which he was in fact supreme in his day; they wished to kill him in envy, but Cassandra (*q.v.*) revealed his identity and he was welcomed back to his own family. Under Venus' guidance he seduced and abducted Helen (*q.v.*), thus bringing about the Trojan War. He killed Achilles (*q.v.*) by treachery, but was himself slain, by an arrow of Hercules', in combat with Philoctetes (*q.v.*).

Parnassus. A mountain rising above Delphi, sacred to Apollo (*q.v.*) and the Muses.

Patroclus. Intimate friend and companion of Achilles (*q.v.*) at the Trojan War, he was killed by Hector while disguised in Achilles' armor.

Peace. A goddess, the daughter of Jupiter. She carried the cornucopia and an olive branch, and was accompanied by the infant god of wealth.

Pegasus. A winged horse, born of the Gorgon (*q.v.*) Medusa. He belonged to the gods, serving especially Jupiter, Aurora, and the Muses. The spring Hippocrene, on Mt. Parnassus, sprang up where he struck the rock with his hoof.

Peleus. King of Phthia in Thessaly, and father, by the sea-nymph Thetis, of Achilles (*q.v.*). To his wedding with Thetis all the gods except the goddess of discord were invited; she in revenge cast amongst the guests a golden apple inscribed "for the fairest." It was claimed by Juno, Athena, and Venus and was (*v. Paris*) the cause of the Trojan War.

Pelias. King of Iolcus, uncle of Jason (*q.v.*).

Pelion. A range of mountains in Thessaly near Mt. Ossa. The Giants (*q.v.*), in their attempt to scale Olympus, piled Pelion on Ossa.

Pelops. Son of Tantalus, a King of Phrygia (*v.* Table C, p. 194). In his infancy his father, a companion and favorite of the gods, killed and cooked him and served his flesh to the gods at a banquet. The gods, horrified, refused to eat, except for Ceres who, preoccupied with the loss of her daughter (who had been abducted by Dis), ate the child's shoulder. Mercury put the pieces of the boy back into the cauldron, and Clotho (*q.v.*) drew him out alive; while Ceres replaced his missing shoulder with one of ivory (all his descendants carried the mark of this event, having one ivory-white shoulder). Arrived at manhood, Pelops went to Pisa in Elis to woo Hippodamia, the daughter of King Oenomaus, who had promised his daughter and kingdom to the man who could defeat him in a chariot race. This Pelops did by inducing Myrtilus, his charioteer, with the promise of half the kingdom, to replace one of the linch-pins of Oenomaus' chariot with a pin made of wax.

Oenomaus was thrown from his chariot and killed; but Pelops, rather than pay the price, killed Myrtilus, incurring the wrath of Mercury, Myrtilus' father (*v. Atreus*). Pelops extended his power from Elis over most of the peninsula, so that it was called Peloponnesus, "Island of Pelops."

Penelope. The wife of Ulysses, noted for her fidelity in refusing all suitors to her hand and in preserving his kingship for him during his twenty years' absence.

Penthesilea. Daughter of Mars and Queen of the Amazons (*q.v.*), whom she led to the aid of Troy after Hector's death. She was killed in battle by Achilles.

Pentheus. Second King of Thebes (*v.* Table B, p. 192). When Bacchus (*q.v.*) came to Thebes and the women were celebrating his orgies on Mt. Cithaeron, Pentheus hastened out to stop them. Bacchus in revenge maddened his mother Agave and Ino and Autonoe, his aunts, so that mistaking him for a wild beast (*v. Maenad*) they tore him to pieces in their Bacchic frenzy.

Pergama. The citadel of Troy.

Persian. Of Persia, a term often loosely applied to all or any part of that area east of the Euphrates, west of India, and south of the Caspian, particularly to the eastern Aethiopia (*q.v.*).

Phasis. A river of Colchis (*q.v.*), flowing from the Caucasus into the east end of the Black Sea.

Philoctetes. A King of the Malians in Oeta, the son of Poeas, to whom Hercules (*q.v.*), dying, had given his bow and poisoned arrows. Philoctetes was one of the suitors of Helen (*q.v.*), and led seven ships against Troy; but, stopping at the island of Chryse, near Lemnos, he was bitten by a snake. The wound would not heal, and produced such a stench that on the advice of Ulysses (*q.v.*) he was abandoned on Lemnos. When the captured Helenus (*q.v.*) prophesied that Troy could be taken only with the arrows of Hercules, which were in Philoctetes' possession. Ulysses and Diomedes came to Lemnos and persuaded him to accompany them to Troy, where his wound was healed. A famous archer, he killed Paris in single combat.

Philomel. Daughter of King Pandion of Athens, sister of Procne (*q.v.*).

Phlegethon. "Flaming"; a river of the Realm of Dis (*q.v.*).

Phocis. A country north of the Gulf of Corinth, where Delphi was situated. At the time of the Trojan War Strophius was its king.

Phoebas. "Priestess of Phoebus," *i.e.,* Cassandra (*q.v.*) or the Pythia (*q.v.*).

Phoebe. Phoebus (*q.v.*).

Phoebus. Apollo (*q.v.*).

Phorbas. A shepherd of King Laius, who entrusted to him for exposure the infant Oedipus (*q.v.*).

Phrixus. Son of Athamas, King of Orchomenus in Boeotia (*v.* Table B, p. 192), and Nephele, a cloud-goddess. When Athamas married Ino, the daughter of Cadmus, Nephele left him, but continued to watch over her children by him, Phrixus and his sister Helle. In her anger at being supplanted she also brought a drought upon the country. The children's stepmother produced a false oracle that Phrixus must be sacrificed to Jupiter; Nephele saved her son by helping him to escape, with Helle, on the back of a magical golden ram given her by Mercury. Crossing the Hellespont, Helle fell into the sea, giving her name (Hellespont, "Sea of Helle") to the straits, but Phrixus arrived in Colchis (*q.v.*) where he married a daughter of King Aeetes. Phrixus sacrificed the ram to Jupiter and gave its fleece to Aeetes (*v. Jason*).

Phrygian. Of Phrygia, a country of central Asia Minor. Tantalus was its king, and it was the country of Attis. In the Trojan War the Phrygians were allies of Troy; the adjective "Phrygian" is frequently used by the Romans as a synonym for "Trojan."

Pisa. A city of Elis, near Olympia, the site of the Olympic Games (*q.v.*). Pelops became its king.

Pluto. Another name for Dis (*q.v.*) in his aspect of protector of the wealth that lies under the earth; the name "Pluto" is applied only to the god, not (like "Dis" or "Orcus") to his realm as well.

Polites. Youngest son of Priam and Hecuba, slain by Pyrrhus at the altar of Hercean Jupiter, before the eyes of his parents.

Polybus. King of Corinth, the foster father of Oedipus (*q.v.*).

Polydorus. A son of Priam and Hecuba, sent to King Polymestor of the Thracian Chersonesus with some of the treasures of Troy, to keep them safe in case Troy should be taken. When Troy fell, Polymestor killed Polydorus for the treasure; his death was avenged by Hecuba (*q.v.*).

Polyxena. A daughter of Priam and Hecuba, loved by Achilles. At his wedding with her at the temple of Apollo he was treacherously killed by Paris. After the fall of Troy she was sacrificed, at the demand of Achilles' ghost, on his tomb.

Polyxene. Polyxena (*q.v.*).

Poseidon. Neptune (*q.v.*).

Priam. King of Troy, the son of Laomedon (*q.v.*; *v.* also Table A, p. 190). He was set on the throne by Hercules (*q.v.*), who had killed his father and brothers. In his youth he joined the Phrygians in their war with the Amazons; but he was old and feeble at the time of the Trojan War. He was slain by Pyrrhus (*q.v.*) at the altar of Hercean Jupiter, where he had taken sanctuary with his wife Hecuba (*q.v.*). He was the father of fifty sons and fifty daughters.

Priamus. Priam (*q.v.*).

Procne. Daughter of King Pandion of Athens and sister of Philomel.

When Tereus, King of Daulis, came to Pandion's aid in war, Pandion gave Procne to him in marriage, and she bore him a son, Itys or Itylus. Tiring of her, he sent her to the country, and telling Philomel she was dead, brought her from Athens. On the way he ravished her and cut out her tongue to keep her from telling of the deed. Procne sought her out, and Philomel managed to convey the whole story to her by weaving pictures into a robe she was making. Together the sisters killed Itys and cooked his flesh, which Philomel served to his father at a meal. When Tereus attempted to kill the sisters he was changed into a hawk and they into a swallow and a nightingale.

Pylades. Son of King Strophius of Phocis, and friend and companion of Orestes (*q.v.*); he married Orestes' sister Electra (*q.v.*).

Pylius. "Man of Pylus," *i.e.,* Nestor, King of Pylus, who reached a very old age, ruling over three generations of men.

Pyrrha. Wife of Deucalion (*q.v.*).

Pyrrhus. The son of Achilles (*q.v.*; *v.* also Table D, p. 197) and Deidamia, a daughter of Lycomedes, in whose palace at Scyros he was brought up. After the death of Achilles he was brought to Troy by Ulysses because Helenus (*q.v.*) had prophesied that Troy could be taken only by a descendant of Aeacus. At the fall of Troy he was one of the heroes in the Trojan Horse, and killed Polites (*q.v.*) and Priam (*q.v.*) at the altar of Hercean Jupiter. He received Andromache (*q.v.*) as his prize. After the war he married Hermione (*q.v.*) but was killed at the altar of Apollo at Delphi by Orestes (*q.v.*) who had earlier been betrothed to her.

Pythia. The prophetess of Apollo (*q.v.*) at his oracle at Delphi (*q.v.*).

Rhesus. The King of the Thracians, who came to the aid of Troy in the Trojan War. Because there was a prophecy that Troy could not be taken if his horses once drank the water of the Xanthus, he was slain on his arrival and his horses carried off by Ulysses and Diomedes.

Saturn. The youngest of the Titans (*q.v.*) and their ruler. He overthrew and castrated his father Uranus and ruled in his stead, but was himself overthrown by Jupiter (*q.v.*), his son. After his fall from heaven he reigned as king in Italy in a golden age of peace and prosperity.

Scyros. An island in the Aegean Sea, east of Euboea. Here Achilles (*q.v.*) was hidden by Thetis among the daughters of Lycomedes, its king. The island was later taken by Achilles. Pyrrhus (*q.v.*) was brought up on Scyros.

Scyth. A Scythian, one of a nomadic people from north of the Black Sea. The Scythians were neighbors of the Amazons. They were considered cruel and barbarous.

Sigean. Of Sigeum (*q.v.*).

Sigeum. A headland at the entrance of the Hellespont, near Troy, the site of the Greek camp in the Trojan War.

Simois. A river near Troy.

Sinon. A nephew of Ulysses (*q.v.*), he aided him in his plot to get the Trojan Horse within the walls of Troy. The Greeks pretended to abandon the war, hiding their fleet at Tenedos and leaving Sinon behind. He allowed himself to be captured, and pretending to be a friend of Palamedes (*q.v.*) and hence an enemy of the Greeks, persuaded the Trojans to bring the horse into the city.

Sipyl. Sipylus (*q.v.*).

Sipylus. A mountain of Phrygia in Asia Minor, on which Niobe (*q.v.*) was changed into a stone.

Sirius. The dog-star, supposed to bring hot weather to the earth; hence "dog days."

Sisyphus. King of Corinth, fraudulent and avaricious and famous for his slyness and double dealing. For informing on Jupiter in one of his love affairs he was punished in Tartarus by having to roll up a hill a boulder which always rolled down again as soon as he reached the top.

Sminthical. Sminthian, an epithet of Apollo (*q.v.*) as mouse-god, perhaps the protector of crops from field mice.

Sparta. The capital of Laconia, the city of Tyndareus, Helen, Clytemnestra, and Menelaus.

Sparte. Sparta (*q.v.*).

Sphinx. A monster with the body of a winged lion and the head and breast of a maiden, destroyed by Oedipus (*q.v.*).

Strophius. King of Phocis, married to Anaxibia, sister of Agamemnon (*q.v.*). He sheltered the boy Orestes (*q.v.*) after Agamemnon's murder.

Stygian. Of the Styx (*q.v.*).

Stymphal. Of Stymphalis, the lake in Arcadia where lived the monstrous birds dispersed and killed by Hercules (*q.v.*, the Sixth Labor).

Styx. (*1*) A river of the Lower World, over which the souls of the dead were ferried to the Realm of Dis (*q.v.*). (*2*) The nymph of the river, the first of the gods to help Jupiter in his struggle with the Titans (*q.v.*). In gratitude Jupiter made her the goddess by whom the gods swore their most solemn oaths; any god who swore falsely by Styx would be banished for nine years.

Susa. The winter residence of the Persian Kings in historical times. Because its district was called Aethiopia it was thought to have been founded by Memnon (*q.v.*).

Taenar. Taenarus (*q.v.*).

Taenarus. A town in Laconia, where there was a cave, an entrance to the

Realm of Dis (*q.v.*), through which Hercules (*q.v.*, the Twelfth Labor) dragged Cerberus to the Upper World. The name was sometimes loosely applied to the Lower World in general.

Talthybius. The herald of Agamemnon (*q.v.*) at Troy.

Tanais. A river of Thrace, the modern Don.

Tantalis. "Daughter of Tantalus," *i.e.,* Niobe (*q.v.*).

Tantalus. A King of Phrygia, the son of Jupiter and the nymph Pluto (*v.* Table C, p. 194). He was a favorite of the gods, but incurred their wrath by serving them at a banquet with his own son Pelops (*q.v.*), killed and cooked. For this he was sent to Tartarus (*q.v.*), where he was afflicted with insatiable hunger and thirst; he was made to stand in a lake whose waters receded when he stooped to drink, while above his head hung branches of fruit which sprang back if he reached for them.

Tartar. Tartarus (*q.v.*).

Tartarus. That part of the Realm of Dis (*q.v.*) reserved for the punishment of the damned. Here were the Danaids (*v. Danaus*), Ixion (*q.v.*), Sisyphus (*q.v.*), Tantalus (*q.v.*), and Tityus (*q.v.*), as well as the rebellious Titans (*q.v.*). Their torments were presided over by the Furies (*q.v.*).

Telemachus. The son of Ulysses (*q.v.*), who grew to manhood while his father was away at the Trojan War.

Telephus. Son of Hercules (*q.v.*) and Auge. He was exposed in infancy and brought up by shepherds. Having consulted the oracle at Delphi about his parentage, he was directed to Mysia (*q.v.*), whose king his mother had married. He was acknowledged by Auge and eventually succeeded to the kingship; and when the Greeks landed in Mysia on their way to Troy he attempted to repel them. He was wounded by Achilles (*q.v.*); the wound would not heal, and he was advised by an oracle that it could be healed only by the man who had inflicted it. Accordingly, he went to the Greeks disguised as a beggar. Achilles healed his wound with rust from the lance that had made it, and in gratitude he guided the Greeks to Troy.

Tenedos. An island of the Aegean off the Troad, taken by Achilles (*q.v.*) in his raids during the Trojan War. It was here that the Greek fleet lay hidden in order to convince the Trojans that the Greeks had abandoned the siege; this was part of the ruse of the Trojan Horse (*v. Ulysses*).

Tereus. King of Daulis, husband of Procne (*q.v.*).

Thebe. Thebes (*q.v.*).

Thebes. (*1*) The chief city of Boeotia, founded by Cadmus (*q.v.*) and fortified with a wall and seven gates by Amphion (*q.v.*) and Zethus. It was the birthplace of Bacchus (*q.v.*), Hercules (*q.v.*), and Tiresias (*q.v.*). For its kings, *v.* Table B, p. 192. (*2*) A city (also called Thebe) of Cilicia, birthplace of Andromache (*q.v.*). It was taken by Achilles (*q.v.*) in his raids around Troy.

Thessal. Thessalian (*q.v.*).

Thessalian. Of Thessaly (*q.v.*).

Thessaly. A district in the northern part of the Balkan peninsula, the birthplace of Jason (*q.v.*) and Achilles (*q.v.*).

Thetis. A sea nymph, the mother of Achilles (*q.v.*).

Thrace. The territory between the Danube, the Aegean, and the Sea of Marmara. Its barbaric people were led to the aid of Troy by King Rhesus (*q.v.*).

Thracian. Of Thrace (*q.v.*).

Thyest. Thyestes (*q.v.*).

Thyestes. Brother of Atreus (*q.v.*).

Tigris. A river rising in the Taurus mountains and emptying into the Persian Gulf. The eastern Aethiopia (*q.v.*) was located near its mouth.

Tiresias. The Theban soothsayer. Blinded at the age of seven, he was granted in recompense the understanding of the language of birds, the power of prophecy, a magical golden staff to guide his footsteps, and an unusually long life span. He played a prominent part in the story of Oedipus (*q.v.*). After death he retained his power of prophecy in the Lower World. His daughter was Manto, also a prophetess.

Titan. (*1*) A name given to the pre-Olympian gods in general. They seized the power from Uranus (Heaven) and Gaea (Earth), their parents, when Saturn (*q.v.*) castrated and overthrew his father, and were themselves overthrown by the Olympian gods, Saturn's children, led by Jupiter. Those of them who attempted to rebel were cast into Tartarus (*q.v.*); others were allowed to keep at least a part of their divine power and functions (*v. Hecate, Latona, Saturn, and Titan 2*). (*2*) The name is often used for Helios, son of the Titans Hyperion and Thea, who drives the chariot of the sun.

Tithonus. Son of Laomedon (*q.v.*; *v.* also Table A, p. 190). He was carried off by Aurora (*q.v.*), who was captivated by his beauty, and became by her the father of Memnon (*q.v.*). She obtained for him the gift of immortality, but forgot to ask for eternal youth; he became in the end so shrunken and feeble that Aurora changed him to a cicada.

Tityus. A Giant (*q.v.*) who attempted to violate Latona (*q.v.*); killed by Apollo and Diana, he was consigned to Tartarus (*q.v.*) where, stretched over nine acres of ground, he was tormented by two vultures which perpetually tore at his liver.

Troia. Troy (*q.v.*).

Troilus. A young son of Priam (*q.v.*) and Hecuba, he ventured to fight Achilles (*q.v.*), who turned him to flight and killed him as he was taking sanctuary at the temple of Thymbrian Apollo, where Achilles himself was later to die.

Troy. A city of Asia Minor, taken by Hercules (*q.v.*) and later by an alliance of the Greeks in the Trojan War (*v. Paris, Helen, Achilles*). For its kings, *v.* Table A, p. 190.

Tyndareus. King of Sparta, father of Clytemnestra (*v.* Table C, p. 194) by Leda (*q.v.*).

Tyndaris. "Daughter of Tyndareus"; *i.e.*, Clytemnestra (*q.v.*) or (less accurately, since Tyndareus was not her real father) Helen (*q.v.*).

Tyrrhene. (*1*) Of Lydia, a country of Asia Minor. Dolphins were sometimes called Tyrrhene because they were the metamorphosis of the Tyrrhene pirates who kidnapped Bacchus. (*2*) Of Etruria, because the Etruscans were originally a band of colonists from Lydia; hence the Tyrrhenian Sea.

Ulysses. King of Ithaca, renowned chiefly for his cleverness and craftiness. It was he who tricked Achilles (*q.v.*) into dropping his disguise as a girl, persuaded Clytemnestra (*q.v.*) to send Iphigenia (*q.v.*) for sacrifice and the girl herself to come willingly. He brought about the death of Palamedes (*q.v.*) by his wiles. His exploits in the Trojan War were usually somewhat underhanded, as the ambushing of Rhesus (*q.v.*) and the theft of the Palladium (*q.v.*). It was he also who invented the ruse of the Trojan Horse. A wooden horse was built outside Troy and filled with armed warriors, while the rest of the Greeks sailed to Tenedos, pretending to abandon the siege. Sinon (*q.v.*), Ulysses' kinsman, was left to persuade the Trojans to break down their walls and bring the horse inside the city. For this device Ulysses was awarded the arms of Achilles (*v. Ajax*). He also tricked Andromache (*q.v.*) into revealing the whereabouts of Astyanax. He wandered the seas for ten years on his way home from the war.

Venus. The goddess of love. In the Trojan War she supported Troy, both because of the Judgment of Paris (*q.v.*) and for her love for her son Aeneas (*q.v.*).

Vergil. Publius Vergilius Maro (70-19 B.C.), the author of the *Aeneid*, in the Second Book of which he tells of the fall of Troy.

Xanthus. A river of Troy. Its course was choked with the corpses of men slain by Achilles (*q.v.*).

Zethus. Brother of Amphion (*q.v.*).

Zodiac. A band in the sky of twelve constellations which were thought to influence men's lives.

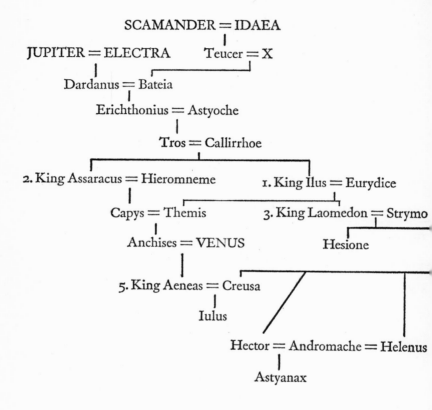

The names of gods are in capitals. The kings are numbered in their order of succession. For Helen, *v.* also Table C.

TABLE A
THE DYNASTY OF TROY

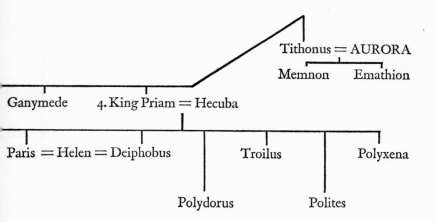

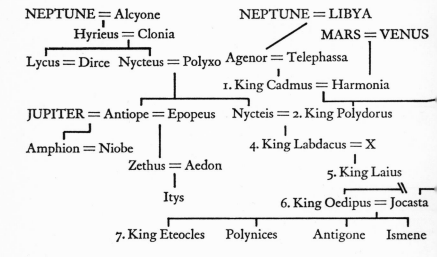

The names of gods are in capitals. The kings are numbered in their order of succession. For Amphion and Niobe, *v.* also Table C.

TABLE B
THE DYNASTY OF THEBES

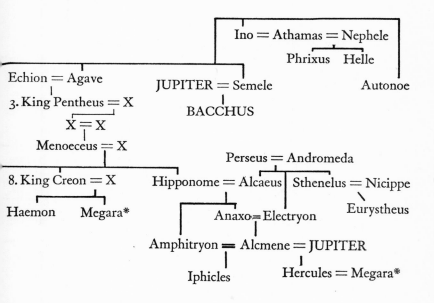

---

* Megara the daughter of Creon is the same person as Megara the wife of Hercules.

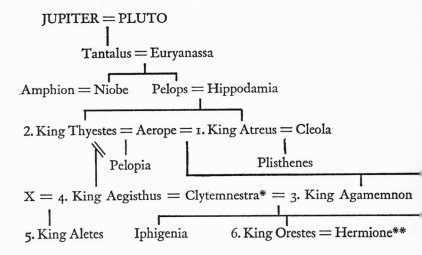

The names of gods are in capitals. The kings are numbered in their order of succession. For Amphion and Niobe, *v.* also Table B; for Helen, *v.* also Table A.

TABLE C
THE DYNASTY OF MYCENAE

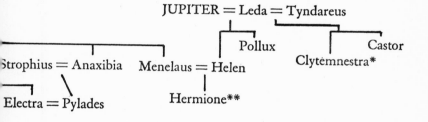

* Clytemnestra the daughter of Tyndareus is the same person as Clytemnestra
the wife of Agamemnon.
** Hermione the daughter of Menelaus is the same person as Hermione the
wife of Orestes.

TABLE D
THE DYNASTY OF PHTHIA

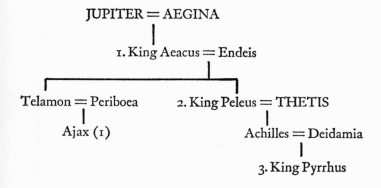

The names of gods are in capitals. The kings are numbered in their order of succession.

BIBLIOGRAPHY

Bieber, M. *History of the Greek and Roman Theatre*. Princeton, N.J., Princeton University Press, 1961.

Bradbrook, Muriel C. *Themes and Conventions of Elizabethan Tragedy*. Cambridge University Press, 1960.

Cunliffe, John W. *The Influence of Seneca on Elizabethan Tragedy*. Hamden, Conn., Shoestring Press, 1965 (reprint).

Lucas, F. L., *Seneca and Elizabethan Tragedy*. New York, Haskell House Publishers, 1922.

Mendell, Clarence W. *Our Seneca*. Hamden, Conn., Shoestring Press, 1968 (reprint).

Newton, T., ed. *Seneca, His Tenne Tragedies*. Bloomington, Indiana University Press, 1966.

Peiper, R., and G. Richter, eds. *L. Annaei Senecae Tragoediae*. Leipzig, B. G. Teubner, 1902.

Spearing, E. M. *The Elizabethan Translations of Seneca's Tragedies*. Cambridge (England), W. Heffer & Sons, 1912.